MUST WIN

MUST WIN

A SEASON OF SURVIVAL
FOR A TOWN AND ITS TEAM

DREW JUBERA

St. Martin's Press ⚏ New York

www.stmartins.com

Design by Meryl Sussman Levavi

Chapter 11, "Rome the Elder and Rome the Younger," appeared in a different form in *ESPN The Magazine*.

ISBN 978-0-312-64220-4 (hardcover)
ISBN 978-1-250-01857-1 (e-book)

First Edition: September 2012

10 9 8 7 6 5 4 3 2 1

To Ann, Andrew, Mary Louise, and Frankie

CONTENTS

ACKNOWLEDGMENTS

The generosity, hospitality, and openness of the good folks in Valdosta is unmatched anywhere. The list of kindnesses goes on too long to detail here. Thanks to all of you.

My experience would have been far less, however, without the astonishing offer of Kay Powell: a whole house! Special thanks also to Kay's sisters Martha Coppage and Mary Frank Wingate for sharing, too, especially that afternoon at Cherry Lake. My kids are still licking the barbecue sauce off their fingers. I am grateful as well for the open arms and open doors of BJ and Larry Sellars, the best temporary neighbors that a temporary resident of South Georgia could have. A key to my house always waits for you in a shoe on the back porch.

Donald O. Davis and his staff at the Lowndes County Historical Museum were tireless as they stacked books on my desk until I couldn't see over them. Mark George, at Valdosta State, and the Rev. Floyd Rose, of the local SCLC, provided invaluable insights. David Waller shared with me both his life and his personal collection of Wildcat history, while his wife Sharon indulged my peskiness. The fellas at Wildcat Central, overseen by Monty Long, provided background and belly laughs, as well as a place to eat lunch. The administrators, teachers, and staff at Valdosta High were always welcoming; and Tracy Williams helped me track down coaches and players when nobody else had a clue. Few in town were as generous as Stan, LaVerne, and Roger Rome, and even fewer as wide open as the Nelsons, Nub and Rena. That steak dinner is in the mail.

I could not have finished without the gift of peace and quiet provided by Bob Longino; Susie and Glenn Jacks; and Tom, Janet, and Nia Junod, all of whom opened up their houses to me when I needed them most. What a gift. Thanks, too, to the good folks at the Buckhead branch of the Atlanta-Fulton County Library, especially James Taylor, who found me space whenever they could.

Marc Resnick is the most patient, encouraging editor a writer could ever ask for. Thanks, man. David Black remembered my name after all these years, then didn't hesitate to become my agent. Thanks also to Kate Canfield and David Larabell and the rest at St. Martin's Press and the David Black Literary Agency who helped guide me along the way. Special thanks to Frank Garland, who knows me well enough to know better, yet toiled through the earliest, worst pages. You're aces, Francis.

Most of all, I want to thank my family. Ann, Andrew, Mary Louise, and Frankie not only endured my absences, they encouraged me to do whatever it took. Their enthusiasm became my own. Nobody's luckier than me.

It had just happened. Nobody knew why or apparently would ever know. He was stronger and faster and meaner than other boys his age and for that he had been rewarded.

—HARRY CREWS, *A Feast of Snakes*

As iron sharpens iron, so one man sharpens another.

—Proverbs 27:17, painted inside Valdosta High locker room

Hey yo, tell him that Pastor Troy and them Down South Georgia Boys said since everybody thank they soldiers then what's up we'll go to war.

—PASTOR TROY, introduction to "No Mo Play in G.A.,"
unofficial Valdosta High anthem

MUST WIN

PROLOGUE

What It Means Here

or Thug Tears

The black kid with the badass tats stood smiling on the practice field sideline. Beat jail. Helmet off, earring on fire in the afternoon sun, he surprised teammates with his out-of-nowhere appearance, as if he'd spontaneously erupted from the heat and the sweat, returned now to this gnat-bitten patch of deepest South Georgia from a biblical-sounding exile of forty-four days and forty-four nights—wandering the wilderness, right across town, inside the Lowndes County lockup.

Odell James took a very deep breath; the still, cooked air never tasted sweeter. Timber trucks rumbled down a nearby four-lane: music. The ink stamped up and down his dark biceps—the numerals 229 and 912, area codes for Valdosta and nearby Homerville, the two addresses the eighteen-year-old had called home—glistened beneath a relentless blue sky.

It was September, but still it was hot. Make-you-stupid hot. A halo of gnats, the state bird of South Georgia, swarmed Odell's head like wild electrons. A handful of teammates banished to the sideline beside him—recidivist goof-offs, including some of the white boys; a few other hard cases trying to make comebacks—quickly formed a semicircle around him, angling to bask in the glow of his by-God sure-enough street cred.

They wanted stories, jailhouse stories. Stories to kill time, stories to retell later. Anything to make bearable this open-air asylum patrolled by a new coach hell-bent on making this strip back into the most fearsome green acre on any high school campus in America.

So far, so good: A month into the season, the Valdosta High Wildcats hadn't lost a game. Beyond a chain-link fence on the other side of the field, a murmuring chorus of parents, retirees, and ex-players idly fingering their championship rings looked on from low wooden bleachers—all of them bunching up and drifting off and then resettling again, like mockingbirds trying to get cozy on a telephone wire. Parked behind them, in the student lot, others watched from inside their pickups, pointed nose-first toward the grass.

"You shiv anybody?" one kid finally asked Odell.

Laughter. *Shiv.* They'd heard it in movies. Or rap songs. Or from somebody they knew who'd, you know, actually shivved somebody.

Odell's full-moon face broke into a crescent-moon smile—nothing could keep Odell from smiling today—and he answered sheepishly, "Nah."

"What you eat, bread and water?"

Bread and water. What're they watching, Turner Classic Movies?

"Nah." Odell kept smiling. "But it was nasty. Nasty meat. Nasty bread. Put me on suicide watch when I wouldn't eat."

"So you eat? Or commit suicide?"

More laughter.

"Yeah, I ate."

They nodded and howled some more. They weren't getting what they wanted, though. Odell didn't seem down with being in jail.

Last season, he was busted for possession: weed. He'd skipped practice with a teammate, and they both got popped while sitting in a car. Technically, Odell said, it wasn't even his weed—the other kid bought it—but he *damn sure* intended to smoke it. Yet unlike his sixteen-year-old teammate, Odell was tried as an adult.

The judge gave him a probated sentence and ordered him to pay a monthly fine. Odell fell behind on the payments and flunked a urine test. So just a couple of days into camp at the start of August, Odell, who the previous two seasons often started and even starred at wide receiver and defensive back, was hauled off to jail.

Not juvie.

Jail.

It was miserable. That's the point Odell was trying to get across as coolly as he knew how. That circle of sweaty faces still stared at him like kindergartners during story hour.

So Odell went on and on about how jail was just hot and dirty and loud. Even worse: boring. Guards woke you up at four for breakfast— "watery grits, nasty eggs," he said, and some kind of stew-and-grits combo that should've gone down like velvet over his Southern palate but didn't, at least not at first. "Had to get used to it," he explained.

Then Odell would go back to sleep until a guard woke him again to take a shower. After that he'd head to the dormitory-like common area and watch TV until it was time for lunch: salami or baloney sandwich, maybe a slice of cheese.

Then back to the common area and more TV. Sometimes he'd play cards, by himself or with a kid he knew from another high school. Dinner was served at four: greens, corn bread, chicken patty, slice of cake. "All of it," Odell repeated, as if he couldn't repeat it enough, "*nasty.*"

Then lights out at ten.

Next day: wake, repeat.

The routine changed only after his cellmate got jumped for doing something silly to somebody else. When a guard showed up, the cell-mate cried that Odell did it, too. No honor among thieves here. That was enough to get him sent to solitary confinement—"the hole," he called it. What that really meant was that Odell's days became even more boring (no TV), the food even less appealing (one hot meal a day instead of two).

Then Odell lucked out the one way that a kid like him can luck out in this town. A guard assigned to the hole belonged to the Valdosta High Touchdown Club. When he learned Odell was a Wildcat, he let him shower when he wasn't supposed to shower, make calls when he wasn't supposed to make calls. Even got Odell out of the hole early. "Wasn't for him," Odell said, "probably still be there."

Odell paused. His teammates didn't say a word. In the awkward silence that followed, one of the white kids piped up, "At least you didn't have to do camp!"

Everybody laughed. Fell out.

The kid meant football camp. This year, with a new coach who wouldn't put up with anybody skipping out to burn a blunt—that's for *damn sure*—camp was four practices a day and lights out at eleven inside the school gym, where everybody slept on air mattresses or sleeping bags atop a tarp-covered basketball court.

The day's first practice began at six, before the sun came up. The last one ended around nine at night, with the sun down and the practice field lights burning for the first time since anybody around here could remember. During the two practices in between (one for special teams), some players spent at least part of their time throwing up. One recalled it becoming almost a scheduled part of his routine. One o'clock: weights. One thirty: run. Two o'clock: puke.

Odell smiled when the kid made the crack about camp; Odell's one of those kids who smiles a lot, even when a smile isn't really called for. He didn't laugh along with everybody else, though.

Instead, he told them that he wished he could've been there for camp—the four-a-days, the 100-degree heat, the hurling—just to be part of the first game of his last year as a Wildcat.

There was something about this new coach, too. He was different from the other coaches who'd been through here lately, all now fired and gone. They don't call it Winnersville for nothing—it's win or bye-bye. This one seemed . . . *realer.* Odell would call him sometimes from jail (thank you, Mr. Touchdown Club). Coach told Odell he could come back whenever he got out. As far as he was concerned, all that other stuff happened before he took over. If Odell kept his nose clean and worked his ass off, he said, everything was cool.

As it turned out, Odell wasn't released in time for the season's first game. So he did the only other thing he could think of: bought a radio and some earbuds from the jail store. Then at eight o'clock that Friday night, while the other inmates still stared at some mindless TV or played cards or argued about stuff so stupid you wouldn't believe how stupid it was, Odell found a secluded spot in a corner of the dorm and pulled a blanket over his head. There he played with the radio dial until he finally heard the drawling voices of Bobby Scott, Guy Belue, and Monty Long, the announcers bringing Wildcat fans the season opener for storied Valdosta High.

Next thing he heard: the frenzied, alley-fight crash of a hundred helmets beating against the tin roof that runs the length of an enclosed walkway from the locker room to the field. Monty Long's handheld mike in the end zone let radio listeners hear the coming storm. The whole jacked-up bunch, gripping their face masks like nightsticks or bottles for a barroom brawl, massed at the end of the tunnel the same way Valdosta teams had massed there before games for decades, beating the corrugated metal above their heads as hard and as many times as they could—some left both feet to hit it even harder—in a kind of ecstatic, tribal tribute to all those hallowed 'Cats who'd dented and damaged the roof before them.

Inside the stadium, the noise they made rolled like thunder up the stands and down the field until finally, and this was the point, it ran through the hearts and minds of the visiting players, who looked on wide-eyed from the other side.

Yet the most profound effect was on the home team. To stand there banging the tin in that dark, deafening tunnel, invisible to everybody but each other and unable to hear anything else, was to be part of something almost evangelical, something that lifted you outside of yourself and that ran deeper here than any lime sink or swamp bottom for a hundred miles.

Odell had hardly gotten over the thrill of finding the game and hearing that tin before Bobby Scott was already yelling from up in the press box into the hot August night. A Wildcat had just caught a quick pass near the line of scrimmage and raced 46 yards down the visitors' sideline for a touchdown.

In the suffocating air under the blanket, his face lit by the cheap radio's glow, Odell saw in his mind's eye a black-and-gold blur cross the goal line. His ears filled with the full-throated roar of 10,000 fans jumping and stomping inside the stadium, accompanied by the brassy blare of the school band. Whoops and hollers seemed to come from everywhere and anywhere. It was as if the random yells of folks listening to their radios all over town were being picked up by satellite from inside living rooms and truck cabs and late-shift work sites—the lumber yard, the pecan plant, the break room at the medical center.

It was too much for Odell. So he stayed huddled under his blanket, wishing he could be with his "boys," kids he'd grown up playing football with every recess, every Saturday at the rec center, every time they ran into each other on the street or in an empty lot.

He stayed under the blanket because, at that moment, in that place, tears streamed down his face.

"I cried," Odell told his teammates, "like a baby."

They just stared. Then they waited for Odell to break into one of his big gotcha smiles, letting them know that the joke was on them.

He never did. It wasn't a joke.

The black kid with the badass tats who stood smiling on the practice field sideline—whose year was blown before it even started and who wouldn't play a single minute until the regular season's next-to-last game, the same week that somebody he loved like his own brother would be shot to death in nearby Homerville—had sat alone that Friday night under a government-issue blanket, inside the Lowndes County lockup, listening to the Valdosta Wildcats play football.

Bawling like a baby.

1

Welcome

or Your Grave Is Ready, Coach

On a blustery winter afternoon nine months earlier, before a round of meet-and-greets with a bank president, a business-running benefactor, a one-legged booster, and the pastor of the biggest Baptist church in town, Rance Gillespie stood in the middle of an empty cemetery for his unscheduled Tour of Dead Coaches.

The only other living thing around was the pumpkin-shaped man who drove him there in his neat white pickup, and who now went on in vivid, if sometimes surreal, detail about the legend buried right under their feet—the last Valdosta High football coach who wasn't fired.

He'd died instead.

Gillespie leaned in. For the newest coach of this once-mighty high school dynasty, the graveyard tour led by the program's most powerful booster was a not-so-subtle reminder of just what was at stake.

This was more than high school football, son, it seemed to signal. How much more, the red-state kingmakers who'd long nurtured this program to national prominence were only now beginning to fathom.

They'd come to a crossroad and they knew it. Their town, their team—hell, even their president (though, for the record, white folks here voted against him by almost three to one)—had all gone black. It was Friday night in the Age of Obama, and this quaint Deep South outpost of 50,000, just a dozen miles above the Florida line, was in the roiling hot middle of it. Once a metaphor for everything that was unchanging in America, Valdosta now stood for all that had changed.

So this morning inside the cemetery—cold, damp, wind gusting all the way in from the Gulf—took on the air of an over-the-top, spirit-conjuring ritual, like a river baptism, or a Sunday night snake-handling service back up in the piney woods.

"I could see why some guys would've run for home," Gillespie would say later, smiling. "I just took it for what it was: Valdosta."

Escorting the youthful Gillespie—a fit, churchgoing, tobacco-dipping fan of Metallica, Guns N'Roses, and "maybe a little Van Halen"—was seventy-seven-year-old David Waller, a self-made heating-and-air-conditioning millionaire who'd missed only five Valdosta High football games since 1947.

Back in the segregated '60s, this white sharecropper's son from out-past-nowhere Georgia, whose father once whipped him for returning home from a dinnertime hunt with nothing more than a "skinny rabbit," had proclaimed that the first time a black kid pulled on a Wildcats uniform would be the last day he ever gave the school a dime.

That was then. Now, all Waller wanted was for Valdosta's fractured legacy to mend itself and win state once more before he died. White kids, black kids, it didn't matter anymore. Winning football games had carried Waller's conscience a long, long way from its ancestral home.

That was true for much of the town. It's hard to imagine a place where winning has ever meant more than it has in this place, bounded by cotton, pine, and swamp, the air charged with a native trinity of God, Family, and Football.

The result: Valdosta had won more football games than any other high school in the country. In fact, Valdosta had won so often, for so long, it could lose every contest for the next sixty-five seasons and still stay above .500. Playing in a region so brutal it was deemed the South-eastern Conference of high school football, Valdosta also boasted twenty-three state championships and six national titles—a brag plastered across the taxpayer-funded green road signs that welcomed visitors to town. A dozen Wildcats had gone on to play in the NFL.

Off the field, season tickets inside the 11,349-seat stadium were handed down in wills and quarreled over in divorce settlements. During a wake for one recently deceased fan, in a little town more than an hour away, six tickets for the next home game were displayed inside an open casket, clutched for all eternity in the man's dead, frozen hand.

Meanwhile, the Valdosta head coach had a weekly TV show taped at the team's 3,500-square-foot museum, ran a weekly game-highlight review for boosters inside the school's performing arts center, and was featured during a live hour-long radio broadcast every Wednesday night from the Smokin' Pig, a red-roofed, log-sided barbecue palace run by one of the twenty-one former Wildcats descended from the same O'Neal. Only complaint ever voiced by fans: The radio show conflicted with Wednesday night church services.

The coach also took home a six-figure salary from the school board and a free truck from the Touchdown Club, provided by a local dealership run by a former 'Cat.

On it went. While other schools had their eras, Valdosta had dominated the whole modern history of prep football, winning its first championship in 1940 and last playing for state in 2003.

So it's little surprise that the three coaches who preceded Gillespie were all fired, or skipped town, when they failed to win that one more title that Waller and other loyalists here wanted before they perished. With a largely desperate black majority and a fearful rush by white families to newer, safer suburbs—forces pounding once-proud powerhouses all over the country—folks here worried that Valdosta High might soon disappear and, by extension, erase them along with it.

An unlikely cabal of white business leaders and black megapastors was even at work to abolish the city schools' charter and merge the system with the county. Its leaders insisted they only wanted to rebalance the schools' racial disparity to better educate low-achieving students, attract new businesses, and keep the place breathing far into the future. Valdosta High was now three-quarters black, crosstown rival Lowndes High three-quarters white.

Others saw more nefarious agendas: a payoff, a power play, a back-door real estate scheme. One prominent black lawyer, a fifth-generation Valdostan, called the impulse to consolidate "the monster under the bed," a strategy to dilute the power of the city's narrow black majority by buying off a few and keeping race in its proper place. Eventually, city and county governments could merge as well.

Real estate agents, who many believed segregated the landscape in the first place by steering white home buyers to new developments in the county with asides about Valdosta's black-and-getting-blacker schools (a tactic locals called "fearing"), now seemed eager to cash in again on a single, rejiggered district.

"There's something here that somebody's not telling people," Sam Allen, retired as Valdosta's first black superintendent, said of the richly financed push by the city's business elite to combine the two systems. "There's something they're not willing to say out loud."

If it did happen, Allen believed, not only would Valdosta's children be no better served, it would mean the end of Valdosta High football as anyone had known it, with the school absorbed and marginalized by its whiter, wealthier, on-the-make county brethren.

The county high school had already taken full advantage of this demographic shift. Lowndes High now had a thousand more students than Valdosta, and its football Vikings, who had won three titles in the last six years, had emerged as perhaps the state's most dominant program. Even worse for fans of the town's school, separated from its rival by only a few miles and a mall, was that Lowndes had beaten Valdosta six straight games, including the previous season's 57–15 drubbing—worst loss in Wildcat history.

Just four days after that midseason embarrassment, Valdosta's head coach was summoned like a teenaged truant to the superintendent's office and fired. He became the third coach axed or pushed out in just seven years.

So Gillespie, an intense young white guy with a guru's rep from the cool blue mountains of North Georgia, was now seen as the school's last, best hope. Only football, folks here reasoned—with its historic power in towns like these to inspire, unite, and protect—could save them.

Standing in the cemetery's early-afternoon chill, the grandfatherly, God-fearing Waller just wanted to make sure Gillespie got all that.

●

First stop on the Dead Coaches Tour: the grave of Nick Hyder.

Wind swirled through the monuments inside Sunset Hill, final resting spot for a century-and-a-half-long parade of random townies. These included mayors, judges, Civil War vets, parents of the Wild West gambler and gunfighter Doc Holliday, infant quintuplets, an air force major killed in Iran during the attempt to rescue American hostages, and an animal trainer from New Orleans crushed to death in 1902 by an escaped circus elephant named Gypsy.

Waller and Gillespie stared together at the iconography that stretched across Hyder's double-wide tombstone. Words and images bloomed everywhere: a black-and-white photo of the animated coach clenching a whistle between his bared teeth; an inscription that noted his THOUSANDS OF VICTORIES FOR CHRIST; his mission—some would say missionary—statement of priorities: God, Family, Country, Friends, Academics, Team; and his most oft-repeated exhortation, running the length of the monument's granite base: NEVER NEVER NEVER NEVER NEVER NEVER NEVER QUIT.

The gravesite rested just beyond the shadows cast by a grove of towering oaks, draped in green-gray Spanish moss that fell in ragged sheets, like uncombed hair extensions, and nearly brushed the mowed grounds below.

"I'm surprised," one fourth-generation Valdostan mused of Hyder's site, given the place its occupant held in this town, "they didn't bury him in a pyramid."

Waller came here often to talk with his old best friend. He knew he was mostly talking to himself, of course, but being in the presence of his soul mate's mortality helped him to curate his thoughts. He'd done it since the day he buried Hyder, fourteen years earlier.

It was the funeral service preceding that interment that everybody here still talked about. Held in the stadium just blocks from where Waller and Gillespie now stood, it was still the most marveled-at spectacle in the town's long history.

●

The coffin sat on the 50-yard line. It was open. The man in repose—who just three days earlier slumped over a lunchroom table in the school cafeteria, where he'd picked out a piece of baked chicken—wore a smart gold sport coat, a black-and-gold tie, and a faint, proud smile. A football was tucked under his left arm, as if he'd demonstrated some routine ball-handling maneuver at the very moment of his heart attack and now cradled an eternal handoff.

The scene teetered between homespun and South Georgia Gothic. Despite the Sunday afternoon heat (96 degrees and only the middle of May), nearly 8,000 mourners streamed into the same stadium they filled on warm autumn nights to live and die with their Wildcats. Young and old, white and black, land-rich and dirt-poor, they shuffled past tall pines and live oaks and magnolias. It was a second Sunday service for most of them. The town's low-slung skyline was pierced everywhere by needle-nosed church steeples, but Cleveland Field was the only house of common worship that could fit, and would welcome, them all.

They flocked to the stadium from every baked and rutted corner of the region. Many of the men wore dark suits and cinched ties; women wobbled up the ancient wooden bleachers in heels. Politicians and fellow coaches, from both high schools and colleges, drove or flew in on private jets from around the South. The Rev. Billy Graham, unable to scramble his schedule on such short notice, was a last-minute no-show.

Only the visitors' stands, on the north side of the field, were deserted. On this day, everyone sat on the home team's side.

God's side.

A covered stage used by the city for public events was set up behind the casket. It held about a dozen people, including an elderly man on electric keyboard who accompanied the service with hymnal standards like "Sunrise Tomorrow" and "How Great Thou Art." Eulogizers included a former Wildcat quarterback now playing at Boston College, booster club brass (Waller among them), and the minister of the First Baptist Church of Valdosta, where Hyder had served as a deacon.

They talked some about the coach's sideline genius—his 300 career wins, his seven state titles at Valdosta, his three national championships—but mostly they talked about what he meant off the field to players, parents, and the community. The mood was lightened only occasionally inside a stadium that sounded eerily empty rather than filled to the top row.

"Nick said, 'I don't believe there's going to be a North heaven and a South heaven, do you?'" the preacher recalled. "And I told him, 'I believe it's all one—white, yellow, black, together in that great, big Baptist heaven.'"

The otherwise subdued crowd sounded grateful for the inside-joke chuckle, but their sense of loss remained powerful. Some compared the town's reaction to the unexpected death of their vibrant, sixty-one-year-old coach to the shock that followed the Kennedy assassination. Indeed, the lobby of the hospital where Hyder was rushed after his collapse swelled quickly with more than 150 locals, including students who sped there right after the high school's early dismissal. The crowd kept silent vigil until a doctor stepped out to officially announce what they all knew but not a single one of them appeared ready to hear: Their coach was dead.

In that instant, much of the town felt orphaned by a man whose only children were the students and citizens of Valdosta; even the Lowndes coach could be heard sobbing in the hospital's lobby. Many wondered during the days that followed if the community could continue on a righteous path without its paternal, pastoring coach.

"Where do we go from here?" one man cried.

Implored another, "The captain of our ship is gone. Give us the strength to look ahead."

Jack Rudolph, a former NFL player and an architect of Valdosta's universally feared defense, told one reporter that at the school in the days after Hyder's death "the psychologists worked as much with the adults as with the kids."

"Our wonderful coach had become a crutch for us," the Rev. Delos Sharpton allowed during his eulogy that sweltering spring day of 1996—a year near the cusp of a new millennium everywhere else in the world, it seemed that afternoon, but here.

Reverend Sharpton looked out onto the crowd. Folks waved programs to roust a breeze, and opened umbrellas to block the hammering sun.

"As individuals, as a team, as a community, we always depended on him being there," the minister continued. "We always looked to him to be our best conscience . . . looked to him to be the voice of the community in race relations."

Heads nodded.

"Nick didn't see color," he emphasized. "He only saw heart."

Reverend Sharpton hit all the right notes. Yet even he sensed that nothing he could say would ease this gathering's communal grief.

"I'm simply a struggling pilgrim," he pronounced at one point, "with a broken heart like you."

For those who'd played for Hyder, memories throughout the weekend's blizzard of newspaper and TV coverage around the South often centered on the times before or after practices. The games, oddly, now seemed almost beside the point.

It shouldn't have been surprising. With a voice distilled like aged whiskey from his home-place mountains in East Tennessee, the razor-featured, charismatic Hyder (a former assistant described his entrances as being "like Elvis walking into a room") usually saved his best preach-ifying not for Sunday mornings at First Baptist but for those hot week-day afternoons on the bright green rectangle behind the school. There he'd expound on subjects that ranged from developing a relationship with God to daily grooming habits to the avoidable ravages of venereal disease. Assistants sometimes had to remind him in the locker room when he got on a roll before practice that if they didn't get out there soon, it'd be too dark.

"He'd start off talking about football," recalled one former Wildcat, by then a Valdosta businessman, "but pretty soon he'd be talking about how you need to act when you take out a date, what time you should be home, the importance of saying 'yes, sir' and 'no, ma'am' to your parents."

Another ex-player remembered, "There were times we'd get through practice and he'd gather the team and start talking, and the next thing you knew it was dark and the parents in the parking lot were turning the car lights on."

The thousands inside the stadium listened shoulder to shoulder for nearly two hours. Concession stands were opened and free Cokes handed out.

Coach, meanwhile, just lay there in the eternal sunshine. Some worried the pancake makeup that gave his face a rich, golden glow might liquefy in the heat and puddle in the casket's satin lining, but the ol' boys at Carson McLane Funeral Home had prepped and buried this town's sons and daughters without a hitch since 1936. This day would prove no exception.

There'd never been anything around here like it. No senator, no mayor, no sheriff, no *preacher* had ever drawn a funeral crowd as vast and varie-gated as this.

Of course, nobody but the previous coach, by then retired and silenced for years by a stroke, had ever won more games and titles for dear old Valdosta High than had Nick Hyder—now broiling in school colors at midfield.

Waller didn't detail all of that for Gillespie; he didn't really remember what all he said that day. He did tell the new coach one thing as he shifted his weight on the soft cemetery sod: Hyder was buried in Waller's family plot, and Waller planned to be buried right beside him.

When the time came.

Gillespie's sharp dark eyebrows rose skyward in bemusement. His players would soon learn to read in them the whole range of their new coach's emotions, from ecstatic to supremely pissed.

The two men moved on. Thirty paces west, Waller halted in front of a simple gray stone. It contained the dates of birth and death and a plaque honoring naval service during World War II. There was also an open-ended date for his widow, Bettie—for when the time came.

That was it. Nothing to pronounce the deceased, as Hyder's monument did, OUR COACH.

Instead, this stone contained just a name.

AUGUST WRIGHT BAZEMORE.

Wright Bazemore and Nick Hyder, two of the most influential coaches in the history of high school football, who together led Valdosta for more than half a century, marked this town forever with their outsized, largely complementary legacies.

A fierce competitor, Hyder seemed impossible now to separate from the evangelical brand of Southern-style Christianity he embedded in the program, which it still strived to embrace.

A good Christian himself, Bazemore seemed impossible to separate from the Southern-fried ethos of jumping on an opponent early and then pounding him, and pounding him, and then pounding him some more—before leading the team afterward in grateful prayer.

Those were the two ideologies Gillespie had been hired to revive.

Bazemore grew up on a farm sixty-five miles north, in Fitzgerald, a town founded in 1895 as a colony for veterans on both sides of the Civil War. He was an assistant on the Wildcats' first championship team, in 1940, and after serving three years in the navy, he coached his own title team before the decade ended.

From that point on, Valdosta became high school football's gold standard. Team and town virtually merged. Preachers called Bazemore for the Wildcats schedule as soon as he could provide it, to make sure they didn't set their fall tent revivals for the same weekend as a home game.

Crouched during games on the sideline, one hand always twirling a roll of athletic tape, he could detail how virtually all twenty-two positions executed their assignments on each play. Folks liked to say he could take his best eleven and beat your best eleven, then take your best and beat his. (As if to prove that theory, the opposing captains for the coin toss before a Florida–Florida State game one year both were former Bazemore Wildcats.) His pro-style offense featured shotgun formations and quick passes on first downs at a time when most teams considered it heresy to do anything but keep the ball low to the ground.

He was also a master motivator, often getting players, boosters, school administrators, business leaders, and even elected officials to do what they least wanted to do. He was suspected of hiring crop dusters to fly over the school on game days and drop taunting leaflets signed by that night's opponent. He once walked off the practice field, taking his assistants with him. After recovering from their shock, team members pulled together and ran the practice themselves—just as he intended.

Yet perhaps his most profound accomplishment was uniting his many constituencies to help steer Valdosta High through integration, no slight feat in that day's hair-trigger, violence-happy Deep South. As much as it would change his own world, this was one game Bazemore wasn't ready to lose. He'd show up for practice at all-black Pinevale and tell the kids there that one day they'd all win a championship together.

The Wildcats won that championship just two years after a discrimination suit filed by black parents with the U.S. Justice Department shuttered Pinevale and merged it with Valdosta—a largely uneventful, if not always equitable, transition into full integration.

Many consider that undefeated 1971 team Bazemore's finest, maybe the best in the state's history. The whole region, rival towns excluded, rallied around it. Unable to slip inside the perpetually sold-out stadium, kids scrambled up soaring magnolias across the street to cheer from treetop perches for Stanley Bounds and Stan Rome and the rest of their unmatchable 'Cats.

As Hyder would later say, "The Supreme Court told us we had to live together, but they didn't tell us how. That's what football has done for this community."

By then, Valdosta's cult-of-the-coach template was set. Tanned, stocky, and ruggedly handsome, but hardly an imposing figure—a *Sports Illustrated* writer described him during a 1970 pilgrimage to South Georgia as a "moderate to small man with gray hair and batwing ears"—Bazemore seemed to part crowds when he walked into a room with his strong-yet-humble movie star's aura.

There was a downside, though. After Bazemore, success here became romanticized, which is to say, almost unattainable. The first coach to succeed him went 17-3 in two seasons and was fired. The move dumbfounded observers outside Valdosta. Inside the city limits, firing seemed like the only option.

"We hadn't lost that many games in the four years before that," Waller offered.

Bazemore soon righted the problem he'd created. He made the phone call to get Hyder, then making noises up north at a high school in Rome, Georgia. After the run-oriented new coach started his first season with a string of losses—"We both had FOR SALE signs put in our front yards on Saturday mornings," recalled Buck Belue, the freshman quarterback who'd win a national title at Georgia—Bazemore suggested to Hyder that he open up his offense. The newcomer wasn't too proud to listen, and the advice led to successive wins and the salvation of Hyder's job.

Still rolling that athletic tape between his fingers, a silvering Bazemore became a fixture at practices for years afterward. Hyder never appeared bothered by Bazemore's shadow, though privately, one assistant remembered, "Nick was never comfortable. He looked over his shoulder the whole time here. He wanted to be remembered like Baze. In his mind, he wanted to be *better* than Baze."

Unable to have kids of their own, Hyder and his wife, June, approached the job like a mission. Nick arrived home late from practices only to watch more film. June often rounded up kids missing from school or practice ("Some were going out the back door as she was coming in the front," Waller recalled), found players summer jobs, or drove down to the police station when they got in trouble. For a whole swath of the town, the Hyders were the safety net.

Yet for years, Waller said, Hyder came by his house to talk nearly every Sunday afternoon, and his first question was always the same: "David, do you think I'll last another week?" He coached the Wildcats five years before he felt secure enough to buy a house. He told one out-of-town reporter during the 1988 season, "I'm just continuously trying to survive." That same year, he was rushed to a hospital with chest pains. The diagnosis: stress.

Ultimately, one assistant said, all the punishing hours and not-knowing anxiety killed him, not that plate of baked cafeteria chicken. "Nick looked like he was in perfect health, but he wouldn't let it go," he said. "He'd watch the same game film a hundred times. He'd click on a play over and over." Then the assistant repeated, to underscore his point: *"He just could not let it go."*

Bazemore suffered a stroke in 1989. He remained alert and still a regular at practices, but now wheelchair-bound and mostly silent. When he died of congestive heart failure at age eighty-two, three years after Hyder passed, his coffin wasn't wheeled onto the 50 at Cleveland Field, by then rechristened Bazemore-Hyder Stadium and about to undergo a $7 million face-lift. Instead, he was carried one last time inside the simple but elegant sanctuary of Park Avenue United Methodist, a sprawling redbrick church just north of downtown. Carson McLane again took care of the arrangements.

With its two great surrogate fathers now gone and the town already changed in ways both small and profound—its dirt roads turning into paved thoroughfares, its white-collar class swelled by a regional hospital and state university, its public schools getting darker—many in Valdosta sensed something had passed that might not return soon.

If ever.

Waller checked his watch: They needed to get moving, but first he wanted to give a couple of other dead coaches their due.

Gillespie didn't mind. He kind of liked this stuff. Besides, what else could he do? Waller drove.

Waller nodded toward something in the distance: A stone out there belonged to Buck Thomas, who coached the 'Cats while Bazemore served in the navy. He then mentioned another coach not buried in Sunset Hill, Bobby Hooks, who'd led the school to its first title, in 1940, then left for a college job in Macon.

Hooks was one of the early coaches to recognize the special crop of athlete that seemed to grow wild and sweet—like the onions up the road in Vidalia—in the soil here below the Gnat Line, the state's physical and cultural equator that separated the North from the South, the clay from the sand, the pretenders from the players.

Only old-timers like Waller still remembered him, while even kids whose hands were too small to grip a regulation football could recite the legend of Bazemore.

As another old-timer noted, "Everybody looked up to Bobby Hooks as a god. Then Bazemore came along, and he raised godship to another level."

The Dead Coaches Tour ended there, but not Waller's real mission that afternoon. Before they turned to leave, Waller placed a once-strong old man's hand on Gillespie's forearm and told him, "I wanted you to meet these guys. They're here in this cemetery, but they know what's going on every Friday night."

Gillespie nodded and wondered what Waller was talking about.

Waller then added that his family plot still had extra spaces and that Gillespie, his wife, and his young daughter were all welcome to them.

When the time came.

"Win two hundred games the next twenty years," he said, only half-joking, "and you can be buried here, too. On Friday nights you can lay out here and listen to the games. If you hear boos, you'll know the ref made a bad call. If you hear cheers, you'll know Valdosta just did something good."

The Spanish moss in the oaks whipped around soundlessly.

Waller added, "All you'll have to do is listen."

No telling *what* Gillespie's eyebrows did when he heard that.

The two men walked back across the winter grass to where Waller had parked his pickup, then rolled on to meet the bank president.

2

Hand Me My Traveling Shoes

or Home

Just months before Waller offered him those free, good-for-forever holes in the ground, Gillespie was out of a job.

He'd spent the previous three years on what could've become a very fast track: offensive coordinator at small-college power Georgia Southern, in Statesboro, a sweltering burg surrounded by cotton, corn, and beans, as well as inspiration for Blind Willie McTell's "Statesboro Blues," the sweaty little number the Allman Brothers covered to the delight of drunken house partiers everywhere (*"Wake up mama/ turn your lamp down low!"*).

Gillespie got the slot there as reward for winning two straight titles at smallish Peach County High, just south of Macon, where he was widely considered one of coaching's big young brains. College was a logical next step—even if he had to work under somebody else, take a 20 percent cut from his nearly six-digit deal at Peach, and leave a house he couldn't sell in a collapsing real estate market.

Gillespie had pondered college coaching since his days as a walk-on scout team player at Georgia (both Gillespie's dad and uncle also walked on there). Getting run over every practice for three years by NCAA-certified freaks will make you figure out an alternative to playing. So Gillespie, who'd briefly flirted with becoming a doctor, instead turned his laser smarts on coaching.

He scratched out detailed notes from every practice and stashed away plays of Georgia opponents that he had to imitate. By the time he left UGA, Gillespie had accumulated enough three-ring binders to fill more than twenty of the boxes that his produce-brokering father used for shipping cabbages.

"That's where I learned," Gillespie said of those scout-team days, "that football was who I was."

He just never knew if he could square college coaching with the years of indentured servitude it often required. The college game looked glam on Saturdays, all those HDTV shots of hot cheerleaders and chest-painted frat boys and the blimp's-eye views of stadiums overflowing like kitchen-counter Roach Motels. Yet back then, as it still is now, the reality was that for most young sideline assistants—meaning those not at a major school or in an elite conference—it wasn't as lucrative as running a solid high school program in South Georgia, where top coaches can command $90,000 to $100,000 or more, plus perks like a truck.

Gillespie got a taste of that life as a graduate assistant at Gardner-Webb, a private college on a sweet little campus in Boiling Springs, North Carolina. His endless days there wound down late each night in a bunk bed in a tiny room that opened onto the locker room urinals.

"You think, 'How am I going to support a wife and kids?'" he said.

Still, Gillespie kept an eye open for the right chance while he scrambled up the high school ladder. After his second title at Peach, when he was named the state's best coach for a second straight year, he networked in earnest.

"We'd won two state championships and I'm going, 'What next?'" he said. "I don't want to say I was professionally stifled. I was just looking for . . . something."

A call came from Georgia Southern's just-hired Chris Hatcher, a next-level up-and-comer who'd won his own national title at Valdosta State. The 12,000-student institution, as it happened, rented Valdosta High's 11,000-thousand-seat stadium for its home games.

Gillespie said he'd have to talk the offer over with his wife.

◆

Rance and Claudette fell for each other in the seventh grade, in tiny Tiger, Georgia, just outside Clayton, tucked in the state's northwest corner amid mountains and trout streams and dam-made lakes. Developers have since turned much of that corner into a second-home retreat for Atlanta's corporate cheese, as well as big-time college coaches like Nick Saban and Vince Dooley.

Before that it was a mostly hills-'n'-hollows boondocks that drew its share of tourists each fall, eager to peep at the leaves and pick apples, yet was probably best known outside the region for supplying subjects in the bestselling Foxfire books. A series that published stories collected by local school kids, the books celebrated a fading Appalachian culture: faith healers, fiddle makers, moonshiners, witches. The books were later turned into a Broadway play, then adapted as a TV movie.

"It was like a little quiet secret we had in the mountains," Claudette said wistfully of the place before the outsider invasion began in earnest, "that we didn't know the rest of the world wanted."

Rance remembered weekend nights spent cruising downtown's Main Street—starting at the Dairy Queen, heading to the red light, then turning around in an empty store parking lot and doing it all over again, "all night long," he said, "bumper to bumper, every kid in town."

Claudette remembered wanting to be a cosmetologist when she was in grade school because "it was a big word and sounded important." In high school she worked at the KFC. Rance recalled that her car always smelled like chicken.

There was no McDonald's, no Walmart (now there are both). There was a Reeve's Hardware and a Harper's five-and-dime and a little shoe store and that DQ and a handful of other storefronts. It was plenty.

"I can't ever remember growing up thinking that we were missing anything," Claudette said. "It seemed like everything was there."

Rance's family attended the big red Methodist church; Claudette's went to the little white Baptist one. They drove thirty-five miles each way to watch a movie. Their curfew was eleven o'clock sharp. They couldn't talk on the phone past eight.

Claudette can't remember her whole family ever not sitting down to-gether for dinner. Her father had died in Vietnam while she was an infant, and her mother married the plant manager at a clothing factory, a tenderhearted local who lived to fish and "fell in love with Claudette," as one close friend recalled, "before he fell in love with her mother."

Rance's folks split up when he was eleven; his hard-charging father, he said, who built his own produce brokerage business, ultimately lost his marriage to his work. Still, even after his father expanded the business and moved downstate to Moultrie, he remained a strong presence in his children's lives. He imparted to Rance his dawn-to-dusk work ethic, as well as a passion for football. Rance bagged vegetables at his grandfather's farmer's market as far back as he can remember, drove a tractor through his uncle's cabbage fields by the time he was seven, and later unloaded produce trucks all day long.

"Rance was never told he had to work," George Gillespie said of his son. "He always *wanted* to work."

Rance played just about every sport in the one corner of the state not known for its obsession with sports—except among the Gillespies and their friends. He was a decent enough football player who liked contact, worked hard, and studied the game. As a kid, he devised offensive formations on a checkerboard. His dad would set up defenses opposite him.

"It was just in his blood," his dad said.

◆

Claudette's mother sometimes babysat Rance when he was little—they lived only about a mile from each other, their houses connected by a snaking mountain two-lane—but the kids had never really talked until they went to the same middle school. In eighth grade, Rance asked Claudette to the homecoming dance.

That was that.

"She was everything I was looking for in a girl," he said. "She was pure, innocent, beautiful. She was physically attractive—she's still a beautiful woman—and that's what gets your initial attention. But the thing that made me keep going back is how, when you get to know her, you see how pure her heart is.

"That's what I wanted," he added. "My number one goal in life was to be a husband and a daddy. I wanted those two things above all, and she was everything I was looking for, as far as who I wanted to spend my life with.

"It's unique that it happened at thirteen," he said. "Any relationship takes some work, but ours has been relatively easy. I found my life's companion at an early age. It's such a part of who I am. We've done everything together—grown up together, gone through life together."

"Together" is an easy concept to lose in many coaches' marriages, because if his job doesn't come first, he probably doesn't have a job for long. Claudette got that, but Rance got that there were limits to that setup, too.

A few years before his offer from Georgia Southern, it was Claudette who had a college chasing her. Petite, blond, personable, with three education degrees, Claudette was courted by Johns Hopkins. They wanted her to train educators in school districts across the Southeast in a reading literacy program the university had developed. Claudette would fly out three or four Sundays a month, work out of town until Wednesday or Thursday, then fly back home.

Hopkins brought in more than fifty applicants to interview for the job, culled them down to three, then picked Claudette.

It was a dream come true—from little Tiger to a top national research university. Claudette had piled up experience and degrees in each rural outpost where her husband had coached. Up to that point, every decision the couple made was to advance Rance's career.

Starting with the first one.

●

Rance never seemed to crack open a textbook yet graduated from Georgia a semester early, in December 1991. Claudette, who never seemed to be without a book, graduated the following May. They planned their wedding for that August.

During a Sunday lunch that spring in Claudette's little house at the end of an unpaved drive, with friends and family around a table and the wedding invitations ready to be mailed, her father asked Rance how things were going.

In the manner of most men in that part of the world, Rance tended not to say a whole lot. So he answered that things were going just fine, thanks, and oh, by the way, he'd just accepted an assistant coach's job at a high school in Thomasville, in South Georgia, about forty miles west of Valdosta. He then asked Claudette's father, as Claudette remembered it, if he could please pass another plate of food.

It was the first Claudette had heard of the job. Her reaction: *"What?"* She added, "You did *not* just do this. You're moving me *six hours* from my parents?"

The more she thought about it, though, the more she came around.

"It was probably the best thing in the world," she'd say later. "We had to totally survive on our own."

Claudette grabbed the wedding invitations before they went out the door and moved the ceremony up to June. She still didn't have a job and he still hadn't gotten a paycheck when the two of them packed up (no furniture but twenty cabbage boxes' worth of practice notes) and headed together down to Thomasville. They never looked back. Their first Christmas, they walked into a Family Dollar store and bought a two-dollar table tree. After they got it home and set it out, Claudette disappeared into another room. She returned a minute later with bows and hair ribbons, and together they hung them on the tree.

"We had, like, no money. Period," Claudette said. "There wasn't one present under the tree. It was the best Christmas ever."

Now, years later, the job wheel had come around again, and this time it landed on Claudette. When she told Rance about the Johns Hopkins offer, he said it sounded great. They'd work out the logistics, no problem.

Yet the timing, for Claudette, couldn't have been more problematic. After years of mapping out the professional life that got her the attention of a place like Hopkins, she wanted more than ever the one thing that so far had eluded her.

A baby.

The previous six years had been one long, swelling heartache. Claudette spent hours driving from whatever outback Rance happened to be coaching in to get to her appointments at an Atlanta fertility clinic that pioneered Georgia's first in vitro baby. After the initial six or seven months proved unsuccessful, Rance suggested they look into adoption. Claudette said she wanted to keep trying. Years dripped by.

They took their toll. Claudette was exhausted, emotionally whiplashed, desperate. "I feel like I dealt with multiple deaths each time it didn't work," she said.

The last time she visited the clinic after yet another attempt at in vitro, the lab results showed that she was pregnant. Yet there were no vital signs of a fetus—a false positive.

Claudette came apart. She left the clinic office, walked down the hall, and stepped into an elevator. That was it. When the doors closed, Claudette couldn't breathe, couldn't hear; the world telescoped into a dark pinpoint, into "some tunnel," she said, "and I could not find my way out." Somehow she did get out of the elevator and made her way to her parked car. She then sat in there without moving for the next three hours.

Just sobbed. Tried to breathe.

When the attack finally lifted, when she could breathe again and hear again and see what was in front of her again, Claudette drove the hour or so back to her home in rural Banks County. She stepped inside her house about seven that night, closed the door behind her, and collapsed on the floor.

Rance walked in minutes later. When he saw her, he got right down on the carpet, and the two of them lay there together for what felt like forever. Rance gripped her tight, then tighter. He told her he wasn't going anywhere, that if she wanted to lie on that floor for the next five minutes or the next five days, it didn't matter. He'd lie right there with her as long as he had to. He'd do whatever she needed him to do.

"I'm done," Claudette told him, meaning trying to have a baby.

Rance asked her if she was sure.

"I'm done," she repeated.

"Okay," Rance said. "Let's adopt."

"I thought, 'Wow,'" Claudette remembered. "'How did I get so lucky at the age of twelve or thirteen to have this man come into my life and care this much about me, and us, and our family?'"

Claudette politely turned down Johns Hopkins.

Not too many years later—after Claudette had cut the umbilical cord during the birth of their adopted daughter, with her husband standing a little queasily behind her—Rance and his wife sat down to have another conversation. This one was about Rance's offer from Georgia Southern.

The conversation didn't go on long.

Rance recalled, "She said, 'If it's something you want to do, we can do it.'"

So he jumped: won that second title at Peach in December and was gone the next month. He didn't even go back for the team banquet; the NCCA warned it could be a recruiting violation. Claudette, who stayed behind with Kennedy until the end of the school year, went to the team's dinner in his place. She picked up his championship ring and delivered his farewell speech herself.

Gillespie barely had time to unpack when he got to Statesboro; he hit the recruiting trail and stayed on it for more than a month. His territory was West Georgia and Alabama, except when it extended to someplace else. He'd often be in one nowhere Southern burg wooing some kid when Hatcher would call out of the blue and tell him to "shoot on down to . . . ," and then he'd have to jump in his leased Saturn and shoot on down to some other nowhere burg hundreds of miles away, woo some other hotshot kid.

It wasn't always easy. Four years later, Gillespie still had the message from Kennedy's first missed phone call saved in his BlackBerry.

"Let's see if I can do this without crying," he said as his thumbs punched the phone's buttons.

A moment later, up came his daughter's voice. She was five. She'd just gotten her report card.

"Dad, guess what?" she began brightly, then moved into a serious-sounding recitation of her grades: "I made several A's and two B's and a 100 in science."

Pause.

"Aren't you proud of me?"

Pause.

"Call me back when you get a minute. Love you."

Pause.

"I miss you when you're not here. It's so *boring* when you're not here. I want you to come home one day. *Okay*?"

Pause.

Silence.

It's a little while later. Kennedy's message has clicked off. Gillespie allows, "That being said . . . I loved it."

He did. He loved recruiting. Loved walking through the high schools, getting to know the kids, talking football with the coaches. Loved meeting with Mama and Daddy and, especially with a lot of the black kids he was after, Grandma and Auntie.

He loved the whole high-stakes game of it—competing against this vast army of other fast-food-eating, khakis-and-polo-shirt-wearing, texting-and-driving road warriors, all in pursuit of the same prize.

"You had the chance to go out and pick your football team," he said. "It wasn't that simple, of course, but you got the opportunity. I loved that part of it."

Back on the grass, he had to mind-meld with the head coach and produce the kind of spread offense Hatcher had become regionally famous for, while not appearing to go rogue. Not the easiest dance after running your own show, but he adapted.

Claudette and Kennedy also came around to college football's rhythms, especially off the field—better, in some ways, than Rance did. While there were those couple of months when he had to stay on the road recruiting, during the season he was usually home at a decent hour for dinner. That was a rarity in high school, where the real work for most of the staff didn't get started until midafternoon, after classes.

Claudette thought the trade-off worked in her favor. Better overall, she figured, to put up with her husband not being there to brush his teeth before bed and say good morning at breakfast during those few months he traveled, than to deal with half a year when he didn't get home from the high school most nights until after ten, when she and Kennedy were already asleep.

"For me," Gillespie said, "to walk into the bedroom at night and give her a kiss, and pat her on the butt in the morning, it made a big difference. I was the one who was lonely."

Overall, college was a charged, cool scene. The Gillespies liked Statesboro, with its ramped-up atmosphere. Kennedy, who otherwise couldn't care less about football, rooted her heart out for her daddy's Eagles.

On the field, things didn't quite click.

At least for the head coach—which meant, finally, for the rest of the staff, too.

That was another drawback to being an assistant: You didn't control your own destiny. Somebody else's destiny controlled you.

Georgia Southern had an oddball football history. The program began in 1924, was suspended at the start of World War II, then disappeared for the next forty-one years. After raising it from the dead in '82, the school won a record six Division I-AA championships (and played in two other title games) between 1985 and 2000. Their trademark: an old-school triple-option running attack installed by bullet-headed legend Erk Russell, the longtime defensive coordinator at Georgia who'd coined the phrase "Junkyard Dawgs." His game-day ideology was simple: "If we score, we may win. If they never score, we'll never lose." His way became the Georgia Southern Way.

Two of the first three coaches to follow Russell won titles sticking to that basic schtick, but even one of those coaches was fired after winning only one title and not another. The next two coaches were less successful and quickly fired or pushed out. The last one was gone after a single season: He dumped the triple option, then went 3-8.

Six years after their last title, Georgia Southern was a major rehab project with sky-high expecations—very South Georgia. It finally looked like a great time to blow it all up and start over. So the school brought in Hatcher and wanted Gillespie to help execute the wide-open "Hatch Attack" that had worked so well, and brought Hatcher so much notoriety, at Valdosta State.

Still, it was a risky play in these parts.

"We were the third coaching staff in thirteen months—not an ideal situation," Hatcher said. "You couldn't imagine how bad a shape that program was in. I had no idea myself until I got down in it."

The first season promised better days: 7–4, including two overtime losses and a road defeat at Division I Colorado State. The Gillespie-managed offense delivered fireworks, averaging almost 37 points a game. To make the transition to college, Gillespie just did what he'd always done: watched game film every free moment he had and generally buried himself in the job.

"He doesn't have many hobbies," Hatcher allowed, "other than football."

However, after the Eagles went a middling 11-11 over the next two seasons, trigger-happy fans, alumni, and administration had had enough.

Hatcher was told he was through right after his press conference following his team's 2009 season-ending victory. He asked the athletic director to hold off releasing the news for a day, to give him time to talk with his assistants. He was given an hour. Gillespie got wind of the sacking from friends who called after hearing about it on the radio.

One coaching buddy at Vanderbilt called and told Gillespie, "Man, I'm sorry. But if you're in this business long enough, you get the opportunity to see all sides of it—from winning state championships to being fired."

Gillespie remembered, "The hardest part was having to call Kennedy and explain it to her. Because she loved Georgia Southern, loved the Eagles. I said, 'I have to coach somewhere else.' How does an eight-year-old grasp that?

"Claudette was fine," he added. "She was about like me. It's part of the business. She'd moved before. We'd go somewhere else."

They weren't the first folks to leave out of this town.

"Reach over in the corner, hand me my travelin' shoes/ You know by that, I got them Statesboro blues."

At forty, Gillespie gazed out onto college football's forever-seeming landscape and thought, *Uh-uh.*

"I didn't really relish jumping back into the rat race," he said. "You ever been to a college coaches' convention? Everybody hangs in the lobby, guys dressed in suits with résumés, and as a head coach walks by, they swarm him.

"I can't deal with that anymore. I realized I like college football. I do. But I like high school football just as good."

There was another thing. Rance vowed then that they'd move to a place their daughter could grow up in and call home—like he and Claudette could with Tiger.

There were several good high school jobs out there, including one outside Birmingham, at a big new school with state-of-the-art facilities.

The Valdosta job was the most intriguing—and potentially, some coaches around the state whispered, the most suicidal.

3

A Brief, 200-Million-Year History

or Beaches! Whales! Gnats! Lynchings!

The Gnat Line once wriggled across the middle of Georgia like the shoreline of Big Sur. From Augusta to Macon to Columbus, it was a kind of wonderful coast from hell, a two-hundred-mile stretch of towering cliffs that dropped off into to-die-for waves. The shifting, gurgling topography was laced with high winds and wild tides and whales.

That was a while ago; things cooled over the next couple of hundred millennia. Cliffs were rubbed to hills, and the salt waters receded to Florida. In their wake, there emerged a Piedmont and a Coastal Plain. The first was formed of rolling clay and hard crystalline rock; the latter was layered with a sandy residue that formed a sort of oceanless beach where gnats could breed and frolic like almost no place else.

Behold: the Gnat Line.

Geologists call it the Fall Line, where the Piedmont literally "falls off" into the Coastal Plain. This geologic stairstep can be observed from the shoals of the rivers whose waters slice through the middle of the state.

Georgia's swellest burgs once bloomed like springtime azaleas along the Gnat Line's juncture with these rivers. It became Georgia's most significant piece of real estate, a twenty-mile-wide wilderness boulevard lined with textile mills and merchant districts and warehouses stuffed with cotton.

The Gnat Line's commercial importance eventually withered, about in inverse proportion to the rise of the railroads and, by extension, Atlanta way north.

Politically, the Gnat Line had long been code for what divides North and South Georgia: Voters reside "above" or "below" it. Now, with nearly the whole length of the state either conservative Republican or Reagan Democrat, it has largely become a distinction without a difference. The two Georgias are no longer the North and the South but Atlanta and just about everyplace else.

So where the Gnat Line once divided the hill cultures from the plantation cultures, it now mostly divides a variation on the same downstate theme. Its cultural significance is mostly confined to odd rites and news items.

How to combat the grain-sized not-quite-'skeeters remains an eternal debate. Most Gnat Landers employ an almost imperceptible blow-and-dry-spit method while they talk—like ridding your tongue of a hair—to keep them from flying into their mouths. Others swear by Skin So Soft, an Avon product that some mamas still slather over their Below-the-Line babies.

A policewoman in Hinesville, home to the largest army installation east of the Mississippi, once said the gnats there were so bad they'd become a traffic hazard. All the swatting she and other officers did in the middle of the road during Fort Stewart's shift changes gave motorists dangerously misdirecting signals.

"You should see me on a military payday," she told a local newspaper. "It gets crazy."

Unable to beat them, little Camilla joined 'em: It hosts the world's only annual Gnat Days festival. Sale items include pinky-tip-sized birdhouses with GNATS inscribed over tiny perches.

Even Erk Russell jumped on the gnat bandwagon. The Georgia Southern coach once sprinkled an Iowa football field the night before a playoff game with water he pulled from a ditch that ran through his team's practice field. He hoped, he said, "some of the gnats would hatch overnight and make us feel at home."

They did.

Georgia Southern won.

◗

Valdosta sits about as far south of the Gnat Line as you can get and not be in Florida.

The town's name is a kind of Italian-for-Dummies reinterpretation of Val d'Aosta, a former governor's plantation whose own handle was lifted from an Alpine region in northwest Italy. For all its relative remoteness, the city has always cultivated an overachiever's impulse for recognition beyond its borders.

Valdosta was virtually citizenless until 1860. That's when a railroad line was laid there instead of in Troupville. The suddenly former county seat hardly blinked: Troupville packed itself up, houses and businesses and all, and resettled in Valdosta, four miles down the road.

The town's 1860 census recorded 120 whites and 46 blacks. As the first train chugged down the new track that same year on the Fourth of July, virtually the whole settlement turned out to watch. Townsfolk prepared a communal supper: barbecue.

Blessed with punishing heat and sandy loam—conditions in which football players would later thrive and throw up—Valdosta swiftly transformed itself. It went from an unsettled pine forest carpeted with wiregrass and palmetto to the world's largest inland market for Sea Island cotton, a luxury variety prized for its silky feel.

The town took off, in both size and eccentricity. Its first full-time Methodist minister was a wounded, partially paralyzed Civil War vet who preached each Sunday from the sitting position. An early music teacher was James Lord Pierpont, who wrote "Jingle Bells." Arrived in Georgia from his native Massachusetts, he also wrote "Our Battle Flag," "Strike for the South," and "We Conquer or Die," all songs penned for the Confederate Army, which he joined as a clerk, even though his Yankee father was a Union chaplain.

The town's first mayor died in Tennessee fighting for the Confederacy in a war whose battles never reached down as far as Valdosta. Its fourth mayor was the father of John Henry "Doc" Holliday, the dentist-turned-gambler-and-gunfighter who died in Colorado years after he fled the Deep South for the Wild West.

By the first decade of the next century, Valdosta had boomed so spectacularly on the back of fine cotton that it claimed the highest per capita income in America. It was a minimetropolis of about 8,000. The local Dixie League baseball team was the Valdosta Millionaires.

For black folks, however, Valdosta was a less quirky, far more treacherous terrain to navigate. Emancipation often seemed like a rumor. Following the withdrawal during Reconstruction of Union troops—an all-black garrison against whom outraged whites filed claims of abuse—the Klan commenced its reign of terror.

One black man was dragged by hooded locals from his home in the middle of the night, toted to a remote spot in the woods, then beaten to death in front of his wife. His offense: encouraging other blacks in South Georgia and North Florida to vote for candidates of the Republican Party—then still very much the party of the emancipatin' Abe Lincoln.

Other blacks in the area just disappeared.

"The land is literally strewn with deceased colored gentlemen," one black citizen wrote in a plea for help to the local paper. "Every log has one behind it . . . every frog pond contains one or more."

So in 1871 and 1872, 112 black men, women, and children—tired, angry, frightened from having had their neighbors' bodies scattered like so much cotton seed—packed up all they owned and emigrated from Lowndes County, in deepest South Georgia, to Liberia, a colony founded by free slaves in far, far-enough away West Africa.

●

By the second decade of the twentieth century, the region's lucrative long-staple cotton vanished: Boll weevils ate up the last crop in 1917.

By then, though, a whole other industry had emerged, and it already was leaving its own complicated legacy on the landscape—one that endures, in ways large and small, to this day.

Slash and longleaf pines were the beating heart of "naval stores," the industry that covered all manner of products made from pine sap. Early on, it mainly meant the stuff used to caulk and waterproof wooden ships, like tar and pitch. It later came to mean products that ranged from turpentine and paint thinner to shoe polish and chewing gum and glue.

The industry migrated en masse to Georgia from North Carolina around the same time those black folks in Lowndes County hightailed it to Liberia. The North Carolina producers came for Georgia's vast virgin forests—it's a rapacious racket—and many brought their own black laborers. By the 1880s, seven in ten turpentine workers in the state were Tar Heels. New camps seemed to crop up overnight, their numbers spreading through remote woodlands with the gusto of the native wiregrass.

Run by hard whites who employed mostly illiterate blacks, these camps quickly established an unsavory reputation throughout Georgia and Florida. Many viewed them as the South's most brutally exploitive workplaces since the abolition of slavery. They were often isolated, mercenary, largely unregulated, punitively credit-happy—and, for almost a century here, insanely profitable.

More humane camp owners resented these depictions, claiming a few rotten apples gave the whole business an undeserved bad name. These operators say they looked upon their workers as part of an extended live-in family. A hard-nosed family, to be sure, but one where they were all together in the middle of nowhere, making it as best they could, trying to scratch out a tough, uneasy living.

"I never beat one out of a dime in my life," insisted Lloyd Powell, who ran one of the last turpentine farms in the state, in Homerville. "I don't have that on my conscience."

Yet the worst of them were fueled by greed, ignorance, sadism, and woods-stilled liquor. Relics from the region's slave economy loomed everywhere. Armed guards patrolled some camps' perimeters at night to keep laborers from running off. Other camps chained workers to their beds.

More profoundly ordinary holdovers from those pre–Civil War days endured as well. Pine resin, for instance, was graded for sale by color— the lighter, or clearer, the better. The highest grades were X for extra pale, WW for water white, and WG for window glass.

Muddier grades are believed to have corresponded to the skin color of the plantation slaves who first tapped them. These slaves' passed-down first names, often designated by an initial, remained part of the industry's color-coded grading system for decades: "Nancy" (or "N," the lightest), "Mary," "Katie," "Isaac," "Harry," "George," "Frank," "Edward," "Dolly," and "Betty" (the darkest).

Or, as they once were known to family, friends, loved ones: Nancy. Mary. Katie. Isaac. Harry. George. Frank. Edward. Dolly.

And Betty.

Long-gone Betty.

The darkest.

●

Work on a turpentine farm began before dawn and ended after dusk.

"Chippers" removed the ornery bark and cut long notches, or "faces," into the sides of the trees. They then attached boxes or clay and tin cups below to collect the sap that oozed out in snowy sheets. Woodsriders clopped through on horseback in the early-morning darkness to coordinate the work and check the boxes. The harvested resin was refined in copper stills, much like bootleg whiskey, and hauled off to markets. By 1890, Georgia produced more naval stores than any other state in the country.

Camp life was usually self-contained—and wild. Most operations had their own shack housing. Some added churches that doubled as one-room schools up to sixth grade, and cemeteries. Turpentining became a womb-to-tomb, generation-to-generation affair.

Workers bought food, clothes, and supplies at company commissaries, often derided as "robbersaries" because of their high prices and unchecked credit in lieu of wages. Debts piled up so high, so quickly, that many workers could never pay them off.

Or leave.

So they ran, slipping out at night after rubbing turpentine on their bare feet or shoe bottoms to confuse the dogs that woodsriders or sheriffs sicced on them. Some owners exploited their own peers' exploitative impulses: They sent out recruiters, or "'cruiters," who sneaked into rival camps at night and won laborers' loyalties in card games. Others bribed them to switch camps with booze or offers to wipe their debts clean.

Then the cycle started all over again.

"When I got to Georgie," one workers' dirge began, "I didn't have long to stay./ I got in debt/ and had ta run away."

Other camps swelled their workforces with leased convicts. Local vagrancy laws were so arbitrary that blacks could be arrested for something as simple as walking across town without proper ID. Camp owners then "leased" these prisoners, who weren't paid until they worked off their sentences.

As outrages mounted, outcries against the industry grew.

"There are more white people involved in this diabolical practice than there were slaveholders," the Georgia Baptist Convention declared in 1926. "There are more Negroes held by these debt-slavers than were actually owned as slaves before the war between the states. The method is the only thing that has changed."

Reforms, however, were few and far between. So workers made the best of it. Drinking and gambling flourished, often encouraged by camp operators who sold liquor or had kickback deals with moonshiners. Deep-woods juke joints overflowed at night, with itinerant piano players brought in for entertainment. The "boogie-woogie blues"—hard-pounding, wildly danceable—originated in the camps of East Texas and roared across the Turpentine Belt long before the rest of the world ever heard it.

Some workers sought more psychological forms of escape. They created in their minds what the writer Zora Neale Hurston, who visited a North Florida camp during the Depression for the Federal Writers' Project, called "Negro mythical places"—wondrous dreamscapes free of all trials and tribulations. They resembled the hobos' vision of the "Big Rock Candy Mountain," a Depression-era paradise filled with "cigarette trees" and "lemonade springs" and hens who "lay soft-boiled eggs."

The fantastical world that black turpentine woodsmen called "Diddy-Wah-Diddy," Hurston wrote, "is a place of no work and no worry for man and beast . . . where even the curbstones are good sitting-chairs . . . If a traveler gets hungry all he needs to do is sit down on the curbstone and wait and soon he will hear something hollering 'Eat me! Eat me! Eat me!' and a big baked chicken will come along with a knife and fork stuck in its sides. He can eat all he wants and let the chicken go and it will go on to the next one that needs something to eat."

Eventually these laborers woke from their reveries.

"If a person could work anywhere else," acknowledged John W. Langdale, who leased a camp in 1894 that morphed through the generations into a Valdosta-based timber conglomerate, "he would."

*

A center tied to this sometimes perverse, often perverting system of debt peonage and hands-off government oversight is a center that won't always hold.

One example: the "tick wars" of the 1920s. These were skirmishes, sometimes lethal, that erupted with the invasion in Georgia and Florida of a cattle tick from Texas with a Latinate name that sounded better suited for one of Hank Williams's backsliding offspring: *Boophilus bovis*. To combat it, governments stretched a barbed-wire fence across the border shared by both states like some cattleman's premonition of the Berlin Wall.

Dipping vats were dug or built behind the fences and filled with an arsenic-laced solution. No cattle could pass from one state into the other without first going through the inspection process. This federal eradication program also required ranchers and small farmers to dunk their herds every few weeks.

By 1922, farmers in Lowndes and adjoining Echols County were dynamiting the vats and cattle pens and roughing up any agent charged with enforcing the program. In response, government agents stood guard over the vats with Browning machine guns. When that didn't slow anybody down, a fort was established on the Lowndes/Echols line and manned with armed veterans from World War I.

Casualties piled up. In Echols County, just east of Valdosta, a federal employee told a farmer searching for his missing heifer that the animal had wandered into a neighboring field and was quarantined. The two men talked amiably for a while, according to reports, until the farmer raised his shotgun and blew half the fed's face off. The farmer later admitted to the killing but was never arrested or tried.

South Georgia was one rough cotton patch, buddy.

It got rougher.

On May 19, 1918, a white mob arrived at the home of a twenty-year-old black woman named Mary Turner. They'd already been on a four-day lynching rampage, which began with the unremarkable arrest of a black nineteen-year-old named Sidney Johnson for "rolling dice." When he couldn't pay the thirty-dollar fine, Johnson was jailed until a white plantation owner named Hampton Smith did what other farmers did all the time for incarcerated black men: bailed Johnson out and put him to work to pay off his debt.

Smith had a history of cruelty to such workers and beat Johnson one day when he said he was too sick to work. Days later, Johnson fired a rifle shot through a window of Smith's plantation house, killing the owner and wounding his wife. Johnson then ran like hell.

To quell what it determined to be an uprising, the mob hanged at least eight black men those next four days—including Mary Turner's husband, Hayes. Eight months pregnant with her third child, Mary refused to stay silent and threatened to swear out warrants on those involved in her husband's murder.

That's when the mob showed up, captured Mary, and carried her to a deserted riverbank. There they hanged her upside down from a tree, doused her with gasoline and motor oil, and set her on fire. Somebody then cut her unborn baby from her stomach and crushed it in the dirt. Afterward, hundreds of bullets were fired into her lifeless body. An empty whiskey bottle plugged with a dead cigar butt marked their graves.

White folks in the area went mute, but a letter written by a state legislator to the white-run *Augusta Chronicle* was reprinted in black newspapers around the country: "Lowndes County—one of the most prosperous and progressive counties in the state; with as cultured and noble people in it as are to be found anywhere on earth—what will be its answer? What will its good people do to punish this crime of crimes and . . . wipe away this stain?

"Or are such people outnumbered within its borders? Must its law officers give more heed to the ignorant and lawless of its population than to those who have made Lowndes County what it is—one of the best counties in Georgia?

"It remains to be seen."

For black citizens, that question was open-and-shut: Five hundred of them fled the county as fast as they could.

●

Ninety-one years later, on a Saturday in the middle of May 2009, a long caravan wound its way like a mechanical ant trail through the two-lane roads of rural Lowndes County. In the tradition of the region, other cars on the road pulled over or stopped to let the caravan pass.

"White folks, they thought it was a funeral procession," chuckled one black preacher who made the trip. "I was amused to see them stop. Mary Turner got respect in her death that she didn't get in her life."

The caravan rolled on until it came to the fork of a still-unpaved road near the banks of the Little River. Everyone stepped from their cars and trucks and gathered in a circle. One of Mary Turner's relatives stepped forward to speak, but choked up before he could utter a word and sat back down. A wooden cross was later hammered into the soft dirt to commemorate the long-buried tragedy.

"Some may wonder, why bring up the past?" the *Valdosta Daily Times* editorialized about the event. "Why dwell on such a terrible thing that happened generations ago? Why commemorate crimes committed by people who have likely long since passed?"

The editorial then attempted to answer its own questions, echoing Faulkner's famous "the past isn't even past" characterization of the South:

"The past lingers. It haunts the present. [It] hangs heavy on the possible dialogue between black and white even in the 21st century."

●

By the second decade of the twenty-first century, Valdosta had evolved into a town big enough to get lost in but still small enough to find your way back—just keep turning left. Many of its civic leaders harbored visions of it becoming something grander, while many of its residents longed for the days when it was too small to care.

"We lost all the Mayberry we had," lamented one longtimer.

Valdosta's population indeed had mushroomed, from about 15,000 when Bazemore began coaching to about 50,000 in 2010. (The county had swelled to more than twice that size.) About a third of the town's residents lived below the poverty level—twice the state's rate—while agriculture and timber still accounted for much of a tight clique's considerable wealth.

Those push-pull tensions between what the place was and what it should be seemed embedded in Valdosta's 150-year-old DNA. They gave even its wealthiest citizenry and sizable professional class both an outsized outlook and a short-sleeved down-homeness. One millionaire tobacco farmer in jeans and muddy boots stood for several minutes in a local diner one Saturday morning picking the pennies out of his pocket to give the cashier exact change.

First lesson an outsider learned: Underestimate folks here at your own peril.

The town's biggest employers were the state university, the regional medical center, and Moody Air Force Base. Yet men in their thirties and forties still debated over lunch counters and steam tables—and in the upscale taqueria across from the Walmart—which summer job was harder: baling hay or cropping tobacco? (Consensus: cropping tobacco.) The seasons still flipped by for many here on an agricultural calendar.

"Whatever that pesticide is they spray on the cotton, when I smell that in the air, to me that's fall," Dirk Harrell, a dental equipment salesman, mused one October afternoon.

Cotton fields still spread far and wide outside of town, but only a handful of working farms remained inside the city limits. There was a patch near the high school, another beside an elementary school. Both bloomed each fall like prickly, snow-white reminders of the town's complex agrarian past.

Despite the sprawl of chain stores and franchise restaurants that accounted for much of the last decade's commercial development, those days didn't feel all that far removed. Any table could suddenly feel like a farm table; families and even young couples out for the night still bowed their heads in prayer inside Sonny's Real Pit Bar-B-Q before digging into their All U Can Eat Sweet & Smokey Rib plates and Gone Fishin' platters.

●

Moody Air Force Base opened just north of town in 1941 and soon established itself as a major post (George W. Bush trained there in the '60s and dated a former Wildcat mascot). It injected the area with a steady stream of new, outsider blood—and a ready pool of football talent, if Valdosta's rivals were to be believed.

Interstate 75, much like the old rail line that created the town, opened on the city's far west edge a few decades later and became a kind of endless, if mostly drive-by, lifeline to the outside world.

It rebranded Valdosta as a convenient regional way station for tourists traveling south to Orlando, for manufacturers looking for cheap land and nonunion labor in the middle of resource-rich countryside, and for cocaine cowboys eyeing remotely convenient landing spots to refuel or unload between Miami and points north. Rumors still persisted of prominent businesses in town founded on start-up money made from daring one-and-out drug hauls.

Big busts in the early '90s slowed that trade. Now the major drug distributors came from Mexico. They wound their way up from the border, moving stealthily through Texas, like *Boophilus bovis*, until they reached Florida and hooked up with I-75. Valdosta became this cocaine corridor's default pit stop.

Of course, legit businesses thrived here because of that proximity to Florida, too. Even with a strip-mall-sized airport that accommodated three commuter flights daily to and from Atlanta, Valdosta could feel more North Florida than South Georgia, more Spanish moss than kudzu. Unlike in the days of those long-ago tick wars, the state line just south of town was now largely invisible; dozens of Wildcats had lived and played at one point in Florida, with relatives on both side of the line.

That porous back-and-forth between the two states had made the city a capital of the borderlands between Tallahassee and Jacksonville, giving Valdosta more of North Florida's restless energy than South Georgia's find-some-shade pokiness.

The two regions even shared a prejudice.

"We like North Florida," one Valdostan explained. "It's South Florida we hate."

●

A two-story monument of Italian-quarried white marble rose from the old courthouse lawn. Loitering on top since 1911, the year it was dedicated by the United Daughters of the Confederacy: a life-sized Johnny Reb in all his frozen-in-time glory—uniform buttoned, weight shifted to his right leg, hands gripped around the business end of a musket.

Inscribed beneath his boots: "LEST WE FORGET"/ COMRADES/ OUR CONFEDERATE DEAD.

On the back: THE PRINCIPLES FOR WHICH THEY FOUGHT LIVE ETERNALLY.

Yet the cozy, low-rise downtown that this infantryman gazed upon today looked to be doing its darnedest to forget all that. Even in the middle of a recession, its two main streets were lined with plum-colored banners—not the Stars and Bars—hung from old-timey streetlamps. Their casual logos featured a cup of steaming coffee, and each banner contained a single word that encapsulated an action civic leaders hoped that today's comrades would take up: DINE, SHOP, LIVE.

The small-town South isn't what it used to be in much of the South. The rest of the world is now just a tweet, iPhone finger tap, or TiVo'd episode of *The Real Housewives of Orange County* away. You'd be hard-pressed to arrive these days in even the remotest settlement below the Mason-Dixon Line, let alone below the Gnat Line, and not find a spot where you could order a skinny latte, a sesame-encrusted yellow fin tuna, or some buttermilk fried calamari.

Within a block of Valdosta's Confederate memorial stood a café that served chocolate martinis and South Beach tacos, a combination hot dog stand/vintage vinyl store, and a pub with microbrews and sculpted burgers. There was even a hookah lounge that advertised fifty varieties of flavored *shisha*.

Or, as it used to be called in these parts, "tobacco."

4

The Trinity

or Gucci Mane, Young Jeezy, Eminem

Just days after students returned to Valdosta High from Christmas break, Reggie McQueen, a rising senior and aspiring rapper, did what he usually did at school: strolled the halls, his long dark dreads swaying around his shoulders like Rasta jump ropes.

Until somebody stopped him.

It wasn't a teacher, Reggie didn't think, though by then he'd missed enough school—including much of November and December after a shootout left his cousin dead and Reggie shaken—that he couldn't really be certain. It wasn't Principal Boling, either. He'd seen Boling plenty the past few years.

Yet the white dude with the brainiac's forehead, sharp nose, and neatly barbered hair sure acted like he knew Reggie.

"Why weren't you at school yesterday? I don't want to hear any excuses. Don't miss any more. Here's my number. Call me if you don't think you can make it," he told Reggie, just like that.

Almost as quickly, he was gone.

Left standing in the hallway to process the guy's no-bull delivery and bird-of-prey stare, Reggie now had a pretty good idea who the white dude was: new coach.

New coach got his attention.

If he hadn't been a football player, Reggie wouldn't have stood out all that much in the halls of Valdosta High. They looked and sounded like the halls of most city public high schools: crowded, loud, teeming with teen drama and affected cool. Packs of kids sported dreads, cornrows, faux-hawks, buzz cuts, frat shags, dyed extensions, white-bowed pony-tails, goatees, soul patches—you name it. Each pack seemed forever headed in its own direction and nowhere in particular.

All at once.

Kids said "yes, sir" and "no, ma'am" a lot more than in almost any other part of the country; when one player posted a raw Lil Wayne lyric on his Facebook page about "bitch niggas," Wildcat radio announcer Monty Long posted an admonishing "easy," to which the player responded, for all the thuggin' world to see, "Yes sir mr long."

Kids here did, to a greater or lesser degree, what kids do: hunted and fished, partied and hung out, listened to music and played video games, studied and slacked, smoked dope and had sex, read the Bible and went to church. Everybody knew everybody. The most common cultural touchstones were God and hip-hop. Kids here saw little irony in quoting Gucci Mane, Young Jeezy, and Eminem in the same breath as God the Father, God the Son, and God the Holy Ghost.

Beneath the polite, raised-right, media-saturated surface, though, things could get messy, as they did at any school of 1,800 kids, about two-thirds of whom qualified for free or reduced lunches (that number jumped to more than 70 percent of the black students), and almost a third of whom wouldn't graduate.

School social workers drove each day to kids' houses to talk with parents they couldn't call: Parents with drug problems either didn't own phones or used prepaid cells whose numbers changed continually. Social workers performed what one staffer called "Band-Aid therapy."

"Kid comes in with bruises, we document and move on to the next case," said Deanna Folsom, the Valdosta schools' social services coordinator. "Child is found cutting herself in the bathroom, we document and move on to the next case."

A problem that had become epidemic in some neighborhoods but remained largely contained on campus was gangs. Local police had identified several dozen different gangs in town, most of them affiliated with the Crips or the Bloods, with names like 9 Trey, SMM (Sex Money Murder), and G-Shine. While a lot of the supposed gang activity was wannabe, rap-influenced posing, there was enough of the real thing that the cops now had a gang task force.

Yet school grounds were recognized as neutral territory. Colors were banned, though that sometimes got squishy.

"Wearing a red bandanna [Crips] out of their pocket? That's too far," said one social worker who'd had arguments with local cops over football players she believed were gang members. "But show up wearing red pants, what can you say? A tattooed six-point star [Folk Nation symbol]—what can you say?"

A bigger concern, especially as the recession hardened and jobs disappeared, was that more students' homes lost their power or water because of unpaid bills and kids showed up at school unwashed and wearing dirty clothes.

Or students simply lost their homes. There were more than a hundred homeless kids throughout the system. Those families often lived in hotels that rented by the week and didn't require a deposit—many of the same hotels, social workers sighed wearily, occupied by registered sex offenders.

"The economy effects everything," Folsom said.

There had also been an uptick in students who showed up at counselors' offices and announced they'd been "put out"—kicked out of their homes without anywhere to go and living from friend's couch to friend's couch. Many of them fell through the cracks in the social safety net and couldn't get or afford follow-up help.

"Sometimes you hope a child commits a crime so they'll get the help they need," one social worker admitted. "It's sad, but it's a daily thing with us."

A lot of kids worked and just hoped to have a meal at night, or a place to sleep, and didn't see much down-the-road value in an education. So they left before they graduated. It had gone on like that for generations; go back far enough in many of these kids' family trees and there was a turpentine camp somewhere.

The challenge for teachers, counselors, and administrators was motivating students from unmotivated homes.

"There are some who have that initiative from the inside, who say they want better," said Helen Jackson, a veteran Valdosta counselor. "And there are some who say, 'This is the way it is, and it's just going to be this way.'"

A dozen or so high school girls got pregnant every year. Often they weren't the first in their families to have a baby at that age. There was even a saying among some boys, recited like a quarterback barking out a count over center: "sixteen, thirty-two, forty-eight"—ages of the new mother, her mother, and her grandmother, all sixteen years apart.

Many of the girls informed their counselors that they were just going on maternity leave and would be back to school soon to pick up where they left off.

"And I have to say," Helen Jackson said, "'There is no maternity leave, my dear.'"

●

"The lure of the street here is really strong," said Dr. Bill Cason, the school system's seventy-year-old superintendent. "Keeping kids separated from that street environment is a challenge.

"It's not a lot different than Detroit or Chicago or San Francisco. You'll find pockets in those cities that are the same way. Kids come from housing projects, multiple families living in one residence. It's a breeding ground for trouble and crime and drugs—you name it."

Yet in the last few years, the day-to-day threat level inside Valdosta's halls had dropped dramatically, while an us-against-them camaraderie among the students had grown. With the hiring of Cason and the arrival of a new principal two years earlier, rules had been tightened and consequences for breaking them upped.

Both students and teachers griped about some of the excesses. Principal Gary Boling often walked the halls with a whistle and a walkie-talkie, for instance, and he'd sometimes dress down a teacher in front of students and colleagues. Still, the new regime generally had been effective at making the school a more livable, cohesive place.

While Valdosta High's overall results on the state's standardized tests ranked it in the bottom third of Georgia's public high schools, and its average SAT scores in reading and math didn't add up to 900, graduation rates and reading scores were up, truancy rates and on-campus fights way down.

"Four years ago, it was a different school," Cason said. "Discipline was out of control; there were fights every day. Now you'll find some disrespectful kids like you'll find anywhere, but for the most part, you'll see kids in proper dress, kids interested in learning. There's been a cultural shift there."

These days, the halls were more likely to erupt in more typical teen disquiet.

"One day, everything will be chill and okay," explained junior cheerleader Morgan Long, daughter of the Wildcat radio announcer. "Next day, all kinds of drama will happen and that's all you'll hear all day— how someone was hanging out with someone else's boyfriend, how that person found out about it."

Her tone as she described these serial melodramas: bored, bored, bored.

The whimsies of many students—at least students not scuffling for that night's dinner or a place to sleep—sounded like a timeless mix of Eisenhower-era banalities and Obama-era technology. Their constant texts, tweets, and Facebook updates were unlocked, open-to-everyone diaries.

Strung together, they formed their own kind of poetry:

"jersey shore:)"

"just got pulled over:("

"sooo my toe nail just randomly fell off?"

"soooo tired of hearing about lindsey lohan"

"should I wear my hair straight or curled for my senior picture? In a dilemma!"

Yet there was always the other side:

"wen yu raised da wrng way yuh kan die anyday"

"The Good Weed Smoke make the bullshit go away"

"Im Just Tryna Beat The Odds"

More to the point:

"shit just got real"

From the outside, the school's 1973 building on the scrub-pine edge of town (the old in-town school, across from the stadium where the team still played, burned down) was a mostly windowless, featureless single-story study in poured cement and confused geometry. Stretch some razor wire around the grassy perimeter and it would look like the most accommodating medium-security prison in three states.

A hulking performing arts center, beautiful on the inside, dwarfed everything else, including the front-lawn trailers. A pair of transplanted palm trees, propped up by a couple of wooden poles beside the school's front entrance, did their haggard best to give the place a bit of subtropical panache.

Inside, it was a Pentagon-like maze of perpetual turns and unforeseen dead ends. One recent graduate said he *never* figured it all out, that "there are parts of that building I've never even seen."

The walls were cinder block, the floors linoleum, the lights fluorescent. It was hard to walk from one classroom to the next in the constantly veering-off maze and not think you were getting a gurney's-eye view of a big-city hospital.

To dress it all up, inspirational slogans and Twitter-brief testimonials were on a wall around every bend.

DON'T COUNT THE DAYS, MAKE THE DAYS COUNT. THE GREATEST ABILITY IS DEPENDABILITY. IT'S BETTER TO BE ALONE THAN IN BAD COMPANY.

Near an entrance to the cafeteria: HEADS UP! PANTS UP! GRADES UP!

Other posters featured a range of celebrities (country singer Taylor Swift, basketball star Vince Carter) who asked the question around every bend, GOT MILK? Among the snack machines' classic go-with-milk offerings: Skittles, Hot Cheese Curls, Pop-Tarts, Brownie Crisps, and Rice Krispies Treats.

Despite the PANTS UP! exhortation, dress was all over the map: jeans, shorts, khakis; heels and flip-flops; pressed shirts and ties, right next to tees.

Some kids looked on top of the world—not much matched the confidence of a confident seventeen-year-old—while others plainly looked lost. Kids with disabilities, unable to see well or walk at all, were greeted or ignored like everybody else: mainstreaming at its tough-love finest. One legally deaf football player had a specialist who accompanied him all day; she signed for him from his first class in the morning to the end of football practice that night.

Yet most kids appeared oblivious to this crucible's competing, intersecting forces: white and black; country club and projects; two-parent and no-parent; daddy's girls and baby mamas. They relished the moments when it all worked.

"It's not like I like it," one kid said of the school's odd, even intoxicating allure, despite everything it had going against it, "but I don't want to leave it."

●

Students tended to self-segregate by race ("It is a black school, so when you see a white kid you wonder, hmmm," one black student said), but there were so many exceptions it could hardly be called the rule. There was the usual breakdown of high school cliques, but these kids often segregated as much by motivation and ability as by race or income level, a pattern that had grown most among black students.

The advanced placement (AP) classes and International Baccalaureate program were whiter than the school overall. In fact, IB had been instituted three years earlier as a clear lure for white parents reluctant to send their kids to a school that hadn't met the state's Academic Yearly Progress standards for four years. Yet even those classes had their own Colors of Benetton quality.

"We were sitting at a table one day and we all looked at each other and said, 'Wow,'" said Ellen Chiang, an IB student who was half Asian, half Brazilian. Her tablemates that day: two Indian nationals, a Puerto Rican, a mixed-race African American, and a couple of Vietnamese. In general, though, Valdosta's diversity didn't extend much beyond black and white.

The n-word—that old Southern bugaboo—was common currency among black kids, as it was everywhere, to the constant befuddlement of older whites who'd tried to excise the word from their own vocabularies, or at least stash it someplace safe while outsiders were around.

Yet the word was hardly taboo among white kids. They used it almost exclusively when they talked to black classmates, and particularly in texts and bromantic exchanges on Facebook and Twitter (White kid: "you my nigga boy!" Black kid's reply: "you my nigga bro").

"If you walk up and call a black kid a nigga, they'll call us crackers," said junior Cole Emmons, who was white. "But we make sure and call them nigg*as*. There's a big difference between nigg*a* and nigger."

James Eunice, a white reserve on the football team and the only Wildcat senior in the IB program, added, "I end up talking more like them than them talking like me."

This mix-'n'-match signifying was summed up by the hallway greeting that tight end Jay Rome, who was black, reserved for Eunice, a longtime friend: "My brutha from another mutha!"

Race jokes were constant and offhanded. These were sons and daughters of the Deep South who'd been raised virtually their whole lives on a mash-up of explicit hip-hop lyrics, Black History Month field trips, and HERITAGE NOT HATE bumper stickers.

There were still what one counselor called "outliers"—students, both white and black, who were unrepentantly racist or still angry about the past—but they were now more sect than consensus.

As much as blacks and whites mixed in all sorts of settings, however, interracial dating was still largely frowned upon.

"Most girls I know text message their black guy friends, hug them when they see them, but their parents will have a problem if they date one of them," said Lindsey Parker, a white junior. "It's always the girls who are looked at more negatively because of it. People say they're doing it to get attention, or they have bad reputations, or they couldn't find anyone else. People are going to talk about you. I can think of several girls who like black boys," she added, "but they won't date them because of what their parents will say."

Still, most students here occupied a kind of post-post-politically-correct universe: a place that at once exaggerated and obliterated their differences.

In one history class, a black kid asked a white kid for a piece of paper. When the white kid said he didn't have one, the black kid shook his head and sighed, "It's 'cause I'm black, isn't it?" The whole class broke up.

When a black girl showed up after school at an Asian girl's house, she was greeted by her friend mock-announcing from behind the door,

"No blacks allowed!" A few minutes later, the two headed out together for something to eat.

That kind of racial vaudeville rolled right onto the football field, where there were about a dozen white kids—and only two starters who weren't kickers—out of around a hundred varsity players. On the sideline during one steaming afternoon practice, a half-dozen Wildcats, white and black, engaged in a kind of joke-telling one-upmanship to pass the time.

White kid: "What's the difference between lynching black people and dog fighting? Dogfighting's still legal."

Black kid: "Whaddaya call a white person you set on fire? A firecracker."

White kid: "What's the difference between a park bench and a black person? A park bench can support a family of four."

White kid: "What's the difference between a white Jew and a black Jew? The black Jew has to sit in the back of the oven."

They howled and howled.

"White, black, Asian, Hispanic—everybody's fair game," said Joy Fondren Eldridge, a popular AP history teacher who graduated from Lowndes High in the mid-'90s.

"The first few times it happened, I found myself holding my breath, waiting to see what happened. But these kids see nothing wrong with it. It's kind of a free-for-all. They have fun with it.

"Some of the teachers and I have talked about it—it's different than when we were coming up. It's like they're on a completely different level. They realize how they're perceived in the community, and they make light of it. They kind of embrace it.

"For a lot of people, there's definitely culture shock," Eldridge added, saying that there were teachers who had fled to whiter schools, like Lowndes. "It's a unique place to be."

There was still a line that couldn't be crossed. It was just harder to find it or even know it was there, movable as it was with the day, the mood, the circumstance.

It lurked.

As one junior girl put it, "In an instant, it can change from being funny to throwing punches."

So while Valdosta High's hallways were locker-lined crucibles for all things teen, they turned mostly quiet now after the classroom doors closed, except for a few stragglers and dodgers.

Like Reggie.

That early hallway encounter with Gillespie came at a providential time for Reggie. He appeared to have the athleticism, dedication, and football IQ to play college ball, but he needed to get more motivated in the classroom to step anywhere near a college campus—something no one in his family had ever even considered.

His mother was pregnant with Reggie at thirteen, had him four days after her fourteenth birthday. Reggie remembered his father in and out of jail, mostly on drug-related charges. Neither his mother nor his father finished high school.

Reggie had already contemplated big life changes before Gillespie stopped him. He'd missed most of his sophomore season after a burglary arrest (he said he was just a lookout). The arresting officer recalled that the dreadlocked, tatted-to-the-max Reggie cried real tears as he was taken out of the school, asking over and over, *"Can I still play football?"*

He returned to play his junior season. Only weeks after it ended—and about two months before he met Gillespie—Reggie watched as his cousin was shot to death in a hail of bullets at a housing project across town from the one in which Reggie then lived.

One minute, Reggie stood beside his cousin. Next minute, somebody started shooting, his cousin went down, and Reggie looked up to see a gun pointed between his eyes.

In all, eleven people were hit that afternoon. Only Reggie's cousin died. A few days later, Reggie eulogized and buried his best friend in the world.

Shit'll make you think.

"I been in this black world," Reggie said matter-of-factly. "It's hard."

5

Building a Team

or Anybody Eligible?

Reggie was just one of dozens of projects on Gillespie's headache list since he was named coach two days before Christmas.

He had to hire assistants, update equipment, comb through budgets (he was also athletic director), fill holes in the schedule, generate goodwill in the community—and get enough players academically eligible to field a team. The day he arrived at Valdosta, he said, twenty-seven kids couldn't play because of failing grades.

Tucker Pruitt, a young assistant Gillespie hired from Georgia Southern to coach wide receivers and be academic coordinator, said of the situation they faced, "It was astonishing the number of guys failing. Not one or two classes, but sometimes three and all four classes. Some weren't even borderline F's—they were twenties and thirties. It was eye-opening for me.

"They'd been in that period where one coach had been fired and there was almost two months before Rance was hired and here," Pruitt added. "So there was nobody pushing them, talking with them every day, emphasizing their grades. Kids are kids—if you ain't putting your thumb down on them all the time, they'll take advantage of it."

This was especially true, he said, at the winningest high school football program in America.

"At a place like this, a lot of them don't care about anything but football—the dream of playing for the Wildcats," said Pruitt, a former Valdosta State quarterback whose father coached seven Florida state title teams before he left to coach in Fitzgerald, Bazemore's hometown.

The first thing Gillespie instituted was mandatory study hall after school ended and before practice began. He also required weekly updates from teachers on grades and behavior.

"They all want to go to college to play, and football is a great tool to keep them in the classroom," Pruitt explained. "It gives them hope. It pushes them. You use their ambition to get them to do what they need to do.

"The reality is most of them are not going to go to college," he said. "But if at the end of the day it pushes them to have some success academically, then I think it's worth it."

●

Gillespie's list went on.

At the top: quarterback. Last year's starter, Dashay March, was tossed out of school after the season. Dashay now was trying to get eligible at the system's alternative school, where he'd also soon be suspended.

As for the returning backup: same thing. He'd been suspended and sent to the alternative school, too. By summer, he'd be arrested and sent to juvie.

Gillespie knew things had gotten crazy at Valdosta, but *man* . . .

Yet Gillespie didn't let problems sit. He was like a shark that way, continually feeding on whatever obstacle stood in his path. So not long after students returned from Christmas break, around the time of his verbal drive-by with Reggie, he fetched Ryan Whilden, a rising senior he hoped might be his new quarterback.

On the surface, Ryan seemed an unlikely choice. He was a laid-back white kid whose dad raised bees to pollinate crops. He was a baseball player who transferred into the city system in eighth grade from Lakeland, a rural town of 3,000 in adjoining Lanier County. His close-cropped dirty-blond hair accentuated a pair of pink scars that swooped across his face: Ryan's head went through the windshield of his brother's pickup when they hit a tree riding around behind his house.

Before ninth grade, football to Ryan was "something you did in somebody's backyard," he said. Baseball was his sport; he'd become a go-to pitcher and clutch third baseman during the high school team's deep run into the playoffs. He did play JV football as a freshman and sophomore but didn't go out for the team his junior year. The previous coach had told him to run fifty gassers—sprints from sideline to sideline and back—before a summer workout. In his mild, understated way, Ryan told the coach, "Well, that's okay." Then he left practice and didn't return.

"That's fifty gassers I'm never going to run," he said to himself on his way out.

Yet despite his lack of speed, strength, and body tone—you didn't have to squint much to picture him sweating through an afternoon on a riding mower—Ryan was one of those kids who just seemed to have a feel for the way games were played. A lot of kids around here were like that. Hand them a ball, any ball, and they'd figure out a way to throw it, hit it, catch it, kick it, shoot it, stop it, or score with it. It's the quality that Bobby Hooks, the old coach who led Valdosta to its first championship back in 1940, spotted in the local gene pool more than seven decades earlier.

"I've been playing sports since I was walking," Ryan said. "I think I can pick up any ball and be good at it—tennis, soccer.

"The only thing I can't do is play guitar," he added in the slow drip-drip-drip of words that for him passed as normal conversation. "I play piano a little bit. But sports just comes natural."

Then, as if noting one more victory for nature over nurture, Ryan added, "That's just how it is around here."

Gillespie also knew that Ryan had decent grades (*eligible!*) and seemed up to the task of learning his wide-open spread offense, a Byzantine assortment of multiple formations, men in motion, and defensive reads codified in language that even the football literate could find tough to decipher.

So, sitting in Gillespie's temporary office one of his first days back from break, Ryan heard the new coach out. His first impression as he sat across from Gillespie: *really* smart. He also caught a good vibe off him. The guy knew football and football players, especially quarterbacks. Every quarterback he'd coached at Peach County went on to play college ball.

Gillespie didn't sugarcoat anything, but he also had a sly, easy wit honed from a lifetime spent in locker rooms and coaches' offices and on the punishing side of the scout team. He understood Man Code. He was both comfortable in and able to confront the new world that Ryan and his fellow twenty-first-century teammates lived in: a tattooed, always-texting, hip-hop-listening, self-involved, softening world that drove most adults nuts.

Gillespie believed football was one of the few ways left to counter all that. He was old-school tough but new-school adaptable. He wasn't one of those guys who longed for the days of no water breaks. This was a coach who'd run you ragged in practice, tell you to suck it up when you came limping out of a pile, but then later call you into his office to show you something cool on YouTube.

Gillespie was the new breed.

Hardass 2.0.

As he sat with the new coach, Ryan knew one thing that Gillespie also knew: This team had a ton of senior talent that hadn't come close yet to realizing its potential.

The 'Cats' run of fallow years wasn't because Valdosta's soil had turned barren and stopped producing great football players; there wasn't a strain of weevil that had devoured all the athletes following the school's last title, back in 1998, like it had all that Sea Island cotton back in 19-whatever.

As far as athletes this coming season, Valdosta was loaded. Of the more than thirty seniors who'd form the core of a still-unsettled team, there were as many as a half-dozen Football Bowl Subdivision (what used to be called Division I-A) prospects, and potentially that many more who could go on to play at smaller schools—providing, of course, they qualified academically.

Among the standout seniors: Freak, Bee, Swoll, Poo (that was Reggie), J-Will, Jarquez S. (as well as Jarquez B.), C-lo, and Yontell. Most of them had played together their whole lives.

The kicker was back, too. A soccer-playing, sun-bleached Widespread Panic freak with a skater's 'tude and Eminem's baby face, Zach Wang returned for his senior season with redemption on his mind. Zach had missed three field goals last year during a 3-point loss to the eventual state runner-up. When Zach walked into school the following Monday, every kid in his first-block class stood up and imitated the referee's hand-crossing signal for "no good."

"I had to walk out," Zach said. "It's Valdosta—they just expect you to go out and win a game. You feel like you have to be perfect."

He shrugged. "At least I didn't miss four."

There were juniors who'd also have an impact. Among them was a deli-tray sampler of nicknames: Meat, Ham, Cookie. Others included Wake, Jarvis, Hester, Fason, Tyran, and can't-miss-him Terry Allen, whose water-balloon shape and pitch-black complexion would prompt some highbrow heckling later in the season from opposing fans in suburban Atlanta. They'd reference the title character from the film *Precious*.

Long after that, in response to something else, Terry would tweet: "lite skin people are overated #teamdarkskin."

The cream of the Wildcat crop was two of the country's most sought-after players.

At 6'6" and 240 pounds, with good speed, pillowy hands, and an impeccable pedigree, Jay Rome was listed by ESPN.com and other recruiting sites as the country's best high school tight end. Every college had a crush on him: Alabama, Notre Dame, Florida, Oregon, Michigan.

Jay was smart, with a better than 3.6 grade point average, including a year in the IB program. Personable, too. One white teacher joked with Jay's mother that she wanted to adopt him, that's how much she liked just being around him.

A naturally fluid athlete—"He looks effortless compared to other guys his size," enthused Georgia coach Mark Richt, an early suitor—Jay also was one of the state's top basketball prospects.

Yet he'd remained largely unchallenged and unrefined because of his size and native talent. Few coaches, it seemed, were willing to push him.

That made Jay ripe for a brainiac taskmaster like Gillespie. He craved somebody who'd drive, sculpt, and tweak him into what he yearned to be more than anything else: heir to his father's legacy as the greatest athlete South Georgia had ever seen.

Stan Rome was a two-sport *Parade* All American in high school, an NBA and NFL draft pick, and then a four-year wide receiver for the Kansas City Chiefs. He still held Valdosta records for most pass receptions and receiving yards in a season, set back when he was a sophomore in 1971, Bazemore's last, best year.

The only part of his father's story Jay didn't care to replicate was the cocaine habit that blew up Stan's pro career and left him with a bullet in his head.

Stan survived that. Now he worked to make sure Jay didn't screw up, too. So without a word from anyone, Stan became a kind of unofficial addition to Gillespie's staff. Ball cap pulled over his graying head, tobacco bulging in one cheek, he stopped in Gillespie's office anytime he was up at the school. He also crab-walked with his crooked cane out to the middle of practice and sat in the locker room during halftime of every game.

Didn't bother Gillespie a bit. He read several things in Stan right off: a deep knowledge of the game that you only acquire from playing it at the most competitive level; a natural bond with the bulk of Gillespie's players, who grew up poor, black, and fatherless, like Stan; and a profound link to Valdosta's glory years, a connection that had been neglected or broken for too long. Gillespie believed that link had to be mended if the school's glory was ever going to be reclaimed.

There was one other thing. Gillespie never mentioned it, but any smart white coach at a majority-black school had to be aware of it. Stan was widely respected throughout the black community, and having him on your side didn't hurt, especially during a time when the town's racial politics were in flux.

The previous fall, Cason, the white, rattlesnake-hunting superintendent, who worked summers as a teen on a turpentine farm, refused to let students watch a back-to-school speech beamed live into classrooms by the country's first African American president.

The black community hit the roof. They packed school board meetings and demanded Cason's resignation. Some asked Stan's wife, LaVerne, to lobby the football team to boycott a game (she declined).

Others wanted to form their own search committee to find a black head football coach.

So Gillespie could use some backup, and Stan had no problem providing it. White officials had courted him before for the same reason—get a prominent, well-liked black guy on your side and you're given the benefit of the doubt. Stan went along with it when he thought it benefited the whole community.

"I played that game all my life," he said. "You got to be able to deal with it. You have to use it when you can to bring about the greater good, while at the same time not be a token, or be part of the problem."

Besides, Stan liked Gillespie. The two bonded over their shared passion for football and the confounding needs of many of Valdosta's players. Each admired the other.

As Gillespie put it, "Stan is a huge asset. He and I never really sat down and talked about our values. It's just one of those things where you know we're on the same page. He loves these kids, and what he does he's doing for the right reasons."

Gillespie added, "Stan cares about this program on a level a whole lot deeper than the fact that his son plays here."

So Gillespie embraced a fact of Valdosta life, circa 2010: If you have Jay Rome, you have Stan Rome, too.

And vice versa.

He could win with that.

*

The Wildcats' other senior prodigy, Malcolm Mitchell, was an even more beguiling prospect.

Known to teammates as Tampa, where he'd once lived, Malcolm was a lightning-fast, bully-tough wide receiver who just might be the best pure athlete in the state. He was a ropy 6'1" 187 pounds, with 4.4 speed and a heat-seeking missile's instinct for the ball.

Beyond the physical attributes, Malcolm was a kind of classic abstract expressionist. His laid-back manner masked a complex grid of influences and experiences—single mom, gone dad, stint in juvie, troubled-history brother—that he seemed to channel each time he went up for a ball. That's when he released all his . . . *stuff* in a knowing blur of spontaneous, uninhibited athleticism. He controlled his chaos. Malcolm could deconstruct it all in the retelling, could talk about the strange, clear voice in his head that foretold his every move, but during games he didn't overthink it.

On the field, Malcolm just "did."

What that meant in ballspeak to Gillespie and Ryan: There wasn't a pass Tampa couldn't get, a tackle he couldn't shed, a defender he couldn't outrun.

Yet he'd started most of the previous season at defensive back, where "'cruiters" from Alabama, Florida, and nearly every other SEC school saw him as a four- or five-star prospect. There just weren't that many speed demons out there who could change direction on the defensive side the way Tampa could, like a bat, and who enjoyed contact as much as he did. The kid was an assassin—a bright, handsome, self-effacing assassin.

It didn't make sense to Gillespie to leave him out there on defense, where he'd get the chance to change a game maybe a half-dozen times a Friday night. Out in space as a receiver, Tampa could change a game every time he touched the ball. Gillespie planned to get him the ball early, often, and every other chance he got.

Before he could do anything with him, though, Gillespie had to earn Malcolm's trust—no easy task. Like many of the other kids who played for Valdosta, Malcolm had no relationship with his birth father and wasn't eager to get close to a new, surrogate one in the form of a coach, even if it was just temporary. After all, the last surrogate-dad coach was already fired and gone.

"I ain't too good on the trust thing," Malcolm explained, in the same just-chillin' tone he used when he talked about how he slept on the floor when he and his mother lived in his grandmother's house, and how that arrangement had felt "just like sleeping in a bed to me."

He continued, "People tell you something and don't do it, that's what makes me mad the most. By him [Gillespie] telling us he was going to do all this stuff, it didn't mean anything. Him saying it, I didn't listen.

"To me," he said, "you have to show me something. I can look some-one in the eye—my mom does it to us—and I can look at them and say, 'No. You're not telling the truth.'"

Earning his best player's trust was a big hoop for a first-year coach at Valdosta High to jump through. With most players, a little Psych 101 worked just fine, but Malcolm was a more evolved breed of cat. Malcolm had some graduate-level stuff going on.

Meantime, Gillespie had a team to put together, a brotherhood to create, kids to get eligible. By spring, however, more and more of his time was eaten up by recruiters who went through him to get to Jay and Malcolm and a handful of others. So after he flailed around for a few weeks and failed to gain Malcolm's trust, Gillespie took another tack.

He demanded it.

"I called him into my office, closed the door, and told him, '*You better trust me,*'" Gillespie said.

"At that point, I didn't have a year to gain his trust. So basically what I told him is where he was, and asked him where he wanted to be. Malcolm's smart, but like a lot of kids he's not real focused on where he wants to go. It all sounds good, but they wonder, 'Is it really going to happen with me?'

"Athletically, he's as talented as anybody I've ever coached. But I told him he'd have to do some other things, and he'd have to *trust* me."

Malcolm had to trust him, Gillespie said, to show him how to work even harder, run routes even better, see even more of the field—in short, to comprehend the whole football universe, on and off the field. Having just spent three years as a college coordinator, Gillespie didn't want Malcolm to arrive at his first SEC practice, with Nick Saban or Urban Meyer deep in his face, and wonder what the hell he'd gotten himself into. It was too easy for a kid as talented as Malcolm to slide by on God-given ability. At the next level, everybody had God-given ability. The backup to the backup had God-given ability.

As Gillespie talked, Malcolm looked him in the eye. Gillespie looked right back.

That went on for a while. Finally, Malcolm decided he liked what he saw: Gillespie passed the no-bullshit test.

Malcolm got up to leave.

Okay, he told his newest coach.

I'll trust you.

●

"Street kid" is an overused term applied to any black kid with an earring, a tattoo, and a healthy ego.

Dashay March, last year's starting quarterback, was straight-up street. As talented as he was unpredictable, he'd been touted around the town's black barbershops, fish houses, and front-porch dominoes games as the "next Michael Vick."

On the white side of town, meanwhile, he was widely demeaned as "pure thug," at least when he wasn't called much worse.

With his dark chocolate complexion and long Betty Boop lashes—as well as an earring, a tattoo, and a runaway ego—Dashay appeared unconcerned with what anybody called him, good or bad.

"I just do me," he said, as if there wasn't one more thing you needed to know. "Whatever I think is right, I do. Most people, they say stuff and they be talking to me and I'm like, '*What?*'"

"The porcupine lets his spines out to protect himself," said one person who knew Dashay well. "That's what he's doing." It was a pose, but it was a pose that Dashay had held for so long that it now looked like his natural posture.

Dashay was raised by his grandmother. She got legal custody of him while his mother weaned herself off drugs and tried to get her life together. His mother also had three younger kids, including a girl born months premature who was now, at age seven, autistic and blind.

Dashay inherited several things, good and bad, from Yolanda March, better known among family and friends as La La, a nickname tattooed in script above her right breast. Inked just below the nickname was a bullet.

Best thing La La passed on to her oldest child: speed. She ran track when she lived in the Philippines and Germany, where her father was stationed in the army before her parents broke up. Back then, she ran like the wind, exhilarated as her legs moved and everyone else just fell away. "I'd finish," she remembered, brightening at the thought, "ahead of *everybody*."

La La gave up running and most everything else positive when she returned to the States as a young teen. She met Dashay's father, dropped out of Valdosta High, and said she dealt drugs when she wasn't doing them. She was one tough chick in one rough business, and she earned a reputation on the street as somebody not to mess with—another thing, said those who knew them both, Dashay inherited.

La La wasn't proud of all that now. In her midthirties, she was trying to do better. But it was, she said, what it was.

"My children act like me," she admitted. "They got a mouth like me. A lot of Dashay's ways are like mine."

She shook her head. Her own mother, with whom she and her four children lived, was home now from her janitorial job at a technical college. While La La talked, Joyce Williams played on the couch with her blind granddaughter inside the small, dark house on Valdosta's rugged East Side.

Grandma and grandaughter sang the ABCs together. When they finished, they sang the "Barney" song. La La hoped someday to get her daughter into a school for the blind in Macon, but first, she said, they had to get the seven-year-old potty trained. So now she attended a Valdosta elementary school.

"You reap what you sow," La La said, seated in the small dining room off the kitchen, prayer book by her right hand.

That was true of Dashay's father, too. Matt Washington had a string of kids around town with a string of other women—at thirty-seven, he had six grandchildren—and he frequently fell into one kind of trouble or another.

Matt was a lot of fun to be around, but mostly he wasn't around. He'd done hard time twice on cocaine-related charges. When Matt wasn't around while Dashay was growing up, his brother, Bones, sometimes stepped in. These days, Matt had a job cleaning up at a barbershop.

"With his dad locked up and his mama not there, his grandma would call and ask me to buy him shoes and pants," said Nathaniel "Bones" Washington, who once kept an entire room full of shoes before he was slowed by a recent stroke.

"I made my living selling drugs," he put in matter-of-factly. "This is a drug-infested town, man."

Dashay had an up-and-down, suspension-filled junior season that still caught the attention of dozens of college coaches. Opportunity knocked on Dashay's door, but it seemed like his chaotic upbringing left him unable to answer it.

About his father he said, "He was around. I just ain't always seen him."

About his mother, "My mom's cool, but it was my grandmother who was like my mom. My mom was like my sister."

About his mom and dad, "My dad sold drugs. He was doing it, and got her into it.

"It was real stuff they were doing," he summed up. "I had that in my head. So when I grew up and saw it, I wasn't surprised."

Dashay's story was the same one told by a hundred other kids who played for Valdosta before him. Wildcat fans can recite rosters of star players lost to these streets. Most white fans in Valdosta were resigned to the fact that Dashay would wind up there, too.

A lot of black folks preferred to believe that Dashay would somehow beat the odds.

If only, many black fans believed, this new coach would put him back at quarterback . . .

By the time Gillespie arrived, he couldn't even be sure if Dashay would be back for his senior year. While Ryan sat in his office and talked about his own future as Valdosta's quarterback, Dashay had already been kicked out of the high school for his rules-flaunting, teacher-sassing ways.

La La's ways.

Yet by early spring, the question no longer was whether Dashay would be back to play. The question was whether or not Dashay would make it through his junior year alive.

On a warm Saturday that spring, Dashay went to a block party across town, on the city's West Side, where he used to live. A couple of hundred folks, including La La and her brother Emanuel Williams, in town from Virginia, where he was stationed with the navy, stood around outside. They grilled, drank, blasted music, chilled out on the hoods of their cars.

Then Emanuel got a call on his cell from La La, standing somewhere nearby but lost in the crush: Somebody just jumped Dashay. He found La La and her oldest son in the middle of more chaos.

Dashay had gotten into a fight with somebody over a girl and beat that somebody up. Then he got in a fight with somebody else. Shouts and threats followed. Then somebody fired a shot in the air. Folks scattered.

Dashay and his family retreated to his grandmother's little ranch house on Claudia Circle, back on the East Side. Friends and family hung out there under the dusty front yard's sweet gum tree.

As night fell, Emanuel noticed a car that passed the house several times. Then two or three guys appeared across the street. Emanuel walked over to see what they wanted. "What up, folk? Where you been?" one guy asked, a reference to Folk Nation, the gang alliance Emanuel once belonged to as a member of the Gangster Disciples.

Dashay came out of the house and drifted into the yard. One of the guys Emanuel talked with began to walk down the street. Next thing Emanuel heard, he said, "is *pow pow pow*!" He thought the shots were in the air until "my cousin told me to duck. When he got done shooting, I started chasing him down the street. Dashay was in the street with me. Then I heard someone yell, 'Somebody's been shot!'"

It was Emanuel's wife. She'd come outside with their year-old son in her arms to see what all the commotion was about. A bullet went clear through her thigh and into the leg of Dashay's nine-year-old nephew, standing beside her.

Police and an ambulance arrived minutes later. The guys who'd driven by the house and fired the gun were long gone. A few days later, with help from the FBI's gang task force, local cops charged six men with the shooting under the State Gang Crime Act.

That night, though, after his aunt and nephew were rushed to the hospital, Dashay barely said a word to the police.

"Gets that from his daddy," said La La, shaking her head. "You're not supposed to tell on nobody."

●

So Gillespie wrote off last year's starting quarterback. He'd give Dashay a chance to play if he did everything he was supposed to do—got eligible, didn't get arrested—but in his direct, to-the-point way, he let Dashay know he wasn't counting on him to lead this year's team at quarterback. During their initial conversation, Dashay recalled, among Gillespie's first words were "You're not playing quarterback."

"I respected that he was straight-up with me," Dashay said, "but I didn't like it. I didn't like him."

Still, Ryan and Dashay had become friends. At first it seemed like an unlikely coupling between country-mouse and city-mouse opposites: Ryan and his big-ass pickup; Dashay and his saggy-ass jeans.

Those who knew them both said Ryan and Dashay had a lot more in common than met the eye. "Ryan and Dashay, they're like two flat tires," Bones said with a chuckle.

Black kids really liked Ryan. Reggie summed him up as "a white black dude." Another black player referred to him as "my blue-eyed soul brother." Dashay just smiled and said, "He black. I swear to God he's black. He's a little country, but he has a black swagger and black girl-friends."

"Ryan fit right in with everything," Dashay's grandmother added. The white quarterback hung out at her house all the time. "If you didn't know Ryan and didn't see the color of his skin, you'd think he was a black boy."

It didn't get much blacker than Dashay, and Ryan liked the idea of playing football with Dashay when he got back.

If he got back.

So Ryan told Gillespie he was in.

One more headache checked off Gillespie's headache list.

●

When Ryan left the room, Gillespie remained in his temporary office. The regular office still needed work in the wake of the previous coach's sudden departure—furniture gone, cinder-block walls pocked with holes from pictures and plaques hastily torn down. People walking by poked their heads in to check it out and couldn't believe it was the coaches' office of an elite program.

So Gillespie set up shop in a nearby conference room and started work before Christmas break was even over. Claudette and Kennedy were left behind again, this time in Statesboro, until the end of the school year. Gillespie needed an administrative assistant (the previous one was the last coach's wife) and found Tracy Williams in the vocational school of-fice down the hall.

First thing Gillespie said to Williams, an '86 Valdosta grad whose mother was the cafeteria manager who fed Hyder's teams during camp: "Tracy, tell me what I need to know."

Not the first words out of most know-it-all coaches' mouths.

"I knew right then," Tracy said, "we were going to be all right."

Together they lugged two months' worth of unopened mail into the improvised office. Gillespie sat at one end of the conference room's table, Tracy at the other. Face-to-face, the two toiled away.

A few months later—his permanent office finally furnished, his staff hired, most of his players eligible—Gillespie ran into a coaching buddy from Alabama who asked him how things were going.

"I'm about ass-worn-out," Gillespie told him, "and the season hasn't even started yet."

6

Living and Dying in Valdosta

or "What's Going on Down There?"

Valdosta was a mess, on and off the field.

The winningest high school football team in America—and opponents all over the South could not be more sick of hearing that phrase—had gone 22-21 the previous four years.

Lowndes, meanwhile, was 42-8 during those same years and had won a state title. In fact, the Vikings had won state four times since Valdosta's last championship more than a decade ago—once an unimaginable turn of events.

"Lowndes is the standard," admitted Ken Washington, a star receiver for Valdosta in the '70s, whose son was a senior on the 2010 team. "They're the enemy, but they're the standard now."

More doom and gloom lay ahead: On the youth league fields where players were developed here by age eight, kids now dreamed of one day being Vikings instead of Wildcats. It was a psychic shift some believed couldn't be reversed, not with the way things were trending.

Even legacies had turned their backs on the Wildcats. Tyler Hunter was the son of Brice Hunter, a standout Valdosta receiver in the '90s who starred at Georgia and then in the NFL. Brice was killed in a Chicago apartment shooting in 2004. Tyler first played in Valdosta's youth leagues but then went on to Lowndes. By the end of his junior year, the defensive back had signed with Florida State. The message was clear: You want to play football in South Georgia, you best play now at Lowndes.

Hunter even mocked Valdosta with a tweet: "My mama said that if I woulda stayed at Valdosta I prolly would still be in the 7th grade lol."

"His dad," one disgusted former Wildcat said, "would be turning over in his grave."

J. B. Brown was one of the city's most respected youth league coaches. He'd seen the landscape shift firsthand; 70 percent of the kids who played at the Boys and Girls Club, he estimated, now wanted to go on to Lowndes. "It's eating away at the Valdosta system like a cancer," he said.

The Valdosta feeder system was once second to none. During the heydays of Bazemore and Hyder, the middle school teams used the same drills, plays, and terminology as the high school. Kids arrived as freshmen with the playbook in their heads.

"By the time they reached the varsity," one Hyder assistant recalled, "all the coaches really had to do is get 'em on the bus, then have the chicken ready for 'em after the game."

These days, J. B. said, "everybody wants to be a Viking. As a coach, I tell them I like Valdosta. But my son—he's at Lowndes High. It was his decision. My wife works at the middle school in the city, but I live in the county. So my son could go to either school, and he chose the county school.

"There it is," he said, wagging his head. "Even me, I'm a die-hard Wildcat and I couldn't convince my own son to go to Valdosta because Lowndes has been winning so much."

Yet Brown believed the situation could still be reversed.

"I got Coach Gillespie's number in my phone," he said. "He's the only coach who ever gave it to me. Given a fair chance, I believe he's the guy who can right this thing."

●

By the summer of 2009, it was clear somebody had to right something. The problems faced by the town, the school, and the team had converged into a single, public dysfunction.

The six months between Memorial Day and Thanksgiving were among the deadliest in Valdosta's modern history. In a town that generally had two or three murders a year, there were nine homicides in just those six months, and countless other shootings. The town's violent crime rate for the year soared nearly 20 percent above the national average. All but one of the victims and perps were black in a town that's just over half African American.

Though the killings were unconnected, the repeated headlines and funeral processions prompted many folks to look at their town much differently than they had their whole lives. Long an archetype of the small-town South, Valdosta crossed a line in many people's minds, becoming a place where, in some neighborhoods, violence had replaced civility as the response of choice.

"Here we are in little Valdosta, which most people haven't heard of other than for football, and my sister was calling from Atlanta and saying, 'What's going on down there?'" said Jay Rome's mother, LaVerne. "It was a real eye-opener for everyone in the city."

That year's assault on the population's senses began on the morning of May 30, when a man riding his bike near the East Side railroad tracks spotted a partially hidden body in the tall grass. A forty-five-year-old single mother of seven had been beaten to death. Police charged her boyfriend of twelve years with murder.

A month later, six assailants shot two men as they sat in a parked car. Not one of the shooters arrested later was older than twenty. Their motive: robbery. Their take: twenty dollars.

Victims just kept dropping throughout the three weeks after that. A retired professor was beaten to death by his roommate. A seventeen-year-old mother of two was found buried in a backyard. A twenty-year-old woman was shot in the throat. A man shot his wife to death while their children played in the house.

Then, at the end of August, a former Wildcat on his way to playing college football was charged with murder after a gut-shot slaying in an apartment parking lot. He'd turned himself in with a Touchdown Club member's help.

That shooting's cold-bloodedness, the involvement of a former Wildcat, the seven murder victims already buried the previous three months—it wasn't surprising that the killings became the featured topic of many Sunday sermons. Some folks wondered if the end times were at hand.

"Death is here. It is in our city. We've ignored it too long and we need to pray," Valdosta pastor Lee Henderson proclaimed prior to a Day of Prayer observance he led on the courthouse lawn, not many yards from the musket-toting Johnny Reb.

"Something very evil, very ugly has reared its head in our area . . . ," Henderson went on. "We want to say, 'Oh, no, you won't. You can't have our cities. We want our cities back.'

"But the first thing we must do," he concluded, "is pray."

So folks prayed. During the two months that followed, the killing stopped.

Then all hell broke loose.

With Reggie in the middle of it.

It happened on a Sunday afternoon, a week or so before Thanksgiving. The air had finally cooled and the gnats become scarce. Sidney Bivens, Reggie McQueen's nineteen-year-old cousin, was enjoying the day outside at the Ora Lee West housing project, where he walked each morning from his apartment to classes at Valdosta State.

Sidney was something rare on those streets: a kid headed somewhere. Hang around the Ora Lee West streets long enough, though, and chances were trouble would find you, even if you weren't looking for trouble.

It found Sidney. A guy from the neighborhood showed up and told him he'd been jumped at a club the night before by somebody on the South Side.

"I want to go get my one-on-one," the guy said.

So Sidney piled into a car with him and a few others—nothing else going on—and when Reggie saw his cousin, he jumped in, too. They headed to Hudson Dockett, the town's other housing project, on the South Side.

As soon they arrived, Reggie noticed that an older woman was calling the police—noticed that she had the look of someone who knew from experience what she was about to see, and that she didn't want to see it.

She wasn't wrong. A fight broke out, things got hot. Reggie told his cousin he thought the police were coming. "Let's go," he said and started to walk away.

When Reggie heard the first shot, he turned to see his cousin on the ground. At first he thought Sidney just dove out of the way of the gunfire. Then Reggie looked around and saw somebody with a gun firing at him. He took off, bullets flying everywhere.

Police later recovered twenty-two shell casings from three different weapons. Ten other people were hit, including three under the age of sixteen. When the first cop showed up, she reported more than a hundred people running in all directions. Then she spotted Reggie's cousin on the ground.

"I lifted up his hand and it immediately fell back down and his eyes rolled backwards in his head," she later testified in court.

Reggie never heard or saw any of that. He figured everybody made it out like he did.

"At that moment, you don't hear, you don't see, you don't do nothing but move your feet," Reggie said. "When I looked up, I was almost on the other side of town."

Reggie learned what happened to his cousin after he got home and his phone blew up with messages. He raced to the hospital where an ambulance had taken Sidney but left before doctors pronounced him dead. "I thought, 'Sidney's not going to die. He's too strong,'" but when his mother returned to their apartment in Ora Lee West, "she didn't even have to tell me," Reggie remembered. "I could tell by the way she was walking."

Sidney was more than Reggie's cousin. While Reggie's father was in and out of jail, Sidney taught him, he said, "how to ride a bike with no training wheels, how to do a back flip, how to defend myself, how to approach women, how to be a man."

Now, he was dead.

"I just broke out crying. I fell to the ground and half my body just left. I didn't want to live. I wanted to be with him. It was the worst night of my life."

Reggie holed up with a girlfriend in a local motel and didn't answer calls from anybody. He tossed and turned through the night, then drifted off at some point for what seemed like only a couple of minutes.

"Sidney came in a dream and gave me a big smile," Reggie recalled. "He said, 'Everything's all right.'"

That's when it clicked.

"Him being killed changed my whole life," Reggie said. "I had made a wrong turn, was with the wrong crowd doing the wrong stuff. I didn't know how much I had in front of me, that it could all be took away. I'd become immune to this life. I thought the thing I know is hanging with the crowd, representing. But in the end, it leads to nothing.

"That's why I'm not just playing ball—there's a lot riding on this," Reggie said of his commitment to the game he made after that Sunday. "When people see ballplayers they think it's just something they do. I'm there because I love to be there. On the field on Friday night, I'm doing something that loves me back.

"I love it," Reggie said, "and it loves me back."

To Reggie, that's what Gillespie signaled a couple of months later in their brief hallway encounter—the way he talked straight up about what he expected from Reggie, but also how he handed him his cell number, told him to keep it, told him to let him know if he needed help.

Told him that he'd help.

"Coaches last year," Reggie said, "they couldn't get that."

7

One-Armed White Jihadi

or Nub

He tooled up and down town in his white F-150, fishing poles rattling in the back. He wheeled around a corner, blew smoke from a Winston Light, honked at somebody he knew.

Seemed he knew everybody.

All the while he yammered away on his Bluetooth, each drawled word sliding out like it had just been sawed and planed at the lumberyard.

"Well, tell him Mike Nelson called."

"..."

"Right, Mike Nelson. But if you put that down he won't know who that is."

"..."

"Just put down 'Nub.'"

"..."

"Nub."

"..."

"Either way."

"..."

"N-u-b or *K*-n-u-b."

"..."

"Bye."

He baited his hooks, loaded his guns, launched his boat, cut his steak, fried his chicken, unwrapped his barbecue, gassed up his truck, played catch with his son, made change, laid carpet, painted, hammered, unscrewed, uncorked, and cussed—all with one hand.

His left hand.

He hated buying gloves ("*Kills* me I have to buy two of 'em"), hated when he couldn't remember somebody's name ("If they all had one arm I'd know what to call them"). While he texted like a madman, it bugged him when you kept texting instead of just giving him a damn call. "Ever see a chicken pecking corn?" he said of what he looked like trying to bat out a string of one-armed messages.

Not that he minded what he looked like. Or what anybody thought. He barreled into offices and homes and sat down at occupied restaurant tables all over town—"He's one of those people who just . . . *shows up*," a local lawyer said—all the while wagging his abridged right wing and trailing cigarette smoke through Valdosta's azalea-accented neighborhoods like some updated character from a Flannery O'Connor story. When a friend's daughter once asked him what happened to his missing arm, Nub bent down close and whispered, *"Santa Claus took it."*

He's a nonstop gadfly who's not always taken seriously yet never quite dismissed. When actor Woody Harrelson wanted to go fishing a year or so ago while he filmed a movie in Valdosta called *Zombieland*, the first person folks here thought he should hook up with was Mike Nelson, a.k.a. N-u-b.

Not only had Nub fished every inch of the switchbacking, gator-friendly Withlacoochee, which started north of town and ran down through Florida until it merged with the Suwannee, Nub also seemed like the one local best able to deal with Harrelson's fondness for wilderness gonzo and uninhibited crazy. Nub was in the movie, too, as an extra, cast virtually as himself: a guy whose arm the zombies tear clean off (the scene wound up on the cutting room floor).

Nub had never heard of Harrelson—he couldn't name you three actors from the last twenty years—but when he was ushered onto the set to meet the famously pot-loving Hollywood star, he took one look at

Harrelson's wild, jittery eyes and told him maybe this wasn't the best time for fishing in these parts after all.

"I don't know what he was on," Nub recalled, "but no way was I getting in a boat with *him*."

The story of Nub snubbing Woody soon spread all over the city. David Waller, shaking his head like the father of a wayward son, conceded, "Every town has a Nub."

Nub isn't just some midway curio, though. When he solemnly proclaimed, "I'd give my left arm for another state championship," folks here took him literally.

His love of Valdosta and hatred of Lowndes knew no bounds. Some thought he'd gone around the bend; he'd brought his newborn son, John, home from the hospital in a Wildcat football helmet. One longtime Valdostan who knew him well and didn't much like him smeared Nub as "a true fanatic—a jihad-type fanatic." Nub took that as a compliment.

At fifty-four, there was still something gleefully bad-boy about him. He was all bright squinty eyes and toothy, hidden-agenda grins—a grown-up version of the kid your mother told you over and over not to play with anymore. That air was underscored by a raspy, cartoon-villain smoker's laugh that escaped in rapid-fire *heh-heh*s, accompanied by soggy gasps that sounded like a bream or carp or old nicked-up catfish flopping around on a dry dock.

One thing was for certain: Nub showed up, people noticed.

"I can tie my shoes at the cash register at Winn-Dixie and everything stops," he said. "Been the case since day one."

So it made a kind of cosmic, slightly comic, even southern Gothic sense that the guy everybody in town just called Nub—"Hi," his teeny wife, Rena, introduced herself, "I'm Mrs. Nub"—stood up in the middle of a Touchdown Club meeting hastily convened after Valdosta's last coach was fired and ignited an upstarts' insurrection.

❦

It was time to shake things up, Wildcat fans believed, and the "one-armed white painter from Valdosta"—Nub's words—seemed like just the sort of over-the-top, crazy-like-a-fox jihadi to do it.

After all, 'Cat diehards believed, this hire could be the most critical coaching decision since Bazemore picked up the phone and got Hyder on the line back in the '70s.

Hell, with school consolidation's dark unknowns massing on the horizon, it might be the *last* coaching hire that mattered. The planets over South Georgia had aligned in strange and unpredictable orbits. The way some people in town talked these days—school board meetings were still packed with folks calling for Cason's head over the Obama incident— Valdosta might even wind up with what was once the unthinkable: a black head coach.

Wouldn't that be a kick in the old guard's pants. First Obama, now . . .

So Nub stood up.

About three dozen Touchdown Club board members—all men, most of them white, their ages ranging between midforties and midseventies— shifted their broad bottoms on rows of metal folding chairs inside the stadium's gleaming, relic-stuffed Wildcat museum. Many of them now stared at Nub the same way those shoppers in the Winn-Dixie checkout line looked on openmouthed whenever he whipped out his one hand and magically tied . . . *a shoe!*

"One group there didn't know what was going on. They got snuck up on and surprised," a booster who was there recalled of Nub's unscheduled ascension. "The rest of us—we couldn't believe he was freakin' doing it!"

Observing it all from the walls in the room: portraits of every previous head coach, photos of almost every team, head shots of every Wildcat Hall of Famer. Arrayed around them: helmets, letter jackets, signed footballs, and yellowing back issues of national magazines trying to decipher Valdosta's otherworldly gridiron success (legendary Arkansas coach Frank Broyles gave his own deeply thought-about explanation to *Sports Illustrated* back in 1988: "It's just *unexplainable*").

The museum's shelves were lined with an endless booty of silver- and gold-plated hardware from dozens and dozens of titles captured over nearly a century. Included was a mounted, outsized pewter legume from the Wildcats' victory over a team from Tennessee in the 1953 Peanut Bowl. Missing for more than fifty years, the trophy was exhumed from a

Valdosta pawnshop, where a former player's daughter-in-law and grandson rescued it for twelve hundred dollars.

Yet to an outsider, the air that November evening inside the museum, with its room-length window that looked out onto a dark, deserted stadium, seemed filled only with anticlimax. Moments before Nub rose, the Touchdown Club president announced that the school board wanted the group to provide two representatives to serve on the search committee for a coach. He'd be one, the president said, and the vice president would be the other.

Nub knew the nominations already had been okayed, if not choreographed, by David Waller, who presided over the museum like a father over a son and who reigned as the Touchdown Club's overseer-for-life.

The choices surprised nobody. Both officers had worked hard for the organization. They'd solicited memberships, sold game programs, organized team meals—all the unglamorous, time-consuming, nuts-and-bolts stuff grown men do in towns like these so kids can play a first-rate brand of football. That they didn't have long football résumés didn't matter. They were good Christian men and loyal lieutenants of David, who clearly expected them to run unopposed.

That's how it had worked around here for as long as anybody could remember. David or one of his surrogates put forward a proposal, then tapped his feet until it was passed. Afterward, everybody gathered in loose circles and talked about next Friday's opponent. David's gracious wife, Sharon, along with a handful of other spouses, would then serve covered dishes or carry-out pizza.

Critics only had to look around at the room's stacked treasures to see how well this oligarchy had worked. While many privately grumbled, few openly complained—until three coaches came and went in the span of seven years and Valdosta appeared to be on the verge of something worse even than extinction: *irrelevance*.

The time was now. With his metal chair close enough to scrape the side of David's own seat, the one-armed white guy nominated two very different candidates to represent the club, candidates he'd worked furiously to find, without the knowledge of David or his inner circle, since getting wind of the meeting just three days earlier. Nub had called, cajoled, and strong-armed—with that one strong arm—voting board members all over town, working like a whip in the Senate cloakroom.

One of the men he proposed didn't even grow up in Valdosta.

The other one wasn't even white.

Both had distinguished football credentials, though. The first had been a star quarterback up the road in Tift County, beating Hyder's Wildcats before heading on to the University of Florida. The other had been a star receiver for Hyder in the '70s and now had a son who played on the team.

When he finished putting forth the two names, Nub sat back down and stared straight ahead. He couldn't see David seated beside him, but he could feel him, red-faced and furious.

David didn't stay quiet for long. He jumped up and demanded the vote be a public show of hands. The grown men in the room squirmed. This now was less a tally for competing slates of candidates than a referendum on the old guard's decades-long control—if not on David himself.

David's candidates were voted on first. Hands skittered up furtively, like ghost crabs darting across a beach. Maybe a half dozen in all.

Then came Nub's slate.

One hand shot right up. Then . . . another. Then . . . another, and *another.* Faces relaxed. Some looked almost giddy.

It was a prison break.

"First time anybody ever stood up to that regime and gunned them down," Nub would say later of his ambush, uncoiling his trademark guerrilla rhetoric. "They got their ass completely blown out of the water!"

Heh-heh.

●

No doubt about it, the whole town was in an angry damn mood following Valdosta's blowout loss that year to Lowndes.

The game was played out by the mall at 12,000-seat Martin Stadium, or what Vikings fans lovingly call the Concrete Palace (Wildcat fans' epithet: the Concrete Spittoon). It's a straightforward, does-the-job facility connected to the team's state-of-the-art coaches' offices and weight room on Lowndes High's sprawling green campus. Unlike the Reformatory Chic evoked by Valdosta High, Lowndes is bursting at the seams with 3,000 students who shuttle through junior-college-like buildings surrounded by landscaped entrances and plazas that open onto acres of playing fields. The overriding aesthetic is Soccer Mamas Gone Wild.

Built right off the interstate, the place looks like what you'd think the home of the winningest football program in America would look like, not the home of the come-lately usurper. In fact, motorists who whiz by on I-75 and catch a glimpse of the five state titles painted atop the stadium's west stands—four of them won since the Wildcats' last title—often assume it's Valdosta High.

On that warm night in early October 2009, the Winnersville Classic between Valdosta and Lowndes, played as always before a standing-room-only crowd and an ESPN audience, seemed over before it even started. For some, in fact, it was over the night before. At a team dinner the Touchdown Club paid for at the venerable Shorty's Steak House on the north edge of town, some boosters noticed a couple of players showing up late, their eyes so red it looked like they'd smoked up every bud the DEA had ever confiscated in South Georgia.

Valdosta fans' pregame jitters proved justified. The Wildcats got the ball first but lost it on the third play of the game, when Lowndes intercepted an errant pass by Dashay. Lowndes soon scored on a 10-yard run, with the Viking ball carrier seeming to haul the entire Wildcat defense—as well as its coach's future—the last 4 yards into the end zone.

Things nosedived after that. Valdosta got the ball back on its own 3, and Dashay was pulled into the end zone for a safety. Lowndes got the ball again, scored again, then ran for a 2-point conversion.

The Vikings started the second quarter with another touchdown, then appeared to forget briefly that there was another team on the field as Dashay winged a 39-yard touchdown pass to Odell. Suddenly remembering where it was and who it was playing, Lowndes then got the ball back and drove a bruising 99 yards for another TD.

Wildcat Nation sat on the hard concrete stunned. The 30 points Lowndes put on the board by halftime already topped the most points it had scored in one game against Valdosta—ever.

The carnage continued into the second half, though it was mercifully speeded up with a running clock once the visitors fell behind by 40.

The crimson-clad Viking fans hooted, hollered, and danced. Wildcat fans, meanwhile, reeled blindly like wounded animals and started looking for trouble. Nub came close to blows with taunting home-team fans—*that* was a sight folks here would've paid to watch—and was threatened with arrest before he settled down.

Players didn't behave any better. Two were tossed from the game for unsportsmanlike conduct. Others made obscene gestures at opposing fans, laughed on the sidelines, or celebrated like middle school kids when they scored with five minutes left in the game to cut Lowndes's lead to 42 points.

As the final seconds ticked off, one Valdosta assistant turned to another and mumbled, "We'll all be looking for a job."

Dashay's uncle had driven to the game from Newport News, Virginia. A former Wildcat defensive back, he returned for the Lowndes game every October. When the last seconds finally ticked off, all he could do was shake his head.

"There was no heart and soul down there," Emanuel Williams said. "It all had changed. Since I left, they got a new stadium, fly uniforms, coaches had changed—they all looked good, but they didn't play with the same heart as past Wildcats. I didn't see that same Wildcat spirit."

Milling around with other grumbling fans after the game, Emanuel told his nephew, "Y'all kind of made history today—and not a good one."

The 57–15 final scorched the local psyche. One Valdosta fan who worked at the hospital said that in the break room during lunch for months afterward, his Lowndes co-workers asked every afternoon, straight-faced and without fail, "Could you please pass the Heinz 57-to-15 sauce?"

Freakin' plowboys . . .

Dashay's uncle was right about the history making. The game's litany of historic affronts ran on and on: most points ever scored against Valdosta; second-worse loss in Valdosta history ('Cats were mauled 51–7 by Moultrie—in 1914); and, most distressing of all, sixth straight loss to Lowndes, seemingly sealing the Vikings' claim as South Georgia's new dynasty, a seat Valdosta had held, virtually unchallenged, for most of the past hundred years.

Of course, it sealed Rick Tomberlin's fate, too. Detractors were quick to point out that not only had the fourth-year coach been beaten by Lowndes four straight years—no other Wildcat head man could claim that level of futility—but he'd lost three straight games to Valdosta in the early '90s, when he was head coach at Lowndes. He'd now failed to win a Winnersville Classic in seven tries. It was as if he'd torn a page out of Bazemore's legacy and then misread it: He could take his best eleven and lose to yours, then take your best and lose to his.

Cason's phone at the central office, across the parking lot from the stadium, rang off the hook beginning early Monday morning, mostly with irate fans who called for Tomberlin's head. Nobody in the building got a thing done.

Cool, calculating, and possessing, as one school system employee described him, "the heart of an accountant," Cason had decided to fire Tomberlin long before the Lowndes debacle. Hired by Cason's predecessor, the likable, flat-topped coach had become a legend at a smaller school in Middle Georgia, winning state three times and making it to the title game twice more. He'd won more games the previous fourteen years than any other coach in Georgia. When he interviewed at Valdosta, his references included Bobby Bowden (Tomberlin warmed the bench at Florida State) and Mark Richt, who told the superintendent back then that Tomberlin was the coach he'd want his son to play for.

Those credentials turned stale fast in Valdosta, and Cason concluded Tomberlin wasn't up to coaching at this level of competition and obsession. ("People come up to you and want to talk about a receiver's *footwork*," Tomberlin had once marveled. "They might not know who their state representative is, but they know the Lincoln score from ten years ago.") Only in hindsight did most fans see his earlier incarnation at Lowndes as a demerit. After all, who *didn't* lose to Valdosta every year back then?

When he arrived in 2006, Tomberlin had inherited a talented but diminished roster way down from the more than one hundred kids who dressed out less than a decade earlier—and promptly went 1-9. He followed that with 9-3 and 5-5 seasons and was 4-2 before he made the five-mile bus trip over to Lowndes.

It wasn't what Valdosta expects for the more than $100,000 in salary and perks it lavishes on its head coaches, especially with its overhauled stadium two-thirds empty for some games and Touchdown Club membership skidding. That salary was at the high end even in Georgia, where an *Atlanta Journal-Constitution* report once discovered that the average football coach in the state earned 55 percent more than the average teacher. Coaches' teaching contracts also ate up about $80 million in state tax dollars—even though a third of them had minimal or no teaching duties.

So if 17-3 got the coach between Bazemore and Hyder fired, 19-19 would practically get you strung up—especially in a place where, in the past, folks had been hanged for a whole lot less.

At a school where football players already walked the halls like princes and kings, some now acted bulletproof—flaunting dress codes, cussing out teachers, often with little or no consequence. Spotting Dashay stepping down a hallway one day with his pants sagging below his ass, one teacher stopped him and told him to pull up his pants. Dashay had hardly acknowledged her before an assistant coach who taught in a nearby classroom called Dashay over, told him how much he liked his new sneakers, then pulled him safely into his room.

End of lesson.

"I truly believe with all my heart that he lost control and respect of some of the kids. There were more than ordinary discipline problems," Cason said. "He did have some support to stay here, but I knew the program needed to head in a different direction."

Cason considered waiting until the end of the season, but the drubbing by Lowndes made waiting any longer out of the question. So he fired him but let him finish out the season.

🏈

Tomberlin called Cason's comments crap and said Valdosta's preoccupation with winning titles "borders on insanity."

The experience left him disillusioned.

"I felt betrayed. I felt expendable. I felt insignificant. They make you feel that way there," said Tomberlin, who found another job at a school near Savannah. "It hurt me to the point where I don't even correspond with people there. I've taken all their numbers out of my phone.

"I won't even take a call," he added, "from the 229 area code."

🏈

After Tomberlin's axing, the town seemed weirdly torn by competing forces: its Christian impulse to forgive, and its historic drive, installed by Bazemore and Hyder, to win, win, win.

An online poll taken by the *Valdosta Daily Times,* which published editorials deploring the midseason firing and the Wildcats' winning-is-everything ethos ("There's more to winning than the final score," it chastised, "and there's more to life than football"), showed that more than 60 percent of readers who logged in disagreed with the quick hook given the head coach.

Callers to a local sports radio show broadcast every morning from a double-wide on the edge of town ranted about little else. Even many who thought Tomberlin needed to go believed Cason should've waited until after the season. The team, after all, could still make the playoffs, and a deep run would be just one more embarrassment. Others felt that letting Tomberlin stay on the sidelines for the rest of the season, with players and fans knowing he wouldn't be back, was a too-cruel civic punishment.

That was Valdosta's public face.

Its game face: Talk with the boys who played for Bazemore and Hyder, now all grown, and you mostly heard something else. For them, waiting four days after the Winnersville apocalypse to eject a coach with a losing record was waiting at least four days too long.

"I would've fired his ass," drawled Berke Holtzclaw, quarterback for Hyder's undefeated 1984 state and national title team, *"at halftime."*

❧

Not long after Tomberlin's dismissal, with the Wildcat faithful still reeling, Nub got a call from the Touchdown Club president alerting him to a board meeting in three days. He was told to be there at six.

Board members were usually given more advance notice than that, and the meetings usually started at seven, so everyone had time to eat dinner with the family. When he asked about the irregularities, Nub was told not to worry about it. Just be there.

"I knew then," he said. "I smelled a rat."

Nub suspected the club's top officers wanted to rush a meeting before any opposition could form against their appointments to the coach's search committee. The hand behind it all, he knew, belonged to the man he believed had contributed more than anybody not named Bazemore or Hyder to Valdosta High's place for so long in the national spotlight.

David Waller.

To Nub's mind, David had devoted more time, probably given more money (much of it anonymously), and likely attended more games over the past half century than anybody else in town.

He'd also sat behind more closed doors in important meetings: running interference for Hyder during the coach's early years when itchy administrators wanted him fired; serving on the school board for more than two decades, almost half that time as its chairman; Touchdown Club president for three terms before becoming its permanent treasurer; and a major force behind the old stadium's $7 million renovation.

Through it all, Waller had gained status as a kindly if unassailable dictator whose attitude toward a coach was the final green light needed to hire or fire him. During the last coaching search, leaks about who Valdosta was courting became so rampant that covert interviews were switched from school offices to David's house. While the school board always had the final say, David's imprimatur, issued at the end of the process, was deemed a necessary final step.

During the previous search, one highly touted coach from out of state had everyone on board, it seemed, until David met with him at the local country club. There he questioned the coach about a child he supposedly had with a woman he'd lived with for years but still hadn't married. David thought that might not pass proper Christian muster in this part of the Bible Belt.

He wasn't wild about another high-profile candidate either—Rush Propst, the stupendously successful, outrageously self-promoting coach from Hoover High in Hoover, Alabama. Propst would soon become nationally known through an MTV reality series called *Two-A-Days*, as well as scandals involving at least one extramarital affair and allegations of grade tampering, which Propst denied. Unsurprisingly, Propst proved too rich for David's blood. Three years later, he'd be hired by rival Colquitt County and quickly take his new team to the state finals.

David's choice: Tomberlin, a devout, straitlaced family man.

David sighed and shook his head when his back-room, invisible-hand role was raised. He said it wasn't true. Then he added, "Not really."

Now, with Valdosta's last three coaching hires ending in flames—and

Waller still supporting Tomberlin after the Lowndes fiasco—many fans and boosters were growing weary, too.

Of Waller.

●

In a town full of hardscrabble upbringings, David's was a harder scrabble than most.

Born during the Depression on a farm in the middle of the state, not far from where Herschel Walker grew up, David was raised without electricity or running water. He never had a store-bought toy; he and his siblings made toy trains from string and empty syrup cans.

His hard-drinking father worked on and off for the railroad, and David's chores included hoeing the farm's fifty acres of cotton and peanuts, often beside his long-suffering mother. When he wasn't doing that, he milked cows, picked weevil eggs out of the cotton, and hunted for supper.

"It was a real tough life," he said, "but we were happy. We had a mother who loved us, and Daddy loved us—he was just real hard on us. We got whipped brutally."

His family later moved to a small farm in Valdosta. The first football game David ever saw was at Cleveland Field in 1947, Bazemore's first team to win state. The teamwork, the precision, the way the whole town came out to concentrate its collective will onto that lone lit rectangle—David had never seen or felt anything like it.

He couldn't play, though: He worked. He delivered the daily newspaper every afternoon to 140 mostly black customers over nineteen miles of soft dirt roads—"basically," he said, "the colored route." When he got home he milked the cows and finished his other chores. Then he got back up in the morning and milked them again.

David absorbed his upbringing's lasting lesson: Life was work and work was life.

Then he had a gym class taught by Bazemore. The coach thought he was fast enough to try out for football, so Waller became a Wildcat his senior year. He rarely played, but he was a Wildcat.

Yet that one season was enough for David to absorb another lesson, a kind of addendum to the earlier one: Like life, Wildcat football was work—glorious, blessed work. As Bazemore taught it, the more you worked, the bigger the payoff and the better your life would be. Work wasn't a treadmill. It was a ladder.

That same lesson, Waller said, was absorbed by dozens of other former Wildcats who now served the town as its most prominent lawyers, businessmen, educators, and leaders. So while Waller expanded his own heating and air-conditioning business by working nineteen-hour days and taking calls on Sundays while his family went off to church, Wildcat football became another touchstone in his life, much like the Baptist church he served just as diligently.

Nub respected the hell out of all that. He really did. His own upbringing wasn't nearly that rough. His birth father abandoned him, but he was adopted by a pathologist. His mother was the daughter of Charleston society.

Still, his route had its own ups and downs and detours.

Beginning with that nub.

He lost the arm at thirteen. He was riding a horse one evening that he used to ride all over town because, back in 1969, that's what you could do in Valdosta. When the horse came to a steep bank at the top of an intersection, she couldn't stop and lurched into the road to stay upright. Right at that moment, a pickup barreled by.

"I heard she was killed at impact," Nub said.

As for him, getting hit was the last thing he remembered until he woke up in a hospital surrounded by doctors.

His left arm was busted and in a cast.

His right arm . . . "It was like it was filleted from below the elbow to the wrist. I don't remember any pain. They kept me on Demerol."

A few days later, gangrene set in. He remembered being loaded into a hearse. "Like from a funeral home," he said. The hearse rushed him to a hospital in Augusta, but the arm turned black and it was too late to save it. They operated, he woke up, it was gone.

"Never once have I ever been upset about it," Nub said. "*Ever.*"

What did upset him: He'd never be a Wildcat.

Nub wanted to be a 'Cat the first time he saw old Cleveland Field, then a woodsier site than it is now. His father drove him by it when the family moved to Valdosta from Macon and told young Mike that the greatest high school football team in America played right there. Nub went back for every game he could.

"I remember squeezing into that place, seeing people climbing trees to watch, or climbing on top of a house that used to be right on the corner," he said. "And then I remember coming home and telling Mama, 'The 'Cats won again!'"

Nub played in junior high. He was small but fast and mean, which went a long way in Valdosta. Bazemore could make something out of fast and mean.

Then that truck took his arm.

Bazemore visited him in the hospital. A thirteen-year-old boy in South Georgia could not have been more impressed if the president himself had landed *Air Force One* in a neighbor's cotton field and showed up at his door.

"That was powerful," Nub recalled. "All I wanted to do was play football."

Then his father moved the family to rural Virginia, for a government project to research black lung. Nub now was small and mean and one-armed, plenty good enough for the poor little coal-mining town where they settled. He started at cornerback.

"I was kind of a hated guy, the way I used my nub," he said. "There were always a lot of complaints from the other teams. They thought it was illegal. I learned how to slip my nub between their face mask and their face and pull them down to the ground. Should I be flagged for that or not be flagged for that? It was always a point of contention."

His nub didn't limit him to yanking down receivers one-handed.

"I made interceptions *and* receptions," he said. "They'd put me on offense the first play of the game. Nobody would cover me. But I could catch real good. It was three weeks until the opponents caught on."

Nub and his older brother soon found other distractions out there in the middle of nowhere: guns, pot, a little crime. His brother wound up in jail, escaped, then fled to the house of the judge who'd sentenced him. The judge called Nub's parents over, and they all had a dinner there. Then the judge called the state patrol to carry his brother back to jail.

"My mother used to tell us when we'd go out, 'Be careful,'" Nub said, "and I'd say, 'Mom, *we're* the bad guys.'"

When Nub's brother was released, his family sped back to Valdosta. Nub was still fast and mean, but by now he was mostly a fast and mean delinquent. He was thrown out of a private high school, left Valdosta High, then dropped out of Lowndes.

"Not being able to play for the 'Cats is something I don't think I'll ever get over," he said. "Not playing for the Wildcats upset me as much as people perceive I should've been upset over losing my hand. I was never upset over that. But not being able to play for the 'Cats—there's not anything in the world that hurt me more. I'll never know how I would've done.

"It still haunts me today," he added. "Worst is when some smart-ass who played will come up to me and say, 'You never strapped it on for the 'Cats.' I always tell them, 'You need to feel like you were lucky enough to strap it on.'

"I'm telling you," Nub repeated as he pulled out a cigarette, lit it, and put his lighter back, all with one hand, "it *killed* me."

●

Nub settled down in his forties, married, had a kid. Hasn't touched a drink since.

Yet even during his most delinquent, party-hearty years, he faithfully followed the 'Cats. He loved it. Despite the fact he grew up a certified-organic racist—"Just like any other white guy, I thought we were better than them"—he related to a lot of the players, most of whom by then were black. A lot of them seemed intent on matching him youthful misstep for youthful misstep. Others were determined to make better lives for themselves. Nub tried to help them all.

One morning he drove a former Wildcat on a full football scholarship to the airport for his flight back to college. The kid grew up so poor that some boosters had to buy him a suitcase when he first went off to school.

That same morning, after dropping the player off, Nub drove straight from the airport to the downtown courthouse. He testified as a character witness during the pretrial hearing for another former Wildcat, charged with murder.

"Stories like that," Nub said of that morning's highs and lows, "are everywhere here."

◆

Nub eventually found himself on the Touchdown Club's board. Most of the 1,200-member club's power came from its annual budget of about $100,000, raised mainly from dues, program sales and ads, and game-day parking spot rentals next to the stadium—prime tailgate slots.

The money was spent on everything from new equipment to meals after practice or on the road, hotel rooms if the 'Cats had to stay over-night, bonuses for assistant coaches, and the head coach's truck lease. A few years ago, the club spent $100,000 for new weight equipment. This year they'd spent $14,000 on an industrial washer and dryer.

Waller had overseen, and helped generate, that money for decades. For all that time, he'd been at the center of that powerful club's power.

There is, however, an inevitable arc to the public lives of men like David Waller in towns like Valdosta, where everybody knows every-body's business and everybody has an opinion about it. Stay around long enough, people start to look for alternatives. They get tired of the same old same old. Everybody else gets younger. A pillar of the community, in some circles at least, beomes a pariah.

So David Waller now found himself locked out of having anything to do with the hiring of the new coach.

"This program was in jeopardy because of choosing the wrong coaches, of one person controlling it for too long," a prominent booster said of Waller's eventual exile. "Most of the community, black and white, pretty much felt it was Waller doing the picking almost single-handedly.

"One of the things he always tried to pick was someone who was a wholesome Christian, a man who'd fit in with the South Georgia Bible Belt kind of stuff," added the booster, himself a regular churchgoer. "And that's all right. But he has to be a good football coach, too. Ultimately, it boils down to: Is he winning or is he losing football games?"

David understood what was going on. He didn't like it, but he under-stood it. A man doesn't come from where David came from, and accom-plish all that David has accomplished, without a keen understanding of the dynamics around him.

"Things change," he said. "They wouldn't let me be involved. They looked at me like, 'This is a different era. He shouldn't have anything to do with it.'

"Partly it's my fault," he allowed. "I've done so much of it—I know just exactly how everything is supposed to work. I keep thinking somebody else will appear on the horizon and say, 'I'll take it over.' But it hasn't worked out that way. It just happened I was there a long time. What worries me is I don't know how many more years I can do it."

David paused. He knew the one thing that would fix whatever had gone wrong.

"If they could win just one more . . ."

8

Pick One. The White One

or The Gospel of Football

They really liked the black guy.

Before Gillespie arrived from Statesboro to interview for the Valdosta job, the search committee talked long and hard with Corey Jarvis, a promising young coach at Martin Luther King Jr. High School in Dekalb County, just outside Atlanta.

Jarvis had won forty-nine games and reached the playoffs five times in his five seasons at MLK, a school that didn't exist until 2001 and didn't have all four grades until two years later. Despite his success, Jarvis had grown frustrated at the school. It didn't have its own stadium, it shared ticket revenue with the county's other schools, and fund-raising was rough, even though Jarvis had put two dozen kids on college rosters.

He wanted out, but there were only two exits he really wanted to pursue: a college job or the top spot at Valdosta.

"I don't think there's a coach in the state of Georgia who wouldn't want the Valdosta job," Jarvis said. "There's the legacy of Hyder and Bazemore. They have a winning tradition. They have great kids and community.

"I had the opportunity to play them as a head coach," he went on. "They came up to MLK and we went down there. You'd see how the community comes out and supports that team. It's just amazing."

Jarvis knew Valdosta was no longer the Valdosta of old. There's no grapevine that lights up like the coaches' grapevine. He'd heard all the whistling-through-the-graveyard talk about how Valdosta couldn't compete anymore in the state's largest classification, not with the student numbers it had. He knew that a lot of athletes there now sprinted across town to Lowndes.

"But I never look at a situation as impossible," he said. "You look at the type of kids who come from Lowndes and Valdosta every year, you know there's enough kids down there to be successful. It's just that now there's another big dog in town."

He also wanted the chance to coach kids again from South Georgia, which he did before MLK as an assistant at Crisp County High, north of Valdosta but still below the Gnat Line.

"The kids down there are totally different," he said. "The kids there want it just a little more. They're wanting to get out of there. They play some down-home, hard-nosed football. Football there is like going to church on Sunday. Kids are just raised around it."

So he walked into the Valdosta interview in the late fall of 2009 prepared to get the job. The men who'd assembled to meet him included Cason, the poker-faced, snake-snaring superintendent, and four former Wildcats.

Conspicuous by his absence was David Waller or any of his surrogates.

Three of the men on the committee were African American: Stan Rome, the former NFLer who'd played for Bazemore and whose son was the highly recruited tight end; Kenny Washington, the former standout 'Cat receiver Nub had put forward; and Rufus McDuffie, head basketball coach with a disciplinarian's reputation and an assistant principal at the high school.

The Touchdown Club's other rep was Brian Massingill, the former Tift County and Florida quarterback. Massingill had a tall, poised, and talented seventh-grade son who played quarterback in middle school. Area coaches already salivated over him.

Jerry Don Baker rounded out the football-centric group. He'd played for Bazemore, coached under Hyder, then was an assistant to the first two men who followed them. Jerry Don brought a kind of forensic perspective to the table: He'd seen how the program worked from the inside during its glory days (he was one of those fifth graders Bazemore held back every year or so to "mature"), then watched it up close as it all un-raveled.

Jerry Don knew he was taking a hot seat—another retired coach turned down the committee's offer to participate, saying it was too po-litically charged. Nevertheless, adhering to the motto of "Once a Wild-cat, Always a Wildcat," he felt duty-bound.

"I felt on behalf of all the work we'd all put in over the years that I didn't want to see Valdosta go all the way downhill," explained Jerry Don, now a salesman at his brother's used car dealership. "The last two coaches were hired by people with no football knowledge."

After facing this august, gimlet-eyed group—"Some of the best ques-tions came from the *administrators*," he'd later say—Jarvis felt good about how he performed. In fact, he impressed everybody with his knowledge of the game, his ideas for the program, and his commitment to the kids. One white panelist thought he was "borderline arrogant" but didn't hold it against him, feeling "maybe he has to be that way in that setting [at MLK]."

All in all, Jarvis said, "I think I surprised them."

Then, after he finished the formal interview, one of the men in the room—Jarvis can't remember which one, and nobody in the room re-called it—told him, Jarvis said, "This community isn't ready for a black to be head football coach."

"It was shocking they came right out and said it. It wasn't like they tried to hide it. There was no sugarcoating to it.

"Then two of them asked me if I'd come back to be defensive coordi-nator. I knew what that meant. In the past, when I'd walk in for an inter-view at schools and they'd see I was black, they'd say, 'We didn't know you were so . . . young.'"

Jarvis, who played college ball at historically black Albany State, also in South Georgia, added, "They weren't discouraging. I think they made an honest attempt to find a black coach. But I think maybe I did better than they thought I'd do, that I'd been one of the top three they'd bring back. And I think they wanted to let me know what I'd be walking into."

Jarvis already had a pretty good idea of what to expect this far down in the state. He hadn't forgotten his previous South Georgia experience in Crisp County. He loved the football atmosphere there, but the racial atmosphere was something else. The school still held segregated proms.

White coaches would diss black folks in the community as casually, and almost as impersonally, as if they were talking about the weather. So did people who worked around his wife at the Boys and Girls Club. There was a clear division in town between the races, both physically (the railroad tracks) and culturally. He'd gotten out of there as soon as he could.

So Jarvis talked that night with his wife and two young daughters about what he'd been told.

Next morning, he called Valdosta to withdraw his name. He later was hired at Duluth, a suburban Atlanta high school.

"Everybody knows I wanted that job bad," he said, "but I couldn't bring my wife and two little girls into that situation."

❋

Ultimately, none of it mattered.

Not race, not experience, not how well anybody else presented himself.

Not anything.

Gillespie came in and blew everybody away, including the committee's black members.

"It was a no-brainer," Stan Rome recalled. "The guy from MLK was at the top of my list. He interviewed extremely well. Then Gillespie came in, and whatever you want to call it—God-inspired? the stars aligned?—after we interviewed Gillespie, I was done."

Gillespie had interviewed in Valdosta before, when the job last opened up in 2005, the year he won his first title at Peach.

It was one of the stranger interview processes he'd ever gone through. First, he was asked to come to town on a Saturday. He was also asked to bring Claudette.

"I was like, *o-kay*," Claudette remembered. "I'd never gone on an interview before. I was like, 'Are they going to ask me football questions?' It was like the family was being interviewed, like they were trying to see, 'Do we want this family here?'"

Rance and Claudette were taken to the high school on a Saturday night. The grounds were dark, the hallways quiet and eerily empty. The Gillespies' click-clacking footsteps rang off the metal lockers and cinderblock walls.

Rush Propst, then one of the most famous and soon to be the most infamous high school football coach in America, believed all the furtiveness was by design.

Propst, who'd won state five times in less than a decade at Hoover High in Alabama, also interviewed for the Valdosta job. From his own experience, Propst had a pretty sensitive radar for anybody who wasn't coming clean. He said Valdosta officials knew that their practice facilities, coaches' offices, and even the students' general behavior at the time might shock some candidates who expected Valdosta still to be the cream of the crop.

"I wasn't even allowed to go into the cafeteria," said Propst, who did visit the school while students were there. "I felt like they were trying to hide something."

●

Valdosta still appealed to the Southerner in Gillespie, much the way Catholic coaches are still drawn to Notre Dame. The standard line had long been that the three best coaching jobs in the state were the University of Georgia, Georgia Tech, and Valdosta.

Nobody prepared like Gillespie prepared—just ask his bleary-eyed assistants after a marathon film session—and he was prepared the day of his interview to walk out of Valdosta with the job. He impressed the panel as smart, genuine, confident, and almost spookily organized. "You have any idea how organized he is?" one committee member said. "It's *sick*."

With more mountain twang than plantation drawl, Gillespie told the committee what kind of system he would run, how he would conduct practices, how physical they would be. He broke down almost to the hour what his week would look like. He talked about how he'd get kids to class, how he'd keep their grades up. He'd coached the same kinds of kids at Peach County—mostly black, mostly poor, mostly fatherless—and detailed the success he had there, on and off the field. At its core: tough love with a heart.

He talked about his stint at Georgia Southern and what he could bring to the table from college coaching, not the least being a better idea of what colleges wanted when they recruited high school kids.

His talk was also sprinkled with references to "product" and "brand" and "marketing"; he understood that he was selling his program as much as coaching it. He let them know that he knew his way around numbers and budgets. He came across as thrifty, or at least not looking to exploit anybody's generosity, something that had happened here in the recent past. One post-Hyder coach, now long gone, had groused after the Touchdown Club presented him with the keys to a newly leased truck. His gripe: It didn't have four-wheel drive.

Offered a similar deal when he first arrived, Gillespie would decline the truck altogether. He said he'd hold on to the black Saturn sedan he'd driven at Georgia Southern until the lease ran out. He'd gotten a really good deal on it from an old hometown friend who owned a dealership back in Clayton.

In short, Gillespie told the search committee how he planned to turn Valdosta around.

"The bottom line is, people here want to win," he'd say later. "Along with that they want their kids to act right, to represent Valdosta football in a certain light. They want you to win, but even if you get beat, or if time runs out on you, then you still play your ass off for forty-eight minutes. You're physical. You're a football team. Those are the things they want.

"The positives to coming into a place like this: There are some really good kids on the team. It's a football place. Those kids are tired of hearing you're Valdosta and you're supposed to be the best and you're embarrassing us. They're tired of going into the barbershop and hearing that. So they're willing to do whatever you ask them. They don't want to be in that place anymore.

"The problem is it takes forever for them to understand the speed, the effort, the total work mentality it takes to get to that culture. How do you start? You run around in front of them and do it yourself. They'll follow you. It's called leadership. You've got to do it yourself first.

"You cheat this game if you don't work hard at it," Gillespie said, "and if you cheat the game the game's not going to be good to you."

He paused. Did what he often did when he paused: spit tobacco juice into a cup; any cup; empty water bottle, empty foam container from Chick-fil-A, empty anything.

"There are very few places in our culture anymore where a kid—a young man—can learn toughness and have a place to go and find himself," he went on. "A place where he can be put in tough, adverse situations and be expected to survive. Football is one of the last resorts for that. Football is still a place where it's okay to take a kid every afternoon and be hard on him.

"It's not just a football program," Hardass 2.0 added. "Any real football program is not just a football program. It's a place where kids go to become better people."

He spit.

Grinned.

"Thank God I'm forty-one and not sixty-one."

The Valdosta interview wrapped up so quickly Gillespie thought they were gaming him. "I thought, 'Okay, I know this interview technique. They're trying to piss me off.'"

In fact, the door had barely closed behind him, several members of the search committee said, when McDuffie, the black head basketball coach and assistant principal who'd won five state titles at another Georgia high school, said out loud what every man in there was thinking:

Offer this guy the job before he gets off campus or somebody else will grab him.

9

The Firm

or Feeding His Soul

Claudette sensed something different about the place right off.

A month after her husband accepted the job, Claudette, Rance, and Kennedy rode together to the Wildcat museum for a Saturday night meet-and-greet and dinner with the Touchdown Club board. As the family pulled into the parking lot beside the darkening stadium, Claudette noticed side-by-side metal signs that reserved two prime spaces.

One was for Bettie Bazemore.

The other for June Hyder.

The royal widows of Valdosta.

"I said to Rance, 'These people have lifetime parking here? The *superintendent* doesn't have a space,'" Claudette recalled. "I told him, 'So you have to be a good coach and die—and I'll get a parking space!'"

That was just the beginning of Claudette's initiation into the attention and ritual that accompanied being married to the head football coach at Valdosta High. She hadn't even heard yet about David Waller's offer of free gravesites.

"It's like *The Firm*," she mock-whispered at one point during the crowded dinner, waiting in a line that stretched halfway around the room for potluck dishes prepared by boosters' wives. "I almost expected when I went home that the house would be bugged."

That night, Claudette met Bettie Bazemore—in her eighties, tiny, still a firecracker. "Took 'em long enough," she'd say later of her reserved parking space outside, which she now used on Friday nights to tailgate with her grown kids and grandkids.

The room's light bounced off trophies, helmets, plaques, even the glass eyes of the stuffed wildcat shot on a fan's farm. Preserved in full snarl by the museum's front door, it still looked like something you didn't want to get your fingers too close to.

Men strolled around with plastic cups filled with punch and examined the photographs of players that hung everywhere. They'd go on at length about some play that one or another of them had made back in '59, or '71 or '84 or '92, along with the name of that night's opponent, the game's final score, the weather, and, often as not, what they'd all had to eat beforehand. Many of the men pointed out photos of themselves.

"It's not a trophy case in a school, but a building that's totally about nothing but football," Claudette marveled. "It's like players can't wait until something's entered in the museum about them."

Six months after Rance got the job, Claudette and Kennedy left Statesboro and moved with him into a rented ranch-with-a-pool in an established but unfancy Valdosta subdivision. Rance was done making small-college coordinator money—about $76,000—and back to making South Georgia high school head coach money: $105,000. They still rented; the house they left two jobs ago in Peach County remained unsold.

Claudette also got a job with the Valdosta system: behavior intervention specialist for the five elementary schools. She spent days in classrooms observing how teachers interacted with problem students, then provided a blueprint of cues and responses that might help those teachers work better with the kids.

The students' diagnoses ranged from ADHD to spectrums on the autism scale to behavior that wasn't easily classifiable. She had one kid who wouldn't stop eating inedible objects, and another with echolalia who, after hearing the same words directed toward him at home, repeated "shut the f— up" more than a thousand times in eight minutes.

For Claudette, there was no escaping football. On her first visit to a hair salon, the young stylist who worked the chair beside Claudette realized who she was and told her straight up, "I'm a Viking." Claudette's response: "Does that mean you're going to shave all my hair off?"

The women inside the salon got a good laugh out of that. Another young stylist told Claudette which Valdosta teams her daddy and grand-daddy had played for. She then said that her family's season tickets were in section D. "Where you sitting?" she asked Claudette.

"I thought, gosh, where I grew up they didn't even sell season tickets. You just walked up and bought one. So I told her, 'I don't know.'"

Again the women in the salon laughed. *If her husband wins enough games fast enough,* you could almost hear them thinking, *she might be all right.*

Other folks told Claudette about tickets they'd gotten in their divorce settlements. "It was like, 'I want custody of the kids—*and* the season tickets.' And they're serious!"

She added of the very public place of a coach's wife, "People are looking at you, trying to figure out, 'Is she nice? Is she friendly? Is she genuine?' And I want to say, 'I'm just Claudette. I'm a real momma. A real wife. I have a real job and real problems like you have, too.'

"Sometimes that gets forgotten," she said. "For some people, you're the topic of their dinner table conversation."

◆

One evening, while Rance was still at work, Claudette looked out a window and saw several pickups parked along the curb in the front of the house. She didn't know who the vehicles belonged to and told Kennedy to stay away from the window and not open the door.

Rance pulled up around nine and waltzed right in, a line of polite but eager men shuffling in behind him. Claudette and Kennedy were already in their pajamas.

"And I'm like, 'Who *are* these people?'"

They were youth football coaches who'd come to learn at the new master's feet. The local programs, once unmatched, had suffered from benign neglect almost since the day Hyder passed. Gillespie promised to change that, and these guys, who coached in rec leagues and at the middle school, were eager to start.

"They sat down with Rance and asked him, 'How can we implement what you're doing? Tell us what we can do to start getting these kids to do it your way,'" Claudette recalled. "I was like, 'You guys want something to drink? We're going to bed.'"

Rance sat with them for hours. He booted up his laptop, shuffled through their game sheets, diagrammed plays. It's hard to know who called it quits first: Rance or the guys who came over to talk with him.

Claudette offered, "Rance will talk football with a dead frog if the frog is listening."

Then her smile disappeared. It only went away like that when she was dead serious.

She was dead serious.

"It's truly not just his job," she said. "It's his passion. I won't say it's an obsession, but it's borderline."

She paused. There was something else.

"It feeds his soul."

◆

Claudette had trooped with Rance for nearly two decades through a kind of Who's Who of the Who-Cares South—Thomasville, Douglas, Fort Valley, Homer, Statesboro. Strip out the local accents, the dark histories, and the sweetened iced tea and it's pretty much been a journey through small-town anywhere-in-America.

High school football still centered many of these places. It still provided their spirit and pride; it was still a reservoir for hopes and dreams.

That seemed to be what Claudette witnessed that night when those youth league coaches showed up at her front door after she and Kennedy had already slipped into their pj's. The easy banter and common shorthand of those sun-splashed men around her kitchen table spoke of something genuine, searching, almost desperate.

All they wanted was their identity back. They'd come to the right place: Untangle enough X's and O's and unbalanced lines, it seemed, and you'd uncover strands of Valdosta's DNA—a genetic code twisted up in a century's worth of locker room sermons, brutal practices, last-second victories; cheerleader pyramids, halftime shows, homecoming kings; sprained ankles, blind refs, police escorts; segregation and integration; banging the tin and Pastor Troy. It's all in those looping play diagrams if you stare at them hard enough.

Valdosta's fixed devotion to the very thing her husband was most devoted to was what Claudette quickly came to appreciate about the place. She'd seen intensity for high school football in a lot of the towns she and Rance had lived in, but nothing like here. Valdosta was down, but it didn't seem like it could ever really be out.

"This heritage, this legacy, what people are holding on to—if it dies, people feel like their soul will be buried with it," she said. "There's a deep passion you have to respect, whether you understand it or not. People are just holding on to life support. It's like, 'Don't turn off the life support yet!'

"I know that sounds like a drastic comparison," Claudette added, "but for a lot of people here it's not. For them to go to Bynum's Diner on Saturday morning and talk about some football, or hang at the Waffle House after the ball game every Friday night and talk about plays they didn't think were called in our favor or to talk about a play that they thought was awesome—I could live here a hundred years and never pull together what it means to each person. But at some point you just jump in and embrace it.

"That's what people have done here. People are on the same page on Friday night. Nobody wants to be left out of it. Democrat, Republican, whatever—we're all Wildcats at that moment.

"So many people here are like, 'Please don't let this die. This is the heritage. This is where it all started. If we don't keep that, we're forgetting our roots.' That's what they're saying. 'Don't forget us. We don't want to be forgotten.'"

When Rance got on a roll, his features concentrated into a dark sharp thing beneath his forehead that you didn't really want to mess with.

When Claudette got on a roll, she was wide open. You wanted to sign up and join her cause—whatever it was.

"I love this little school system," she said, almost like she was tugging one of its ears. "It's pretty neat."

10

Do It Again!

or Hell

On a dog-day Monday, the second of August, at 5:51 A.M., with the sky still black, the moon still bright, and crickets and coaches already in full-chirp, two things took place on a freshly mowed field that still glittered with overnight dew: Summer officially ended for anybody standing on that wet grass, and Valdosta's last-chance, must-win future officially began.

"They say it's going to be hell," senior offensive lineman Darrien Green mused the night before, lying shirtless on a mattress thrown down inside the school gym, where players and coaches set up camp for the week.

Green fooled with some music until he found what he wanted. Then he added, already resigned to his fate, "I'm just going to go along with it."

Yet as Gillespie stood in the middle of the lit-up practice field behind the deserted high school that Monday morning, he announced unnecessarily to all the scared-straight faces around him, "Men, summer's over."

An assistant heard that and exhaled into the warm, moist air. "Man," he murmured under his breath, "summer's been over since spring." Then he corrected himself. "Really, it's been over since *Christmas*."

That's when Gillespie landed in Valdosta and began to assemble a ten-man coaching staff as unrelenting, single-minded, and seemingly tireless as he was. Saturday staff meetings often ran from noon until midnight. He handed each coach a three-ring binder that detailed his expectations, then added new pages almost daily.

On the field, he wanted his coaches to run as hard as his players. Off the field, they'd do the team's mountain of laundry, grade out each player's performance, and break down film on Sundays. From August through November—and into December if a playoff run went that deep—they could expect to put in twelve- to sixteen-hour days, including their classroom duties.

This was old-school, naval-stores Valdosta: Outwork the rest of the world.

Now, almost ten minutes before this first morning practice's scheduled six o'clock start—a two-hour workout followed the players' arrival the night before—they were ready to go.

"Don't you just *love* this," exclaimed Alan Rodemaker, the exuberantly tough-talking defensive coordinator who'd left a six-figure sales job to get back into coaching and rejoin Gillespie, whom he'd worked with at two other schools. "You get to be with these kids, wear shorts . . . It doesn't get any better."

Tyrone Lucas, a defensive line coach who'd roomed with Rodemaker when both played at little Presbyterian College, stomped onto the field in construction boots, picking up stray blocking pads and looking like he was ready to pave a road or lay track.

"This is great!" he rasped with the same shredded vocals as Rodemaker—apparently an occupational hazard of defensive coaches—except Lucas's voice registered a deeper black bass than his old roomie's white baritone. "I love it. I *luuuv* it!"

At sixty-two, Al Akins was the staff's last coaching link to Hyder. He assisted on five state and three national title teams. He came by his tough-as-dirt reputation honestly: He'd been a bouncer before he became a coach.

"I agree with everything he's doing 200 percent," the raw-boned, beak-nosed defensive ends coach observed of Gillespie, "but old as I am, it's about to kill me."

The workload was nothing new to those who'd toiled under Gillespie before. In a profession stacked with workaholics, nobody claimed to work harder or more efficiently. Gillespie spent hours in front of his computer writing down-to-the-minute scripts for each day of off-season conditioning, spring practice, summer camp, game week. He was almost always first one in, last one out each day at school. On Thursday mornings, he assembled his assistants in an empty biology classroom at 6:30 to listen to a retired coaching friend read from the Bible and connect its lessons to their lives and their profession. They went straight from there to school, then from school to practice, and from practice to Gillespie's office—to watch film of practice. On Monday nights, Gillespie jogged from his weekly Touchdown Club game review inside the performing arts center back to his empty office for more late-night tweaking.

Some mornings Gillespie drove Kennedy to school. Often he'd drop her off only to remember a radio interview he'd promised to do. He'd call the show and answer questions while he wheeled his way back to the high school.

"When he first moved here we thought he was going to lock up and die," one Touchdown Club member said. "The hours he's keeping now weren't any less in February. It's just how the guy's wired. He does all the wrong things: doesn't sleep, eats salt like it's sugar. He burns the candle at both ends.

"Know how dogs in their sleep will be chasing rabbits?" the booster added of Gillespie. "When he's sleeping, he's chasing officials."

Gillespie was as much on display as his most sought-after players when he made his on-field public debut at the team's ten-day preseason workout. He'd already won over the old guard by bringing back small traditions that, nevertheless, were considered sacred in a tradition-rich region like this. Before every practice and game, for instance, the Wildcats would again form a menacing circle that covered half the field to begin warm ups. They pounded their thigh pads and clapped their hands in a rhythm passed down, until its recent interruption, for decades.

Observers also noticed a startling new energy. At one practice, which Gillespie scheduled on a Saturday to get his kids maximum exposure, more than a dozen recruiters ringed the field from places like Florida State, Florida, Georgia, and Alabama, as well as one-tier-down schools like South Florida and Marshall. "You recruit Valdosta," South Florida assistant and former NFL receiver Phil McGeoghan said of the turnout, "or you lose."

Some of the recruiters were as blown away by the tempo and organization of Gillespie's practice as they were by the raw talent flying around the field. These were guys who stopped at as many as fifty high schools a week. They liked to parachute in and slip right out—be seen and be gone. That wasn't possible that Saturday.

"It was a college practice," said Kirby Smart, Alabama's defensive coordinator and a Georgia grad who had known Gillespie for years. "After two hours, other coaches were coming up to me saying, 'Is he done?' No coach wants to be the first one to leave. And I'd say, 'No. You're going to have to wait.'

"I knew right away," Smart added of Gillespie's talented but still un-formed Wildcats, "these guys had a chance."

For Gillespie, the method to his madness was simple.

"It's all about programming these kids," he said one late night while he tweaked a script on a desktop in his fluorescent-lit office. The night's spittoon of choice: plastic water bottle. "Every day, every minute, you're constantly trying to modify behavior. Does it happen in a year? I don't know." His dark eyebrows arched. "I hope it happens enough."

A whiteboard with the team's depth chart hung on a cinder-block wall. A bookshelf next to his desk included *The Education of a Coach* by David Halberstam and *Winning Every Day* by Lou Holtz. A storage closet was piled with game film and team files and—buried in there somewhere, he thought—some of those twenty cabbage boxes' worth of notebooks that he'd filled after practices back at Georgia.

An old letter from Kennedy, scratched out in pencil, was taped to the closet door. "Dear Dad," it began, "I love you. Jesus dide on the cross to pay for our sins . . ."

He talked about programming kids "on multiple planes": physically, mentally, emotionally.

"Before you even get to the mental part of toughness, the pure, body, physical toughness has to be established. They have to be reprogrammed to run into each other in practice, to the point where they don't say, 'Okay, we hit during this drill, but in this drill we don't.' Uh-uh. We're going to run into each other at practice. They didn't expect that before. Now they do. So that physically, even if their body doesn't want to do something, mentally they're expecting it. It's a fine line crossing over from one to the other, but there is a line.

"It's a mental capacity for work and for performance. It's what you do when you're fighting the battle to win the game. I want them to feel like when we line up we're going to win because we're Valdosta. That's the way it used to be here. I felt like we lost that.

"It's a fine line between 'We're Valdosta and we're going to win' and being arrogant. You get those two things in line, you got a good football team."

He reached for the water bottle.

Spit.

"Sometimes you get a group that won't let you push them over the hump," he went on. "It's frustrating. I've had groups not as talented as this one that have won championships. It's why we drive them, why we demand excellence on every single play. If you play your best on every single play, good things happen."

He paused.

"What's that sound a lot like?" he asked.

He didn't wait for an answer.

"Life."

Alex Stephenson emerged from the locker room Monday morning with his helmet already strapped on, the first Wildcat to step into the morning's presunrise darkness. The sophomore quarterback had transferred to Valdosta in the spring from Ware County, sixty miles east. His goal, beginning with today and continuing the rest of camp: Make Ryan Whilden his . . . well, make Ryan his backup.

A sturdy, dark-browed Mark Sanchez look-alike (his mother is Puerto Rican), Alex jogged onto the field at 5:35 A.M. and grabbed the first ball he found. Ryan shuffled out fifteen minutes later, helmet off, still fiddling with his jersey and tugging at his pants.

"This is my week to shut the door," Alex announced in the gym the night before, seated at the end of his mattress. "This is when I show I'm better than anybody."

With a confidence at once matter-of-fact and camera ready, the fifteen-year-old explained why he transferred.

"I was going to be the man at my old school," he said, "but it was a 4-A school [Valdosta is 5-A, the state's highest classification], and only two kids in its history played at Georgia. The coach there thought it was okay to lose. The coach here is here for the same reason I am. To win.

"Hopefully, then I'll move on to college."

Despite his outward certitude, Alex seemed at a slight remove from his teammates. He spent much of the evening alone, texting his girl-friend. Most of the other players had known each other their whole lives. Parents had dropped some of them off that afternoon straight from church. The seniors, especially, sounded anxious for a change from the way things were this time last year, and the year before that, and the year before that.

"I go to church, I go to the barbershop, and all I hear is how Lowndes looks good again," Green said. "I'm tired of it."

Many of the fathers who dropped players off were former Wildcats. Most sported championship rings. They sounded as enthusiastic as their sons about the new season.

"I can't wait to get my Friday night clothes on," said Robert Morri-son, an ex-'Cat who played running back for a season under Bazemore and whose son, Yontell, was a starting offensive lineman.

His gold teeth twinkling in the gymnasium's hard light, Morrison liked what he'd seen so far of Gillespie. He worked hard, sounded smart, won at a school (Peach County) that was mostly poor and black, like Valdosta, and so he knew all about working and motivating these kids. "If a player ain't here," Morrison said, "he'll go get him."

Morrison believed the vibe already felt better than at last year's camp, when players didn't stay overnight.

"Coach Tomberlin was a good guy, as far as being a good guy goes," he said, "but we want to win some games."

Morrison then spotted Dashay, red underwear peeking out from his low-riding gym shorts.

"Told me he's gonna fool 'em all and play," Morrison said. "Kid needs someone over him to be a manly figure."

That wasn't something Alex lacked.

Alex's father, Matt Stephenson, stood inside the gym as the players arrived. You couldn't miss him: big, dark-haired, dark-eyed bear of a man. Still in his forties, with a GED and two-year technical degree, he'd become wealthy after founding a company fifteen years ago in Waycross that sold commercial laundry equipment, washers and dryers. Origi-nally a one-man shop, it was now a $20 million business with more than sixty employees and another office in suburban Atlanta. High-profile clients included the Atlanta Braves, the University of Georgia, hotels (even a Ritz-Carlton), cruise lines, prisons, and hospitals.

Matt had pushed Alex—didn't mind saying that he pushed him hard—to excel at school and sports since he was four. He coached him up until middle school. Matt was the dad who yelled the loudest at Little League games, upbraided his son publicly when he made a mistake, had him running sprints and doing push-ups in the yard at home. Every minute not spent getting better, Matt believed, was a minute wasted. He grew up hard, so he was hard on his kids. He saw his own business success as proof that it worked.

"I'm tough on all my children," Matt said, easily and openly, "but in a good way. They know they're extremely loved, but they also know my expectations are extremely high. That's the cards they were dealt, and they're just going to have to deal with it. I know I'm a driven person. I couldn't get rid of it if I wanted to.

"I think it'll prove to be a good thing," Matt added. "When Alex was just this big he said, 'Daddy, I want to play with the Georgia Bulldogs.' And I said, 'Son, if that's what you want to do that's what you'll do. Anything's possible.'"

Players kept filing in. Matt nodded in the direction of Phillip Moore, the Wildcats' starting running back. At 5'6" and 170 pounds, he was the team's strongest player, pound for pound—picture a subcompact Humvee. Phillip was known to everybody in town simply as "Swoll," a nickname he adopted after his small body swelled with muscle once he started to lift weights—or, as he put it, "swoll up." Inked across Phillip's broad, muscled back, in case anybody needed reminding: SWOLL.

In his easygoing, soft-spoken way, Swoll was the tough, talented, eternal core of what Valdosta football had always looked like. He'd been the team ball boy as a kid, filled his room with Wildcat paraphernalia, rooted for his Wildcat older brother. He bought into Gillespie's workhorse ways, seeing the new coach as a missing link between Valdosta's gloried past and its resuscitated future.

"Too hyped to go to sleep man," he'd texted before the first spring practice, at 12:49 A.M. "Tomorrow the rising action ends and the climax begin in Wildcats' return to the throne."

Like everybody else in town, Matt was a huge fan of Swoll, but Matt, who wouldn't let his kids dream small, wondered if Swoll dreamed big enough.

"All he's ever wanted is to be a Wildcat," Matt said. "I don't know if his aspirations ever went further than that. Whereas Alex's aspirations"— Matt raised a hand above his dark eyebrows—"are up here."

Matt glanced again around the gym. Players unrolled mattresses, set up PlayStations, nodded their heads to digitized music that only they could hear through their earbuds.

When he looked back at Alex—already set up at one end of the gym, away from all of the clowning and gaming and hanging out—he could see a kid who starred at Georgia, who waited anxiously around a TV with the rest of his family on NFL draft day.

"This," Matt said flatly, "is a stepping-stone."

❦

Six months earlier, Matt, his wife, Janette, and his two younger children and grown stepdaughter, appeared to be settled in Waycross forever. They lived in a big house out in the country, entertained friends, watched Matt's business boom. Janette, who grew up in Puerto Rico and gave Alex his dark good looks, took a class in town to improve her English.

That all changed with one out-of-the-blue phone call.

From Nub.

The Touchdown Club had charged Nub with buying an industrial-strength washer and dryer. It was one of the first things Gillespie said he wanted when asked for his wish list. Players used to wash their own game and practice uniforms, and some went weeks between cleanings. Gillespie wanted his team looking first-class all the time.

So the Touchdown Club agreed to pony up $14,000 to make its new coach happy. It sounded like a lot but, hell, he didn't ask for a new truck.

Nub looked around and finally called a company in Waycross. When Matt learned the Valdosta Wildcats were interested, he called Nub back himself. "I take pride in selling laundry equipment to prestigious places," he said. "So I was really proud hearing Valdosta High was interested."

Matt grew up in Valdosta but never played football. He had to work and tend to his mother, who was in and out of homes and hospitals with a mental illness. Her medical bills and illness-driven spending sprees forced his father to work two and three jobs just to keep up, until finally they divorced. Matt left school before he graduated to join the navy. He wanted out, and in the navy he found his way up.

"I learned if you go in and do what they ask and excel at it, guess what? You get a pat on the back. And that pat on the back felt good to me because then you got a raise. All of sudden, I really started achieving."

Matt left after eight years and eventually landed a job with a commercial laundry company based in Atlanta. He'd worked on missile systems in the navy, so servicing computerized laundry equipment was a snap. One customer was so taken with Matt's work he fronted him a loan to start his own company. Matt opened Tri-State Technical Services a month after Alex was born.

"I promised myself that Alex would have a nice life," he said. "I wanted a lot for my family. My parents did the best they could, but my mom and dad never sat down and talked to me about going to college. They never had that luxury. I want more for my kids."

Then he added, "I don't know if I fall into that classic 'I play ball through my children' thing. Subconsciously, that might be what's going on."

While he never played for Valdosta, two of his uncles are in the school's Hall of Fame. So after Matt and Nub discussed washers and dryers, the talk moved to football. Nub went on about the new coach and his wide-open offense and how the team looked loaded, especially at wide receiver and tight end. Only thing the 'Cats lacked, Nub said, was a proven quarterback. Nobody knew if last year's starter would be back, and the kid most likely to start didn't even go out for the team last season.

"Well," Matt said, "my son's a helluva quarterback . . ."

Nub arranged for Matt to meet Gillespie about the washer and dryer. Talk again shifted to football—and to Alex. Gillespie said he couldn't say much, that there were procedures everybody had to follow if a kid wanted to transfer.

"We knew there was an opportunity there," Matt said, "but I wasn't feeling enough from Gillespie. He can't recruit. Weeks went by. My discussions with Alex got more intense."

By then, Alex had done some research online. He learned a couple of things. All three quarterbacks Gillespie had as head coach at Peach went on to play Division I college football. Also, as a football player, Ryan appeared to be really good at baseball.

"Alex was like, 'Dad, wake up. Do you realize the opportunity this is? I'm willing to do it,'" Matt said. "When I tried to back out of it to make sure he really wanted to do it for himself, he said to me, 'Are you kidding me?'

"There's no denying Alex spotted the target and we were going to go for it," said Matt. "I believe in him and his dreams, and I'm going to give him every opportunity to achieve those dreams. It was as simple as that."

The rest of the family balked. Janette's first response to Matt, in her fast-improving but still heavily-accented English, "Have you lost your *mind*?"

Alex withdrew from Ware County High at 11:00 A.M. on a Thursday in March. He enrolled at Valdosta that same afternoon.

Alex and Matt moved into a rented, largely unfurnished house in town; they had to live there for a year before they could move to another house Matt owned off a lake out in the county, next to his father. Janette and the other kids would come when school finished later that spring.

The move baffled Ware County head coach Ed Dudley, but he'd coached almost twenty years in suburban Atlanta, where kids play musical chairs with coaches and systems. He said Alex told him he was moving to Valdosta to be closer to his sick grandfather.

"He was not in line to start as a sophomore. He was going to have to work his way through the system and earn his playing time," Dudley said. "If that translates into your grandfather being sick, so be it.

"I fully support people trying to do what's in the best interest of their kid. But I do think people make a mistake trying to make high school football more than what it is. It's not a tryout camp for college football. I think some people start losing sight of the value of high school football as a game and a sport, as a place where you learn sacrifice and character.

"You can only push a kid so much," he added. "Colleges spend a billion dollars a year recruiting. If you're good enough they'll find you. Herschel Walker did not go unnoticed growing up in Wrightsville, Georgia."

Alex impressed Valdosta's coaches instantly. Gillespie kept a point system to rank his quarterbacks after each summer workout, and Alex leapfrogged Ryan. He was bigger, stronger, faster. He overachieved in the weight room and buried himself in Gillespie's complex playbook; in the spring, his new girlfriend shook her head during an economics class while she watched him thumb through the offense.

In July, following one of the 7-on-7 passing league games that dominate prep teams' off-seasons, Valdosta's coaches, players, and fans witnessed a side of Matt and Alex's dynamic that folks in Waycross had long gotten used to, if never quite comfortable with.

With his father, grandfather, and girlfriend inside Bazemore-Hyder Stadium, where the temperature on the turf again topped 100 degrees, Alex had a horrible day. His passes were high, low, long, short—"probably," he said, "the worst I ever looked." In a moment of frustration, he glanced up into the stands, looking for a tall, slim coed with long brown hair and a can't-miss-it smile: his girlfriend Lindsey Parker.

Matt saw that and hit the roof.

He disapproved of Alex having a girlfriend in the first place. It would mess with his focus. Matt and Alex had always done everything together: hunted, fished, gone to games. That had intensified with their move to Valdosta. Matt now spent more time away from the office to watch and to be with Alex.

"I never let Alex just run," he said. "I've always kept my thumb on what he's doing."

Now, though, Alex dated a girl who was a year older and drove a car. "It was, 'Hey, Dad, I'm going to the movies with Lindsey,'" Matt said. "'Hey, Dad, I'm going to Lindsey's house to have supper.' 'Hey, Dad, we're going to this and that.'"

It was tough on Matt. He talked to Alex about it, told him, "Man, I'm losing you."

Now that tension came to a swift, furious head. Matt cornered Alex outside the stadium after the game and lit into him, face red, F-bombs flying, poking a forefinger into his son's forehead to underscore his outrage.

"Dad," Alex exclaimed, "I just had a bad day!"

"You don't have bad days when you're the quarterback of this caliber team!" Matt shot back, then roared that Alex had his mind on his girlfriend instead of football. That had to stop now. *Right now!*

Alex stood there paralyzed. Then he started to cry. Matt didn't let up. Folks leaving the stadium looked on for a moment, then turned away, embarrassed for gawking but troubled by what they saw.

"I moved over here for you and you're going to do *that*?" Matt continued to shout. "It's garbage! It's god-awful! You ain't never going to amount to anything playing like that. We can pick up and move back right now if you're not serious about this. Don't waste another minute of my time!"

Later, Matt said, "Emotionally, mentally, I broke him down. But it was something he won't ever forget. It's something that when he thinks about his dad, he'll say, 'He was extremely tough but, man, do I know my dad loved me. My best friend was my dad.'"

At the time, that's not what Alex thought. That evening he fled to his grandfather's house, afraid to confront his dad again at home. Matt, still fuming, came and got him.

Later on that night, overcome with guilt as he slept by himself (Janette and the kids were still back in Waycross), Matt wrote Alex a two-page letter of apology.

I'm sorry, he wrote. *I was angry. I didn't mean all that stuff I said. Please just forget it.*

I love you.

Alex called Lindsey and told her about the note. She told him to reconcile. Alex had come to rely on Lindsey as a kind of safety valve for the pressure he'd felt for moving his family and upending their lives. Lindsey was a bit of a nerd, a grade-obsessed A student in the IB program. She didn't know much about football, a rarity among girls at Valdosta.

"She couldn't care less if I was the starting quarterback at a good college or in the band playing trombone," Alex explained. "She liked me because of me."

Lindsey's own parents were divorced, so she understood the pressure on Alex and how complicated his relationship could be with his dad.

"His dad was open from the beginning that Alex was playing for Valdosta to get noticed and go play college ball," she said. "He even talked about the NFL."

Matt had always pushed him, Lindsey said, and he always would. She was driven to excel at school, so she didn't necessarily see that as a bad thing. She encouraged Alex to accept his dad's apology.

"They get caught up in the moment, say things to each other, go back and forth," she said. "By the end of the day it's usually resolved."

So that morning Alex and Matt hugged and moved on.

"That's my dad." Alex shrugged. Then he made a smile. "I'm used to it. I think it brought us closer together."

So there was Alex, first player on the field, long before the sun came up, the first morning practice of camp.

By the time the black sky turned blue, it was full-on boot camp. Coaches sprinted from station to station ahead of their players, the pace full speed all the time.

"We're going to get from zero to one hundred right freakin' now!" Gillespie yelled at the start.

"You gotta be *shittin'* me!" another coach yelled when he spotted a player walking between the white lines. "I got a running back that won't run! *You sprint!*"

"I didn't like it," a defensive coach called out during a drill after a cornerback made an interception. "He caught the ball, but everybody was going at three-quarters speed. *Do it again!*"

On it went, loud and constant, like the earsplitting rattle of the waking cicadas.

"Eyes on his sternum—*go!*"

"C'mon, boy, extend out. I don't hear no *pop!*"

"Be physical with your hands. *Too high! Too high!*"

Then, to a player ordered to flop on his belly and jump back up a dozen times after he blew an assignment, *"Land on your dick!"*

On it went. Ninety minutes in, players broke an easy, Thoroughbred's sweat and caught their first rhythm of the day. A couple of dozen folks already watched from the bleachers across the field. They nodded, smiled, frowned, and tossed out cold coffee from their takeout cups.

Alex and Ryan alternated running the offense. Both looked sharp. Then, twenty minutes before the end of the session, a harmless-seeming 15-yard spiral fluttered over the middle. Jay Rome went up for it, his long, athletic frame almost blotting the low sun behind him. As he reached for the pass with both hands and pulled it into his chest, a defender flew across low and fast and took his legs out from under him. Jay landed hard on the soft grass. He didn't get up. Then he did the one thing nobody wants to see a football player do.

Grabbed a knee.

The men lazing away the morning on the wooden bleachers quickly rose, craned their necks, murmured among themselves. Teammates and coaches circled Jay. "You okay? You okay?" Jay didn't say a word. Just nodded.

At 7:38 A.M., on the first Monday of camp, Valdosta's season of redemption, possibly of survival, suddenly looked in doubt.

Somebody shouted, *"Anybody seen Stan?"*

11

Rome the Elder
and Rome the Younger

or Royalty

It still looked like the place to get what you want, if what you wanted was cheap and illegal.

There were the boarded-up houses and empty lots. There were the pissed-off dogs chained in the worn-out yards. There was the all-day, all-night crowd on the front steps of closed-up Ray's Food Mart, drinking more than drugging these days, at least since the cops started to watch what folks there did when they weren't playing dominoes.

Across the street from Ray's, taped to the door of a barbershop run by a young black man named Columbus Washington and his mother, Rosa, a hand-printed Bible passage warned anyone about to step inside: "No weapon that is formed against us shall prosper."

Mrs. Washington explained, "You never know how a person is feeling when they walk into a barbershop."

Other warnings were posted on churches that sprouted like wiregrass on almost every corner. "Those who live by the sword," cautioned one sign in front of St. Peter Church of God by Faith in Jesus Christ, "die by the sword."

When the Apocalypse came, the message everywhere seemed clear, it would start here.

Then there were the half-dozen fellas—not one looked older than twenty—who stood around a trash-can fire in the middle of a weekday, like extras from some hip-hop *Rocky* remake, and peered out from hoodies and slouchy wool caps on this played-out West Side street and hungrily eyed anybody who drove by.

It was here that Stan Rome showed up more than two decades ago, "totally out of my mind, totally self-destructing," in search of the cheap and the illegal.

He found both. Yet even when somebody offered him five dollars' worth of crack, it wasn't cheap enough. The greatest athlete in the history of Valdosta High, a two-sport stud at Clemson, an NBA draft pick, and an NFL wide receiver, didn't own a dime. So when the dealer dropped a little something in his palm, Stan calmly closed his massive hand and took off—running for his life, running like the wind, toting his precious five-dollar rock of street-grade cocaine like it was stitched and bound in pigskin.

Stan left that sorry dealer behind in the fall of 1988 the same way he'd once left a thousand sorry cornerbacks shaking their heads on fields across the South.

"Here's what comes to my mind when I think about Stan Rome," recalled Gary Rowe, a teammate on Valdosta's 1971 national title team, who then played defensive back at Tennessee.

"When he'd go out to that wideout position and everybody knew what the play was going to be—they knew we were going to throw that quick out to Stan Rome, and they'd stack two or three or however many players out there to stop him—guess what they couldn't do?

"They couldn't stop Stan Rome," he said. "That's the heart he had. How bad do you want it? Stan Rome wanted it pretty bad."

Well, Stan wanted what he had on that cool autumn morning back in the late '80s pretty badly, too. Even though Stan was thirty-two and hadn't caught one of those quick outs in years, that suckered dealer didn't stand a chance. He had to know it, too, the instant Stan accelerated and made his first cut down one of the neighborhood's dirt side streets.

As one former coach remembered, "Stan didn't move like everyone else. He moved like a panther. A black panther."

So the dealer did what those thousand beaten corners probably wished they could've done when they lined up opposite Stan Rome: He pulled a .22. With that, he didn't need to catch Stan—nobody *caught* Stan—he only needed to get close.

Which he finally did, spotting Stan as he loped with those long smooth strides of his over a short paved bridge that crossed a nearby canal. From 30 yards away, the dealer lifted his gun and fired.

Head shot.

So it was on that hard, cracked, unforgiving bridge, spanning a dismal little ditch in a tough-luck outback not far from the Florida line, that Stan Rome's legacy as this storied town's favorite son appeared to come to a cold, stupid end.

●

Twenty-two years later, the day after Jay went down clutching his knee that first morning of camp, Stan Rome swerved his black Escalade into an open space behind the high school. He unfolded himself slowly to get out of the vehicle, then headed straight for Gillespie's office, wielding his cane like a divining rod as he made his way with wide, zigzagging strides.

Jay looked startled as he lay on the trainer's table the day before, trying to absorb the potential consequences of the pain in his knee. His face relaxed when he learned it wasn't anything serious: just a deep bruise. It would hurt like hell for a few days and then he'd be good to go.

Just to be safe, Gillespie decided to keep his all-state tight end out of the next few practices—until Stan showed up. His appearance wasn't a surprise. Football coaches are used to parents worried that they'll put their own self-interests—i.e., winning—ahead of their kids' best interests, and rush them back from an injury too soon.

This region was different. Mark Richt had coached South Georgia boys since he was an assistant to Bobby Bowden at Florida State. He knew exactly what separated kids here from a lot of kids in other parts of the country: "They're coached hard."

Gillespie knew of high schools elsewhere in the state where if he coached there the way he coached here, kids would clear out their lockers by the end of the first day. In a place like Valdosta he could coach his kids as hard as they needed to be coached because, he said, "Parents here want their kids coached hard."

He had players whose daddies and granddaddies were coached Hyder hard, Bazemore hard.

Hard as it gets.

So when Stan saw Gillespie after the next day's practice, he wanted to know why the coach was keeping his son on the sidelines.

"He said at the next level, and at the next level after that, Jay has to learn to play hurt," Gillespie said of Stan's concern that blazing summer afternoon, three weeks before the first game. "He said if Jay doesn't learn to play hurt, they'll just cut him."

Next day, in pads, Jay took the field.

Stan's narrative was the town's narrative, winding through redemption's classic three acts: up from nothing, fall from grace, rise from the dead.

Or as Stan put it, "How many people get shot in the head and live to talk about it?"

Jay was his story's main target, of course, maybe even its like-father-like-son sequel—minus, locals hoped, the father's facedown second act on that bridge over the canal. Yet its lessons were universal and had been retold all over town. Bent nearly in half, walking with a cane, Stan was both an inspiration and a cautionary tale to any kid who dreamed of being a Wildcat.

Jim Melvin, the former head basketball coach at Valdosta State who knew Stan when he was a skinny grade-schooler dunking with both hands, summed it up, "Stardom has its fallout, and it can be cruel."

No one was a closer reader of the Stan Rome Story than seventeen-year-old Jay. In a town where football was king, the Rome name was royalty. That made Jay successor-in-waiting. Old-timers here often projected one Rome onto the other. It was easy to see why: In a photo of the 1971 title team, standing almost a head taller than everyone else, the young Stan was a dead ringer for Jay. He carried the same alert eyes, the same soft, open face, the same sure-of-himself posture. Even the same number: 11.

These days, however, Stan stood almost a head shorter than his teenaged son. One side of his face was partially paralyzed. He couldn't hear out of one ear. His words sometimes caught in midsentence, like a needle stuck on scratched vinyl.

So when someone like David Waller watched Jay snare a pass one-handed, or break through a pair of tacklers, or stand warrior-tall on the Valdosta sideline, he sometimes saw "the Stan we knew when he played for the Wildcats."

"I think his daddy is going to be awfully cautious with Jay," Waller said, echoing the sentiment all over town. "He knows what happened to him. He understands what can happen to anybody."

Jay didn't dodge the comparisons to his father's greatness or the warnings in his fall. He'd heard about both all his life. They were inspiring and they were sobering. So while Jay worked to forge his own identity, on and off the field, he still paid homage to his bloodline.

Hung on a wall in Jay's bedroom: his father's Clemson warm-up jersey. His Facebook handle: HeirToTheThrone. His Twitter account: @ KingRome11.

"Knowing what my dad's been through, his upbringing and everything, it tells me anything is possible," Jay said. "He's teaching me from his mistakes. I know everything he went through made him a better man, and him being a better man is making me better."

Jay then added, those alert eyes widening as he got more to the point, "I'm just thankful he's still here to help me."

Stan's story begins where a lot of black kids' stories began in the segregated South of the '60s. He was raised in a narrow "gun-barrel" house by a single mother with a seventh-grade education, surrounded by extended family but wholly isolated from the wider white world.

Valdosta's South Side had its own schools, stores, dentists, barbecue stands, poolrooms, and clubs. It even had its own two-street Strivers' Row, out where the grid of wood-frame bungalows gave way to neat, simple ranch houses: Bethune and Bunche were the street addresses of choice for a modest but tight cadre of black professionals.

All that activity crowded up to a very precise line—then stopped. Railroad tracks ran like an electric fence between the South Side and downtown, keeping blacks in and expectations out.

"We really didn't realize," remembered Roger Rome, Stan's older brother by three years, "that we didn't have anything."

Stan and Roger barely knew their separate biological fathers, but with a formidable mother who stood 6'3" tall, they grew like weeds and excelled at every sport. Their reputations jumped the tracks and spread across town.

More than that, the Rome boys' feats on the football field and basketball court became a kind of curative for the utter smallness that their towering mother felt as a single black woman with two kids in that era's repressed, hemmed-in world. As her sons' renown grew, her self-image blossomed.

"They gave me a name," said Roberta Washington, in her late seventies and married to the same man for more than thirty years. "Because all the time before they played sports, my name was 'that gal that got those two boys down there.' But when they started playing, I got to be 'Roger and Stan's mother.'"

Despite Valdosta High football's national reputation by then, however, few blacks even knew where the school was.

"There were imaginary boundaries you didn't cross," Roger said. "So we just made all the games at Pinevale [the all-black high school]. Football was big on both sides of town. Pinevale didn't get the press Valdosta got, but to our minds we thought, 'So what?' We had something good here."

When segregation finally lifted, white coaches found the Romes. Roger became a two-sport standout who'd be recruited for football by Kansas and play basketball at Florida. Stan, meanwhile, was visited by Bazemore in the eighth grade. The legendary coach promised Stan and his teammates a state title when they arrived at Valdosta High.

The whole town seemed to adopt the two brothers. No other athletes bridged the gap between one side of the tracks and the other like the Rome boys.

"Both had that fire in them. You couldn't put it out," said Melvin, who ran a gym where Stan and Roger played basketball every day during the summer. "They wanted to be somebody. They had personality, they were handsome—the world just kind of wanted to be around Stan and Roger."

Stan started varsity in the ninth grade, the first freshman football player in anyone's memory to do that at Valdosta. In his sophomore year, Valdosta won that title Bazemore had promised, with Stan setting school and state records for catches and yards. Far beyond the pine and cotton and swamp, the football world now knew about Stan Rome.

Then, even with colleges around the country wooing him after his sophomore season, things started to jump the track. Stan was at once the king of Valdosta and a stranger to himself.

"I was thrust into a situation where I was a star, everybody was telling me I was great," he said, "and I still felt like that tall skinny kid from a low income family who didn't have a father. So I said, 'I got to act the part.' I started drinking at parties, smoking a little pot. I thought, 'When is everybody going to wake up and find out I'm not all that?'"

In his senior year, *Parade* magazine named Stan both a football and basketball All American; he was its first dual-sport honoree. Recruiters from Miami to UCLA called constantly or camped out in front of his mother's house. In an era before cell phones, and before much NCCA scrutiny, the stampede to Valdosta became a gold rush. Stan often hid out at his girlfriend's house.

It was one wild, disorienting ride. Joe Wilson, a Bazemore assistant who left and coached Lowndes's first championship team, remembered Stan as polite and personable, but also as country as the day is long—just like Valdosta back then. Wilson once flew with Stan to New York for an all-star basketball tournament that featured the nation's premiere young players: Moses Malone, Butch Lee, Skip Wise. As they waited together in front of their Manhattan hotel for a bus to take them to the game, a bewildered-looking Stan watched an endless river of New Yorkers bustle by. Finally, Stan leaned down and told Wilson what was bugging him.

"There's all these people," he marveled, "but none of them has said a word to us."

"There we were," Wilson laughed, "this old white South Georgia coach and a tall black kid—the first time these two country boys ever been up there."

Wilson also remembered the game: Malone scored 2 points; Stan, who didn't play in the first half, put up 14. On the court, he looked as worldly as they come.

Stan chose Clemson. The school told him he could play both sports, and Stan was hot to play basketball in the Atlantic Coast Conference, then home to NC State's David Thompson, that era's Michael Jordan. To compete, Clemson head basketball coach Tates Locke aggressively lured black players to the white-centric school, including Skip Wise, a Baltimore high school legend, and Wayne "Tree" Rollins, a 7-footer from Cordele, ninety miles north of Valdosta, who'd play eighteen seasons in the NBA.

Aiding Locke with recruiting was a wealthy booster named B. C. Inabinet. The running joke at Clemson at the time: How do you know the basketball team is practicing? The parking lot is full of Monte Carlos.

In a memoir Locke wrote after he fled Clemson and the NCAA slapped the school with probation, Rollins estimated that during his four years there he received $60,000 in clothes, flights for his mother, walking-around money—and a '73 Monte Carlo. Rollins's reasoning for taking the gifts echoed the circumstances of Locke's other prized recruits.

"When you come from a poor background, you just have to take the money. I looked at basketball as a job. They were making money off me at Clemson. My mother was supporting four kids at home and we needed the money."

Rollins told *Sports Illustrated* his quotes were accurate, but he later denied them to a South Carolina newspaper. Inabinet also denied Rollins's accusations. He explained, "I gave Locke cash and I didn't ask what he did with it."

Inabinet, who died in 1983, was banned from the program by the NCAA.

Stan's mother still remembered the freewheeling, larger-than-life (6'8", almost 400 pounds) South Carolina hustler. She said Inabinet barraged her with offers of a better life, including a new house.

"I was trying to make up my mind, but I didn't know what I was doing," she said of the whole recruiting circus. "I'd only gone to the seventh grade. Only thing I knew, I was working hard and taking care of my kids."

Stan won't talk much about that period, except to say of Clemson's recruitment, "They didn't do anything a lot of other schools didn't do."

●

Stan's career at Clemson was a bumpy, uneven success.

He only played football one year. The Tigers went 2-9 and rarely threw the ball. Losing was the one thing Valdosta hadn't prepared him for. Its lessons came hard.

"I'd lost four games my whole four years at Valdosta," Stan recalled. "The locker room became really depressed. It really did a number on my head. I was like, 'I'm going back to basketball.'"

Basketball became problematic, too. Locke skipped out after Stan's freshman year, replaced by Bill Foster, who didn't like that Stan played football. Foster also had his own class of favorite recruits, who cut into Stan's playing time.

Stan still averaged almost 17 points a game his senior season, enough, he said, "to get into the fourth round of the draft. But if he'd turned me loose I could've put up numbers to be a first- or second-round pick.

"All the time, I felt I was being mistreated," Stan added, "and that fed into me partying more or doing whatever to escape from what was going on."

Beyond the liquor and pot, Stan acquired a taste for cocaine. It didn't affect his performance.

Not yet.

"I was still in the mix for accomplishing the goals I set for myself," he said. "I wasn't doing anything that was going to completely take me out. I just thought I was being a normal twenty- or twenty-one-year-old athlete."

So did the NBA. Cleveland drafted Stan, and he was the last player cut, just before the season opener. Cavaliers coach Bill Fitch called Stan into his office and said he had a business dilemma: two aging stars, including Walt Frazier, with no-cut contracts. He asked Stan to stay in Cleveland, told him he'd get him a job working around the arena so that he'd be there when a spot opened up.

Stan thought he'd already done enough to make the team. He responded, "Just give me a plane ticket. I want to go home."

◗

Stan had hardly unpacked in Valdosta when the semipro Western Basketball Association called. He flew to Reno, played there a couple of weeks, then was traded to Las Vegas—"the last place," Stan noted wryly, "I needed to be."

By season's end, Stan had offers to visit several NBA camps, but a call came out of the blue from the NFL Chiefs. Unknown to Stan, they'd drafted him in the eleventh round. So without playing a down since his sophomore year at Clemson, Stan flew to Kansas City and signed a four-year deal.

His cocaine habit swelled with his salary. By his fourth season, he said, "I really lost it."

Roger, whose own basketball career was curtailed when a lawn mower lopped off part of a toe, by then had moved to Kansas City for a sales job. Just days after arriving, he remembered, "I had guys calling me looking for money Stan owed. Stan gave me $60,000 in cash, told me to keep it for him. Suppliers were looking for the money. He was out of control."

The Chiefs finally wearied of Stan's erratic play and missed practices, and released him before the end of his fourth year. He played briefly in the fledgling United States Football League (he later pawned his Washington Federals jersey for drug money) before he returned to Valdosta for good, landing a job selling clothes.

He was a mess—a sharp-dressing, good-timing, back-slapping mess.

"I felt like a failure," he said. "I'd let myself down, the town down, my family down. I kept trying to escape who I'd become in a bottle or a pipe. It reached the point where I didn't want to live but I didn't have the courage to kill myself."

Then Stan met a smart-as-a-whip, straight-as-an-arrow country girl from nearby Clyattville. LaVerne Hargrett was one of nine kids raised on a farm by parents who never finished high school but stressed education to their children. Seven would graduate from college, while two others joined the military.

LaVerne was at Valdosta State when Stan showed up. She'd never heard of him. When he took her to a Clemson game against Florida State in Tallahassee, "people kept coming up asking him for his autograph," she recalled, "and I thought, 'Are you kidding?'"

Stan had been in and out of rehab, but LaVerne didn't think he was anything but a recreational user. She wasn't hard to fool. She once found a bag of his and described its contents to a girlfriend over the phone.

"Marijuana," her incredulous girlfriend told her.

Other friends were more incredulous when they learned who LaVerne was dating. "Stan *Rome*?" one remembered telling her. "He's a crackhead!"

Stan behaved though, and they got married. By the end of their honeymoon, however, things already were falling apart. LaVerne would come home and find something new missing that Stan had hocked for drugs: the TV set, his wedding ring.

A dealer once showed up at their house while Stan was out and demanded money for drugs Stan had snatched from him. LaVerne didn't have it and wondered, as the dealer stood in her doorway, if he was "fixing to kill me." Then she recognized him from Clyattville; they'd grown up together.

LaVerne broke down. "I was standing on the porch," she said, "a drug dealer consoling me."

Scared, humiliated, only twenty-four, LaVerne left.

A few months later, Stan got himself shot in the head.

That should've been that . . . but after a doctor removed the bullet lodged behind one ear, Stan was left with a lopsided face, some rotten hearing, and that's about it. Physically. (His crippling back pain came later, a degenerative disc from his playing days. He got NFL disability.)

Emotionally, Stan had hit a bottom that he didn't know existed. He was broke, virtually homeless, and just had a bullet plucked from his head.

"I remember being in that hospital saying, 'God, why don't you let me die? I ruined my life, all this God-given talent you gave me,'" he said. "And it was like God spoke: 'I have a purpose for you. I see something in you that you don't see in yourself.'"

He added, "I was strung out big-time."

LaVerne remembered standing beside Stan's hospital bed "with all these emotions, not knowing what to say."

Stan remembered this: "LaVerne looking over me, like she'd kill me herself if everybody would just leave the room."

Stan told her he was sorry. LaVerne had heard that a million times.

Stan's mother was already in another room at the hospital: After she'd kicked Stan out of her house a few days earlier she thought she was having a heart attack. It turned out to be a nervous breakdown; she'd about worried herself to death.

When she learned Stan was shot, she had the weirdest reaction. "I felt good," Mrs. Washington recalled. "I just said, 'Thank the Lord.' It had got to a place where I was up all night long with him being in the streets and I couldn't be in no worse shape if the Lord took him.

"So I got out of that hospital bed and when I saw him I said, 'Now it's going to be okay.' And he said, 'Mom, I'm through.' He said, 'I've gone to the bottom. I can't get no lower.' And I believed it this time. A feeling came over me I never felt before. I knew it was the end."

Others weren't so certain.

"We were just hoping for the best," Roger said. "He's a good-hearted person, but he had to get that shit out of his system before he could become the person he is now."

If Stan's surviving that head shot was, as everybody here agreed, a holy-mackerel miracle, what came next was almost more implausible.

A couple of days after the shooting, a white, retired military colonel named Mike Stouffer showed up at the hospital—"like an angel," Stan's mother said—and announced that he was taking Stan home and straightening him out.

Stouffer's kids had gone to high school with Stan, and he'd followed Stan's career through Kansas City. When Stan came back to Valdosta, Stouffer bought some clothes from him.

That was the extent of their connection. Stouffer wasn't from Valdosta, wasn't even from the South. Didn't matter. He'd never forgotten watching Stan all those Friday nights at old Cleveland Field, and how just being inside that crazed, packed stadium watching the Wildcats with the rest of the town had finally—after postings in Germany, France, Japan—made him feel like he'd found a home.

"In Valdosta," Stouffer said, "if you don't grow day lilies and support the Wildcats, you're just an outsider."

So when Stouffer heard about the shooting, he headed straight to the hospital. He never planned on bringing Stan home, and the moment he announced his offer, he admitted, he raised his eyes to the ceiling and asked, "Lord, what did I just say?"

His son called and read him the riot act. "Dad," he said, "you're crazy as hell. He'll rob you blind. He'll shoot you. *He's a drug addict!*"

Stouffer didn't flinch.

"I had three wars behind me—World War II, Korea, and Vietnam," said Stouffer, now in his eighties. "I'd been a prisoner of war. I'd been through tough times, and I knew he'd been through tough times. I wasn't worried."

Stouffer and his wife set up Stan in their son's old bedroom. Stouffer then got him back his job selling clothes and handled his money until he paid off the untold thousands he'd borrowed, or ripped off, all over town.

It worked. After six months, Stouffer told Stan it was time to go. Still broke and wary but clean and given a second chance, Stan reconciled with LaVerne, and the two rebuilt their lives. Stan worked as a drug counselor, opened two halfway houses, and became an ordained minister. Jay was born in 1992. Two more children followed.

(Stan also had a daughter from high school and a son, Brandon Frye, from when he played in Kansas City, who also played several years in the NFL.)

His troubles weren't over, though. In 1998, Stan was indicted as part of a national Medicare fraud scheme involving a company he worked for in Florida. He cooperated with investigators and reluctantly pled guilty to one count ("I didn't really think I did anything wrong," he said).

Yet after a parade of former drug addicts and their parents testified at the trial about how Stan changed their lives, a federal judge in Tampa handed him an almost unheard of "zero" sentence—no prison, no probation, no restitution.

"We are supposed to protect the community," the judge told a shocked courtroom. "Protecting the community of Valdosta, Georgia, means letting this man come and go as he wants."

🏈

Stan now came and went in his black Escalade all over town, usually with Jay beside him.

J. B. Brown, the local youth league coach who had known the Romes for years, called Stan and Jay "inseparable." He once watched the two talk by themselves together at a restaurant table for hours.

"They're father and son but they're good friends, too," Brown said. "They seem real proud of each other."

Stan parked at the field's edge for nearly every practice, then crab-walked with his crooked cane out to the middle of the field, where he conferred quietly with coaches, players, and his son.

He was nearly as ubiquitous off the field. On a team where most of the players came from homes with one or no parents, at a school where more than half the students qualified for free or reduced lunches, Stan counseled kids in situations he once was in ("I went home to a baby and a girlfriend"), let them stay at his house when they had nowhere else to go, and bailed them out of jail.

To them he was Mr. Stan.

Stan never discussed this mentor's role with Gillespie. At fifty-five, he occupied a sort of mythical chair as Valdosta's eminence grise. He held the position through the accumulated wisdom of his on-field exploits, his comeback from being left for dead, and his capacity for changing both his own life and the lives of others.

Stan barged cane-first into almost any situation with a kind of unaffected, worldly-wise, slightly loopy-looking saintliness.

"I think Stan is really sorry for the life choices he made. I think it haunts him," Roger said. "He wants to do everything he can to help not just Jay but every kid here. He's trying to redeem himself."

For Jay, Stan's story was inseparable from his own. He'd never felt overshadowed or suffocated by it, even though he said, "every time I turn around, somebody asks if I'm going to be better than my dad.

"I don't mind." He shrugged with a tossed-off confidence he seemed born with. "I like to be pushed to be better."

Part of Jay's acceptance came from his full, frank knowledge of Stan's backstory. As a kid, Jay accompanied his father to the halfway houses he ran and watched him work with recovering addicts. He remembered talks the two had on the drives there and back, Stan telling him "about all his ordeals—getting shot, the drugs, the gambling money. I couldn't have been more than seven or eight. I was an inquisitive kid and asked a lot of questions. He answered them."

As Jay got older and Stan drove him to summer basketball tournaments farther away from home, the talks turned longer and deeper.

"Things that happened in his life, good and bad things," Jay recalled. "His college life. The League. The things he was exposed to once he got money—the drugs, any kind of women you wanted, living the high life just because you had it. And I remember thinking how proud I was that he could come from all that, and talk about it, and help people."

Stan isn't much for parenting's do's and don't's; that's more LaVerne's style. Instead, Stan's stories are their own unspoken lessons.

"It's never actually been spelled out, but it's been understood. He just expects me to do the right thing," Jay said. "If you're going to a party, you don't drink, you don't smoke. I knew what was acceptable and what wasn't."

With a six-figure NFL disability settlement, Stan and LaVerne moved the family just outside town in 2002 into a sprawling ranch house in a gated, virtually all-white community. Physically and psychically, it's about as far as one can get from where Stan grew up, and from where he almost died.

Yet even inside the Romes' upscale subdivision, Jay wasn't sheltered from Valdosta's rawer side. The town was still too small for that. Before football and basketball games, kids who Jay knew growing up, and who now made their livings on the street, had offered him everything they thought he might want—liquor, money, "whatever"—for a win, a touchdown, a 30-point night, a dunk.

That was when he recalled his dad's stories.

"All of it kind of guides my path," Jay said. "I've been around plenty of fights and drugs and even people shooting, police coming from everywhere. I never stayed in the 'hood or ran the streets, but I understand the streets. I understand what you can and can't do.

"As I got older," he added, "it hit me why my dad's been through a lot of stuff. It's there."

Stan steered his Escalade down a West Side alley and slowed in front of a sagging green bungalow: It was where he palmed that five-dollar rock he couldn't afford. A few yards away, the fellas around the trash-can fire in the middle of the day stared at him hard, ready to fetch whatever he wanted—or to run like hell.

The streets were the same as Stan remembered them. Only the faces had changed.

He moved on: This was where he made his first cut after he bolted with the crack; this was where another dope house used to be (it was just weeds now); this was where he headed toward the canal.

Then he stopped: This was where he went down. Stan didn't even know he was shot, just felt a little blood trickling down his neck. People rushed from nearby houses waving their own guns, yelling at Stan to get the hell out, he was bringing too much damn heat down on everybody.

There was a sign now: NO LOITERING ON BRIDGE.

Stan kept rolling.

"It's not that I want to forget it. I'll never forget it," he said. "It's just not something I dwell on."

Stan didn't make his past Jay's burden. He recited it to Jay, chapter and verse, but never as a manifesto against prime-time athletics. When Stan preached football to Jay, it was all technique, work ethic, playing hurt—things to master on his way to the next level, then maybe the next level after that. He didn't want the head games he went through to mess up Jay's last year as a Wildcat.

Football punched Stan's ticket out of all this no-name poverty; just look around these streets. His problems ran deeper than the game, he said. Football was just the stage—a very public, booby-trapped stage— where bigger issues played themselves out.

Those were the issues Stan concentrated on with Jay.

"I see so much of myself in him—some of it scares the daylights out of me—but I also see something better than myself," Stan said. "I grew up without a father I could talk to, who loved me unconditionally. What Jay has that I didn't have is stability and functionality.

"As good as I think my mom did—and she did the best she could, and it was more than adequate—it was dysfunctional. There were things she couldn't give us that we needed. So where I may have projected confidence, or imitated confidence, with Jay I think it's genuine."

So Stan and LaVerne did whatever it took—and it took a helluva lot, considering what they'd faced and what they'd had to make peace with as a couple—to give Jay and his siblings the one thing LaVerne had but Stan did not: a mother and a father, together, at home.

You had that, Stan believed, you already had more than most. You had something that could temper the impulsiveness he said Jay inherited from him. You had something that could get you through those times when you feel less than worthy, those dark nights of the soul. You had something that could see past the seductions that promised escape but delivered something else—in Stan's case, tragedy.

You had that, you could write your own narrative.

"That still doesn't mean he won't make mistakes," Stan said. "I understand he's human like anyone else. He's not immune to all the pressures. I can't control that.

"I want Jay to cut his own path. I don't want him to be dependent on me. I just want to be there for him. No expectations. No pressure."

He smiled his warm, cockeyed, Zen-like smile. Stan now read the Jay Rome story as it was being written.

"Sort of a work in progress," he offered.

Stan wound his way out of the 'hood, away from the bungalow, the fellas, the canal, the bridge. As he did, the greatest athlete in the history of this football-mad patch of the deepest Deep South wished for the one simple thing that every father wishes for his son.

"I just want him to do better than I did."

Then he wheeled back across town.

Toward home.

12

God, Family, Football

or Road-tripping to the Swamp

The month between Valdosta's first predawn practice and its season opener unfolded like a primer on local iconography: full of old-time Southern religion, a Southern summer straight out of the opening pages of *To Kill a Mockingbird* ("a black dog suffered"), and Southern by-God football.

The Lord Jesus Christ was invoked at least a dozen times a day by coaches and players, mostly in hopes that he would give them all the strength, the will, and the reflected glory to knock the holy *sheee-it* out of any opponent who dared stand in their way. While not every player was devout, few harbored much, if any, doubt that this way was the Right Way.

Even Ryan, an irregular churchgoer who didn't "live and die by the Word," as he put it, didn't much mind all the head bowing and Lord lauding. A believer but not a born-again, he viewed the team's constant religious thrum as a kind of spiritual Muzak, something he could tune in or tune out, as needed or depending on his mood.

He'd done it his whole life.

"That's basically the South for you," he explained with a what-the-hell shrug. "You see a church on every corner.

"A lot depends on what kind of family you're from, whether or not your grandma takes you to church. A lot of black people on the team go to church because their grandma takes them, not because they want to."

Valdosta's religious overlay was laid on thick and almost unthinkingly, grandma or no grandma. Hyder used to answer anybody who questioned his open mix of Christian orthodoxy and public-school business by saying simply, "I never once got up off my knees after a prayer and abused a child."

That reasoning was good enough for Valdosta back then, and it remained good enough now.

"It's about as spontaneous as a thing can be," said Boling, the Valdosta High principal and a rare Catholic in this Baptist-dominated, testifying-happy region. "I'd probably have to stop it if someone complained. We can't be seen as endorsing the establishment of religion in school, and I agree with that. But it's a strong tradition in the South. From Texas to Virginia, it's how it's going to be, especially as relates to athletics."

The team's regular hosannas were bolstered during camp with nightly "character talks" from coaches who quoted from the Bible, from Nick Hyder (or from Nick Hyder quoting from the Bible), and from their own experiences with faith's power in helping them succeed on and off the field.

The talks often were salted with the bromides and challenges of a self-help seminar.

"Excuses are monuments of nothingness that build bridges to nowhere."

"It can take a lifetime to gain respect, but only a second to lose it."

"Do you trust every guy in this room? Because on Friday night you better be able to trust every single guy."

The larger goal, beyond eternal salvation, was rewiring the mindsets of the team's more starkly surviving adolescents. The coaches' personal narratives were meant to inspire them, to make them think about their futures and the wider, bigger picture. Football in a place like Valdosta can offer opportunities—college, new lives—that too many kids here let slip by. Its lessons often turn disposable instead of lasting. Gillespie was doing what he could, what he knew how to do, to change that.

While winning a bunch of games along the way.

"It's all about programming these kids. If they hear it over and over, maybe . . ." he said hopefully. "The most frustrating thing is trying to get these kids to think three or four years ahead, instead of just about the next fifteen minutes.

"Most of these street kids, they're survivors, they got to eat. That's how they live life: They meet their needs. You start talking about goals and it's '*What?*' You try to change that mindset, get them to see the big picture, and they're thinking, 'Yeah, look at Coach in his lily-white world. Come down to my world. There's dope, there's nothing in the fridge, we're all living day by day. You want me to see five years down the road? You *kidding* me?'

"You try to save them all." Gillespie sighed, seated across from his office whiteboard scribbled with more than a hundred names. "It's frustrating when you can't reach some of them. So you try to reach as many as you can.

"But more than anything," he added, "these kids are going to take on the characteristics of us. They always do. It's the way the coaches live their lives, and live their lives in front of these kids.

"We coach hard. We're high tempo. We're tough guys. I think we're all confident guys, and hopefully we don't come across as arrogant. You start to watch the kids: Are they playing harder? Are they tough kids? Are they carrying themselves with confidence? The coaches are going to work and bust their tails every day—do you see that transpire all the way down?"

Then Gillespie said, "They'll take on negative characteristics, too. You'll see talented football teams that for some reason don't really work out. That's why."

Ashley Henderson, the young, bright, redheaded tight ends coach, addressed the team in the cafeteria one night after four-a-days—they'd start all over again in the morning before sunup—and bared raw emotion as he told them all about his brother Doug, who died seven years earlier from cancer. He was twenty-seven.

"This isn't a sad story," Coach Hen promised as some kids squirmed in their chairs. "It's a story about fighting."

One of three football-playing boys who moved to town with their parents from Florida, Doug Henderson III played for Hyder's Wildcats in the early '90s. Doug III blew out both knees but stayed on "as a scout team guy," Coach Hen said. "He was proud of it. That was his role. He loved his team. He loved the Wildcats."

Doug III went on to get accounting degrees from Georgia and Valdosta State, then a job in town at the regional medical center. Life was good . . . until he was diagnosed with synovial sarcoma, a rare form of soft-tissue cancer that usually hits young adults before they turn thirty.

Looking out at the sea of indestructible teens being fed and watered in front him, Ashley, who starred at Valdosta and played college ball for Georgia Tech and Valdosta State, then detailed the short eighteen months between Doug's diagnosis and his too-quick death.

He recalled his brother undergoing radiation treatments that "charred his flesh so bad he couldn't sit down." When doctors said there was nothing more they could do, he told them that wasn't good enough. So they sent him to the MD Anderson Cancer Center, in Houston. There he endured a twenty-six-hour operation to amputate a leg.

As he spoke that late night, Ashley knew he wasn't reaching everybody; kids being kids, some fingered their earbuds like rosary beads, just waiting for the final "amen" to plug them back in and get crunk with Lil Wayne.

It didn't really matter. Just telling his brother's story in front of this new generation of 'Cats—and telling it not many feet from the spot where Hyder fell dead and yet continued, it seemed in this town, to speak from the grave—was at once a catharsis and an act of honor.

Doug III would've gotten a bang out of it.

"You think the knots and bruises you have are bad? You have no idea what real suffering is," Ashley went on. Some kids straightened in their seats. Stopped fidgeting. "So tomorrow morning is going to come at 5:15, the lights will pop on and you'll be thinking, 'I'm sore. I'm tired.'

"But my brother was a Wildcat and he's still running in heaven," Ashley said. "He's got two brand-new knees. He's fine. When I think of character, I think of my older brother. Anybody who played for Coach Hyder never, never, never, never, never quit."

The players smiled. They never, never tired of hearing that.

"When life is stacked against you, men," Ashley then finished, his round eyes narrowing, as if now channeling his older brother, his hero, his inspiration, his unfathomable loss, "God doesn't give you more than you can handle. So this week, men: Press on. We're all in this together."

It was after ten. Heat lightning crackled in the darkness outside the cafeteria's glass doors. The clean, well-lighted place, with its buffed linoleum floor and stainless steel kitchen counters, felt filled with ghosts—or at least the words of ghosts.

The young Wildcats shuffled out the door after shaking Coach Hen's hand, crossed a hallway, and filed back into the gym. There they played video games, texted girlfriends, listened to music.

Fell dead asleep.

If the lessons didn't get through that way, of course, there were more traditional methods to drive home a point.

Coaches' voices turned raw over the next few weeks from exhorting players, berating players, and calling out the manhood of players unable to vanquish teammates and climb up the depth chart—words that spoken the same way in some parts of this town could get a man gut-shot.

"Y'all look like little girls!"

"Quit feeling sorry for yourself or I'll give you something to feel sorry about!"

"I'm so sick of telling you what to do. I know it's six in the morning, but there ain't but three things you have to remember. *Now do it again!*"

"Y'all act like you've never seen five o'clock in the morning," one coach teased the second day of camp. "This is twice you've seen it now. It shouldn't be a surprise to you anymore."

During a punt return drill, one kid tried to dodge a horde of defenders. He was smothered in his tracks.

"That," Gillespie said aloud to nobody in particular, "is the most *non*athletic move I've ever seen."

That got a laugh from everybody, including the kid who made the stumbling, bumbling move. They were getting tougher.

During downtimes, players retreated to the locker room or weight room for the private worlds of their iPods and smartphones, looking like third-world UN interpreters as their lips moved silently while the plastic wires from their headphones hung around their necks. The *thump-thump-thump* of beats and rhymes coming through those wires jumped the Jesus track and landed closer to home. Dirty South ditties like Gucci Mane's "Pressure" quickly became team-wide hip-hop anthems, for white players as well as black: "*40 glock you/ double pump you/ F——king f——k ya/ Wacka trunk ya.*"

A-*men* to that, cuh.

Back outside, the sun burned without pity all month long, except for when lightning cracked the sky and sent everybody sprinting for cover. By midafternoon, squadrons of bottle-green and iridescent-blue dragon-flies slipped below a cloud cover of gnats and flew their strafing missions across the practice field, just feet above the grass. Distant booms rolled in regularly from the bombing and gunnery ranges over at Moody AFB, just north. The sounds were indistinguishable from the afternoon thunderclaps and backfiring lumber trucks.

High overhead, red-tailed hawks eddied aimlessly for hours against the sky's vast blue backdrop, riding hot thermals and updrafts with their wings spread wide, less for aerodynamics, one sideline observer reckoned, than for relief from the heat.

That heat never went anywhere, just hung around like a lost dog. There wouldn't be a day the whole month much under 100 degrees. It defined the air everybody breathed, sometimes the water everybody drank.

"Winningest team in the country," receiver Wesley Bee spat with disgust one afternoon during a brief break in practice, slamming down a hose on the sideline as sweat poured off his head, "and the damn water machine don't work."

●

When Gillespie's programming worked, this is what it looked like:

Late afternoon. Practice over. Million degrees. Players and coaches all gone to the locker room.

Except for Randy Cook. Still on the grass, a goalpost wavering in the heat, the dark, shirtless figure sprinted from sideline to sideline.

One time.

Two times.

Three times.

Cook paused, bent at the waist. Sweat streamed off his head and hit the grass like a hard rain. His neatly cropped hair glittered. He straightened up, ran another gasser. Then ran one more.

Not a coach in sight.

"I felt like I owed it to the team," the junior defensive back explained when he finally walked off the field, his cut torso gleaming, toting his equipment in one hand, a gladiator headed for home. "As a starter, I have certain duties, I have to give a certain effort. I wasn't locked in all the time today. I misread some keys. So I had to do this, for all those Wild-cats who did it before."

A player still loitering in some shade near the high school looked out at the field and spotted Cook. His head jerked in surprise. He jogged over and handed him a water bottle. Cook drained it.

"I've always wanted to be a Wildcat," Cook said, sweat still pouring off him. "I've been going to games since I was little. It's in my blood. I want to work like the Wildcats did in the '80s and '90s. They worked harder than we do. When we go out to play, we're playing in somebody else's footsteps and we have to play as good or better. I'm always thinking, 'Somebody stepped foot on this field before I did and they probably won—probably won big.' I have to win as big as them."

Cook swatted at some bugs orbiting his head.

"This town's given me so much," he said before he headed to the showers, almost three hours after he first jogged out there. "It's given me a place to play the game I love. So why not give the people a sacrifice of my own? They sacrificed so much to give me what I have."

Hot, beat, sore, hungry, Cook flashed a bright white grin.

"Least I can do," he said, "is give them a W."

He headed to the locker room. Halfway there, he started to jog, his cleats click-clacking double time.

●

All the God talk; all the four-a-day, do-it-again practices; all the gnats, dragonflies, and eyeballing hawks; all the shouting and belittling and encouraging; all the new schemes and geeky spread-offense nomenclature; and, especially, all the rising expectations that these Wildcats might be, could be, *better be* back—after all that, Valdosta finally got road-tested two weeks before the season opener, at a scrimmage by the big swamp, over in Waycross.

A scrimmage doesn't mean a thing, unless you're from Valdosta. Then it's a combination sneak preview, wine tasting, and initial public offering. It's a big Friday night out in the middle of August.

So nearly a thousand Wildcat fans, including the school superintendent and the Touchdown Club brass, made the sixty-mile trip east for a little friendly head butting with the Ware County Gators. Many fans left town early, alert for speed traps along the plumb-straight highway that skirted the Okefenokee, to set up grills and ice chests hours before kick-off in a parking lot behind the Gators' stands.

For a scrimmage.

The players filled four yellow buses and pulled out of the school a little after 4:00 P.M., trailing a two-car police escort. That's the way Valdosta always rolled—the Boy Kings of high school football, exalted during the '60s and '70s and '80s and '90s by *Sports Illustrated*, *The New York Times*, *USA Today*, and a special Thanksgiving edition of ABC's *20/20*.

Now they'd been uncrowned for more than a decade, the longest drought in school history. Nevertheless, the blue lights and screaming sirens still whirled and wailed at each intersection of the one- and no-stoplight towns that they sped right through in a kind of country-fried motorcade that let the good folks in Manor (pop. 780) and Argyle (212) and Du Pont (139) know that the Wildcats were blowing by.

Players and coaches saw the scrimmage as a marker to evaluate their progress—and hopefully find a starting quarterback. Ryan and Alex came into the game neck-and-neck. The scorecard Gillespie posted in his office each day, which Alex still led, was now less relevant than how they'd perform under live enemy fire. Gillespie, the avowed quarterback guru, was ready to dispatch with all the weights and measures, all the gigabytes and RAM now used to calculate the modern quarterback's bona fides, and go with his gut.

Meanwhile, most of the team's starters had already made their gut choice.

"When he told me he was coming out for football, first thing that come to my mind was 'Ryan will be the starting quarterback,'" allowed Malcolm, who had a bigger stake in who'd be throwing the ball than just about anybody else on the team.

Ryan's astounding lack of game experience didn't matter much to Malcolm. Like other teammates, he sensed that the easygoing son of a beekeeper had that South Georgia DNA.

"My junior year I watched him play baseball, watched him shoot basketball," Malcolm said. "Most people who can throw a baseball and shoot a basketball like that can throw a football. I wasn't worried.

"But a quarterback has to do more than throw the ball," Malcolm added. "He has to get along with people on the field, make good decisions, don't overthink it too much. That's Ryan."

That was definitely Ryan. Asked how a kid who'd never played organized football until ninth grade, and who sat out his junior year before ever taking a varsity snap, could become starting quarterback for the Valdosta Freaking Wildcats, Ryan appeared barely to understand the question.

"It really ain't that hard," he finally answered after a long pause. "Just say hike, get rid of the ball as fast as you can, and throw it to the right guy."

In contrast to Alex's outward, impenetrable confidence—and his father's ever-present prodding—Ryan came into the Ware County scrimmage the same way he came into every situation: looking like he couldn't care less, yet quietly, almost offhandedly cocksure.

Ryan was the king of not overthinking stuff.

"I knew I had the edge," he'd say later, his words sliding out to form another unhurried, hang-loose Ryan-ism. "All I had to do is play good."

Most of the team's other positions were solid. So tonight's scrimmage, more than anything else, would be a welcome chance for these itchy 'Cats to smack somebody other than themselves.

"We're tired of beating up on each other. We're ready to go beat up on somebody else," sophomore wide receiver Devin Bradley mused during the bus ride. "We're hungry and we're humbled. We want to get back to the way it was in the days of Coach Hyder and Coach Bazemore."

Devin was sixteen, just two when Hyder died and not even on the grid when Bazemore retired. Yet he revered both those men, wouldn't dare say Hyder or Bazemore without applying "Coach" before their names, as if they could still order him to run gassers from the Great Beyond.

Devin loitered near the bottom of the depth chart yet spoke with that same reverence about Gillespie.

Coach Gillespie.

"I love Coach," he said. "He works hard. He loves the kids. We see that. He always comes out ready to go. He's committed to winning."

Somewhere east of Homerville (pop. 2,456), some roadkill caught the players' attention. It had been flattened and reflattened into unidentifiable oblivion. Deer? Dog? Armadillo?

Devin didn't look.

"Our goal is a state championship," he declared as the bus sped by that spot in the road. "Anything less will be a disappointment."

●

The Valdosta buses rolled down Highway 84 through country where cotton and turpentine once were kings. The land here was still quilted with cotton fields and slash pines, but fewer people made their living from either. There was more room now for pecan groves and honey farms and blueberry patches, little white churches and unpainted shacks, long ranch houses and pristine double-wides.

The soil under the warm asphalt turned swampy on the other side of Big Alligator Creek. Waycross sat just eight miles north of the Okefenokee, the spooky 400,000-acre wetland whose black waters invited cypress forests and red-cockaded woodpeckers and about a jillion gators. It was a landscape that felt utterly isolated from the known world yet sublimely comfortable in its own skin.

This was Dixie. A bottle tree glinted in the sunlight that slanted across one front yard, the local spirits presumably forewarned. A souped-up pickup idled in a shell driveway, TARA DARA spray-painted in red script on the side. Cattails choked a muddy farm pond.

As they finally entered Waycross, the buses climbed a bridge that spanned a massive freight yard. The only incorporated city in Georgia's largest county, and home to less than 15,000 folks, Waycross was named for those intersecting rail lines that once made it a transportation crossroads. More than sixty trains still rumble through town each day.

Near the stadium, the motorcade turned down a humble residential side street. Two men walking along the road stared for a long moment at the passing yellow buses, then brightened when they saw where they were from. Both shot the Wildcats the finger.

"They know," Devin said proudly.

The sign welcoming visitors to Valdosta trumpets the high school football team as the winningest in America. *(Photo courtesy of Oscar Sosa)*

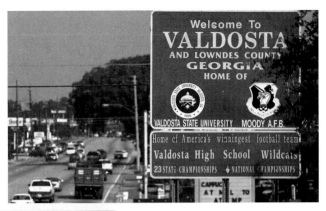

The grave of legendary coach Nick Hyder, who died in 1996 from a heart attack in the school cafeteria. Etched into the base: "Never never never never never quit." *(Photo courtesy of Jefferies Eldridge)*

Valdosta's twenty-three state championship banners and six national title banners hang high from the stands inside Bazemore-Hyder Stadium. *(Photo courtesy of Jefferies Eldridge)*

A Confederate memorial rises on the lawn of Valdosta's old courthouse. *(Photo courtesy of Jefferies Eldridge)*

Mike "Nub" Nelson, self-proclaimed "one-armed painter," led the charge against consolidating Valdosta's city schools with the Lowndes County's schools. Many believed a merger would be the end of Valdosta football. *(Photo courtesy of Michael S. Chapman)*

Valdosta royalty: Jay Rome *(right),* considered by many to be the country's top tight end, played in the long shadow of his father, Stan Rome, an NFL player until his career was cut short by drug addiction. *(Photo courtesy of Colby Katz)*

Stan Rome is seated on the bridge over a shallow canal, where two decades earlier a crack dealer shot him in the head. His story is now both an inspiration and cautionary tale for every kid who dreams of being a Wildcat. *(Photo courtesy of Colby Katz)*

Led by new head coach, Rance Gillespie, the Wildcats stroll to the stadium through the "Cat Walk." *(Photo courtesy of BK Smith, PhotoCR. com)*

Fans greet the Wildcats along the "Cat Walk" ninety minutes before each home game. *(Photo courtesy of BK Smith, PhotoCR. com)*

Student fans gather early and raucously before a Wildcat home game. *(Photo courtesy of BK Smith, PhotoCR. com)*

Wildcat players, led by coach Rance Gillespie, are "banging the tin" of the roof inside the tunnel that leads from the locker room to the field, as Valdosta players have for decades. *(Photo courtesy of Jefferies Eldridge)*

Called "the next Michael Vick" by many Wildcat fans in his junior year, Dashay March *(above)* returned for his senior season after a shootout at his home and suspensions put his status in doubt. *(Photo courtesy of Michael S. Chapman)*

Jay Rome strives to live up to his father's reputation as perhaps Valdosta's greatest athlete ever. *(Photo courtesy of Michael S. Chapman)*

Rance Gillespie with his daughter, Kennedy, congratulates his players in the end zone after his first win as head coach of storied Valdosta High. "His reward if he won 199 more," a booster only half joked, "a free gravesite in the town cemetery." *(Photo courtesy of BK Smith, PhotoCR.com)*

Gillespie is congratulated after his first win as Valdosta head coach by longtime booster David Waller, who'd missed only five Wildcat games since 1947. (*Photo courtesy of Michael S. Chapman*)

Malcolm Mitchell (*right*), who nearly quit football his sophomore season, refocused himself to become one of the South's most highly recruited players and one of Valdosta High's most popular students. (*Photo courtesy of BK Smith, PhotoCR.com*)

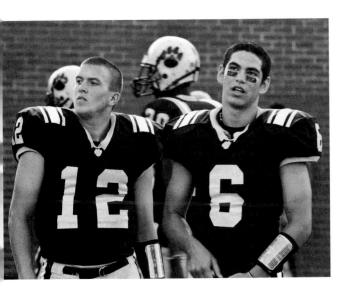

Laidback senior Ryan Whilden (*left*) and ultracompetitive, sophomore transfer Alex Stephenson (*right*) battled through the spring and summer to be the "Cats" starting quarterback. (*Photo courtesy of Michael S. Chapman*)

Gillespie's wide-open, big play offense was put to the test against visiting Brunswick, from coastal Georgia. The shootout continued into overtime and became the highest scoring regular season game in Georgia High School Association history. *(Photo courtesy of Michael S. Chapman)*

Phillip "Swoll" Moore, the team's undersized but tough-yard heart, dreamed of being a Wildcat his whole life. Pound for pound, he's the "Cats" strongest player. *(Photo courtesy of Michael S. Chapman)*

Attendance tripled for the Wildcats during coach Rance Gillespie's first season at Valdosta's over 11,000-seat stadium. *(Photo courtesy of Michael S. Chapman)*

Senior wide receiver Malcolm Mitchell was moved from defense to offense full-time and became one of the state's most electrifying athletes. *(Photo courtesy of Michael S. Chapman)*

The Wildcats posed in the tunnel with their coach before banging the tin above their heads and taking the field. *(Photo courtesy of BK Smith, PhotoCR.com)*

The Valdosta-Lowndes "Winnersville Classic" is perhaps the country's most intense high school rivalry; the last Wildcat coach was fired four days after he lost to Lowndes. Here Reggie McQueen *(left)* lays out to defend against an early Viking bomb. *(Photo courtesy of BK Smith, PhotoCR.com)*

The final play of the Valdosta-Lowndes game is as hard fought as the first. Malcolm Mitchell stretches for a Hail Mary pass amid two Lowndes defenders. *(Photo courtesy of BK Smith, PhotoCR.com)*

Even the youngest Wildcat fans take the field after a Valdosta victory, like the boy here perched on the outsized shoulders of 6'5" defensive lineman Jarquez Samuel. *(Photo courtesy of Michael S. Chapman)*

He didn't play much, yet nobody loved being a Wildcat more than senior James Eunice. He planned to walk on at Georgia, but drowned two months after Valdosta's season ended. Georgia coach Mark Richt put his name and number (23) on the Bulldog roster. *(Photo courtesy of Michael S. Chapman)*

"I remember when we used to play here in the '80s," one coach recalled as he peered out a window. "It was *red*—rebel flags lined the streets."

A couple of blocks later, outside the parking lot, a smiling middle-aged white man waved the buses through the gate at one end of hulking Memorial Stadium. Plastered across his own pickup, parked nearby, was a redneck sampler of Confederate-themed bumper stickers. One demanded that Georgia return its state flag back to the one with the Stars and Bars that the segs put on it back in the '50s.

The Wildcats piled out of their buses and into the woozy heat. The visitor's locker room was an un-air-conditioned cinder-block fortress big enough for maybe half the team; think tight two-car garage. Most players dressed under the spreading live oak beside it.

The home of the green-and-white Ware County Gators was built in 1949 as a 12,000-seat baseball park for the local Georgia-Florida League franchise, but a baseball game hadn't been played there in decades. A sign painted at one end of the reconstituted stadium bragged about the 1,500-student school's recent gridiron glories: REGION CHAMPS '03, '04, '06, '07.

Alex took an easy breath as he looked out at the familiar setting, fiddling absent-mindedly with his Puerto Rican grandmother's rosary beads, a gift she'd given him and which he now draped around his neck.

This was a homecoming of sorts, though Alex had been back to town a number of times since transferring out last spring. His dad's business was still headquartered here. Even so, Alex had spent much of the last week deleting obscenity-laced texts from former teammates who promised to "lay the wood" to him. He took them as a sign of respect and laughed them off. He believed he was the front-runner in Valdosta's quarterback sweepstakes. He wasn't looking back.

"It's not home anymore," he said as he stared a little longer out at the grass now turning green-gold in the lowering light. Trains hooted in the distance, as they would all game long. "I'm glad to be where I'm at. Wouldn't trade it for the world."

Alex and his teammates walked the field's velvety grass before they dressed and warmed up. Dashay bobbed his head to the beats that boomed through his head phones: Gucci Mane's "Murder for Fun."

"Game time," he explained.

Players returned to the equipment truck parked near the oak tree to put on their pads and get taped up. Nub walked over from the nearby tailgate with an offer. Last spring, after Alex left, Nub heard that one of Ware's big sophomore linemen was interested in playing for the Wildcats, so he drove him over to Valdosta to watch a practice. The kid stood around for a while, acted bored, then said he wasn't impressed.

That still chapped Nub's bony white behind. He lifted his snipped wing in the kid's direction.

"Whoever puts the biggest hit on him I'll buy a steak dinner," he croaked. "Whoever knocks his hat off I'll buy *two* steak dinners."

Some players nodded eagerly, but as soon as Nub walked off and returned to the parking lot, senior linebacker Justin Williams told them all flatly, "Everybody just do your assignment."

It was a scrimmage, a tune-up for the real thing in two weeks, but Gillespie stuck by his "every play, every game" credo as he gathered his charges under the oak tree before kickoff.

"Listen, you waited a long time for tonight and now here it is," he began. This was his own dry run, a prelude to what he hoped would be many pregame speeches as Valdosta's head coach. "Let's make sure you lay it all out there. And men, one thing's for sure: You lay that frickin' yellow hat *right on their ass!*"

He then told them to take a knee.

"Dear Father," he began, head bowed, eyes shut, "thank you for this game of football. We pray that we play well and that we play the way a Wildcat football team should play the game."

Then Jay, the knee he bruised that first morning of camp no longer hobbling him, shouted out a call and response from the middle of the team huddle.

"What time is it?"

"Game time!"

"What time is it?"

"Game time!"

"What time is it!"

"Game time!"

One hundred and five black-and-gold-armored kids then sprinted through the gate of a chain-link fence and onto the sun-splashed field. Malcolm stayed back, held out of the scrimmage because of a sprained ankle. He pleaded for several minutes with Coach Pruitt to let him play, but Pruitt stayed firm. "I want you ready for when the games count," he said.

When Pruitt was asked later what he had to do to coach Malcolm, the young son-of-a-coach burst out laughing.

"Just don't screw him up."

The captains returned from the coin toss, the team took another knee—Lord's Prayer—and the game was on.

For a while it looked like it would never end. Alex trotted out for Valdosta's initial set of downs, but three quick, sloppy plays later the Wildcats had to punt. Ryan sauntered out for the second possession and had the ball knocked out of his hands. A Gator ran it in for a score.

Ryan returned in the second quarter, and the offense finally got on track with an eleven-play, 56-yard scoring drive before the half ended. Most impressive: 3 third-down passes that moved the chains, including a 17-yarder to Dashay. Swoll then bullied his way into the end zone from the 4.

The Wildcats gathered under the tree again at halftime. The debut hadn't been pretty—Valdosta was flagged ten times for more than 80 yards' worth of penalties, including two personal fouls—but the 'Cats hit their stride by the end. They finally looked like they were having fun out there, like they remembered why they put up with everything they put up with from the new guy standing in front of them now. They looked like South Georgia boys doing what South Georgia boys like to do most.

Gillespie liked it. He urged them to show him a little more.

"You're a better team than they are," he said from under the rustling oak, an actual breeze finally slipping through as the sun almost set. "Let's make a statement right here to start the second half. Let's go out"—several players grinned before he finished; they'd been with him long enough now to know what was coming next—"and kick their ass!"

Ryan opened the second half under center and again made big plays when he had to. He looked like he'd been a quarterback his whole life, not like this was the first time he'd taken varsity snaps in game conditions. He tossed 3 more third-down passes to keep the 'Cats moving, including another 17-yarder to Dashay. He then finished the rolling 70-yard drive by handing the ball off to his own brother from another mother, Dashay, who indeed looked ready to step up as he skipped behind right guard for 5 yards and a touchdown.

Malcolm liked what he saw.

"Ryan's the man with the plan," he smiled from the sideline.

Alex still looked tight, and his teammates didn't help. One pass bounced off a receiver's hands and into the grasp of a waiting Gator. Alex recovered and near the end of the third quarter lofted a beauty of a bomb to junior Demetrius Melvin, who was brought down on the Gator 5. Reggie took it in from there.

Seated high in the visitors' stands, Matt sounded relieved. "I'm glad he had a good drive," he said of Alex. "He needed that—took a lot of pressure off."

The third-string quarterback finished the last quarter.

"Told you we were hungry," Devin crowed afterward on the bus as the cop cars' blue lights led the 'Cats back through the swamplands' inky darkness.

Final: Valdosta 27, Ware County 7.

Thank you, Jesus!

Matt was less sanguine by the end of the next week. He showed up at Nub's and flew into a rant. Alex deserved to start, he fumed. He still led Ryan in points on Gillespie's chart, and Gillespie needed to honor that. If he didn't, Matt would just move his family back to Waycross.

Nub let him go on. He knew this storm would pass. Sure enough, Matt cooled down, agreed he wasn't moving anywhere, and even found advantage in what he expected would be Alex's backup status.

"It could be the best thing," he said. "Clearly Gillespie saw Alex had some nervous tendencies. By the time Alex is a senior, or even a junior, my goal is to see him head and shoulders above the others. I'm set to bring back that tiger meaner and stronger than ever!"

By the next sentence, he'd already adjusted the new timetable. "I really believe he'll get his opportunity as early as Friday night," he said of the season's first game. "Alex will show them."

Gillespie didn't officially name a starter after the Ware County scrimmage—the 'Cats still had two weeks before their opener—but he'd made his decision.

Ryan.

Ryan had an uneven, mistake-filled game against Ware County, but he never looked rattled or frustrated. If he blew a play he just jogged back into the huddle on those heavy legs of his and did it again, *la-dee-dah*. When it counted most, like on third and longs, his focus turned cool and laser sharp rather than jittery and unsure, the way Alex's did. If things went kablooey, Ryan went back to the basics: Say hike, get rid of the ball as fast as you can, and throw it to the right guy.

It's what Gillespie hoped would happen. It had been a long slog with this bright, competitive, but physically limited dude since their first talk back in January. Ryan might not be Valdosta's next Buck Belue or John Lastinger or Greg Talley—Wildcat quarterbacks who went on to play at Georgia—but he had the sense to get the ball to his most talented teammates and not, as Coach Pruitt said about his own role with Malcolm, screw it up.

"To be the quarterback at Valdosta is not something you just kind of do," Gillespie said. "It's a huge investment. Ryan wanted to dip his toe in it. The question with Ryan the entire time has been 'Is the kid really going to jump in and do it?' And he has. When he makes a mistake, it doesn't faze him. That's the way he is."

Alex was more of an enigma. Part of it was his youth, but something else was at play, too. Gillespie was still trying to figure out which levers to pull to make everything work in sync.

"Alex is a good kid who wants to be quarterback really, really bad," he said, "but he's extremely high-strung and it hurts him, especially in the position he plays. He feels a lot of pressure from somewhere."

The source of that pressure was clear to everybody. Yet Gillespie never criticized Matt. Even after the blowup in the parking lot over the summer, Gillespie said of Matt's reaction, "I have a child, I know the disappointment you can feel. And people express their disappointments in different ways. He's hard on Alex. He has high expectations for Alex. Alex is physically tough, and I attribute that to his dad.

"You have to be careful about the way you react to how people raise their kids. They know their kids better than we know them. We may not always agree, but there's a lot of ways to raise a child. I'd never interfere in that."

Ryan took most of the snaps in practice that first week after the scrimmage. Over the weekend, Matt told Alex to confront his coach. Alex showed up in Gillespie's office at 7:30 A.M. Monday. Gillespie wasn't there yet, but the two met a couple of hours later behind closed doors.

Gillespie did what he does in tough spots: Got to the point. He told Alex that Ryan would start Friday night against Brooks County. He told Alex he shouldn't take it personally, that he was only fifteen and needed more maturing. He added that only one or two underclassmen had ever started at quarterback for Valdosta. It was nothing to get upset about.

It didn't help. Alex broke down, trying to hide his face behind his hands as he started to sob.

"I didn't understand it," Alex said. "Everything I'd worked for—my heart and soul, my blood, sweat, and tears—everything was gone just like that."

He pleaded his case. Said he'd been at every summer workout while Ryan had missed at least half a dozen. Said he'd won the competition on points. Said he'd just plain worked harder.

"It crushed him," Gillespie said afterward. "Nobody worked any harder to be the starting quarterback than he did. It was hard for me to make that call, because of what he did and all that he'd invested. Heck, it was really close.

"But it just became a gut call based on the way they handled themselves in pressure situations, and their makeup and demeanor and those kinds of things.

"Ask me in a couple years and I'll tell you if I handled him right or not."

13

Getting Crunk

or We Ready!

The school fight song streamed through Valdosta High's early-morning intercom like a *Glee*-inspired call to arms.

Suited up in black football jerseys and white hair bows, eighteen wide-awake cheerleaders dashed from homeroom to homeroom to give players game-day hugs and weekly goodie bags stuffed with candy, sports drinks, and Bible verses. Some had to hunt down late-arriving players—no telling where they'd find them—and each girl dropped as much as thirty dollars a week on the five varsity Wildcats she was assigned to serve all season.

An IB psychology teacher, meanwhile, did what he always did in his class on game day: tossed around a miniature football like a fortune-telling hot potato. If a student dropped it, that meant bad luck for the 'Cats, so even the IB nerds took Mr. Day's goofy ritual pretty seriously.

Mike Wakefield, the 'Cats towering, soft-spoken defensive end, had already woken up to his own game-day ritual. His father James, a Valdosta standout under Hyder who played in college and now ran the school system's custodial services, taped a handmade sign from his son's bedroom door all the way down the hall. Printed the length of the sign:

NEVER NEVER NEVER NEVER NEVER NEVER NEVER QUIT!

Wesley Bee, string-bean senior receiver and son of another distinguished Hyder 'Cat, had his own game-day ritual. "I get up," he said, "turn the music up *real* loud, get crunk, wake up my dad and every-body else, then take a shower."

There was more. "After that," Bee added, "I get *really* crunk."

If not crunk, exactly, folks around town did seem stirred up again about a Wildcat season opener. Tickets for the game against nearby Brooks County were almost gone by Friday morning, first time there'd been a rush on seats for an opener in years. Most credited Gillespie; there wasn't a civic group, rec center, grade school, or informal gathering of fans he hadn't visited since he arrived. Locals praised him even as they already handicapped his future, the national sport of Valdosta.

"I think he's going to be okay," said Scott Register, owner of a tire store on Ashley Street, "but time tells and it starts tonight. If Brooks County beats them, they'll fire him. You don't last long if you lose in this town. What'd Charlie Greene lose, two games?"

Greene coached the two seasons between Bazemore and Hyder. A customer overheard Register.

"*Three* games," he corrected him of the old coach's nearly forty-year-old, still unforgiven sins.

Gillespie appreciated the stakes yet was amused by their permuta-tions. The night before, as a summer storm raged, Nub and a couple of friends let themselves into the stadium's deserted locker room. There they sat on the empty benches, in front of the empty lockers, and communed with the ghosts, "all excited about this new coach," Nub said, "finally happy with the way things were, just thinking about what this new season could be."

Nub then pulled out his phone and texted Gillespie.

"You better hang a big number on them tomorrow night," he tapped out, like a chicken pecking corn. "You might be the head coach now but you better make our asses happy."

●

Players began to drift into the locker room early Friday afternoon, loose and loud and playful.

First thing they checked: their helmets. Coaches had stayed late Thursday night to dress the plain, unmarked yellow helmets with stripes and cat paws, a confirmation for any kid who put it on that he was now a real, blood Wildcat.

Dashay sauntered in early. Just months earlier, he was the Wildcat least likely to return—least likely to take his next breath.

He knew it, too. With kickoff still more than six hours away, Dashay sported a fresh haircut, a bright white tee, and, to hear him tell it just outside the locker room door, a new attitude. He'd gone to the alternative school over the summer, gotten himself eligible, survived camp.

"I had to come back and be with my boys," he said of his return. "It's my sport. It's what I do. It's what I'm good at. So I like it. It's all I got."

Behind him, a ladder of mail slots labeled with each senior's name hung from a cinder-block wall. Letters poured into it every day from colleges around the country. Jay's and Malcolm's slots were full to overflowing, like stockings on Christmas. Yet despite his setbacks over the last year, a handful of letters still came every week for Dashay—Alabama, Auburn, North Carolina.

"Got my act together," Dashay went on.

This act was at least his second act. Scripted in ink on one half of his neck: EAST SIDE. On the other half: WEST SIDE. "I grew up. Had to grow up, really. Stuff occurred in my life."

Stuff . . .

"Got a child. Had to step up."

Dashay knew what he faced. He lowered a hand to his knees. "I'm still down here," he said. "I have to earn my way back. I'm a leader, but I have to be led at the same time."

Ryan poked his strawberry blond head out from the locker room door. Spotted Dashay. Grinned. Popped back inside.

"Every day," Dashay added matter-of-factly after Ryan's head disappeared, "I wish I was quarterback."

●

The locker room rocked—a hundred adrenalized, fearless, Friday-afterschool teenagers with hours still to kill.

Some applied adhesive eye black to their faces. Reggie's: RIP JR, a reference to his cousin, shot to death less than a year earlier. Malcolm put on cat paws, ducked into Tracy's office to check himself out in a mirror, and nodded his approval.

"We're way too loose," observed defensive coach Taz Dixon, looking across the room. "Three years from now, when we have the system in place, you'll hear a pin drop."

"Lot of questions be answered tonight," Coach Al added. "Get hit between the eyes two or three times and we'll see."

At 2:45, Gillespie stepped in with a scare-you-straight stare. "Hey!" he shouted, and the room instantly turned pin-drop silent. He told them to get over to the cafeteria for their pregame meal and devotional. The players lined up and shuffled out.

Akins nodded toward the latest coach that he'd worked for here.

"That guy right there's got his s-h-i-t together," he said. "He's already more than answered the question whether he's a leader. He respects what was here before. Some did not."

The players picked up plates of baked chicken, baked potato, green beans, and salad, with iced tea to drink. Most put it all away in about a minute. When they finished, Trea Brinson stood in the middle of the room with a runner's baton in one hand, a football in the other.

"They represent the two things I want to talk about," said Brinson, a twenty-nine-year-old sports chaplain at Valdosta State. "The baton represents transition. The football represents focus."

Gillespie brought in Brinson to talk on Fridays after he heard him speak at his church, the nondenominational congregation housed inside a converted Winn-Dixie. He liked that Brinson was young, had a contemporary handle on scripture, and knew football.

Brinson lifted the baton and dove into the story of Moses and Joshua. Moses was a leader with a "unique relationship with God," he said, and everyone followed his word. Moses died, and there was a "transition to a man named Joshua." Joshua worried folks who'd followed Moses wouldn't follow him.

"Here at school you're at a huge point of transition," Brinson said, and even these young Wildcats, in their shorts and sandals and teen self-absorption, knew what was next. "Tonight you'll play at Bazemore-Hyder Stadium, where those two names have been immortalized. And today you sit in the cafeteria where Coach Hyder—right over there, the second seat at that table—passed away."

Players stared there a minute, like they might see a ghost.

"But we're not going to look back and remember who we were," Brinson continued. "We're going to look forward. Because you're at the point where you're tired of hearing about what used to be. You want to talk about the team today. Someday, you want people to say, 'Remember the *2010* team?'"

Brinson walked over to their new coach, who sat by himself.

"I'm going to give this baton to Coach Gillespie," he said, and the players erupted into a rousing, cadetlike cheer.

"Now, he could hold that baton all day," Brinson closed, nodding at Valdosta's latest Joshua, "but if you don't buy in—if you don't follow—he can't go anywhere."

The players rose from their chairs, cheered again.

Then they pushed their earbuds back in and followed Gillespie out of the cafeteria.

🏈

Gillespie retreated into his office at 3:45 and closed both doors. He then turned out the lights, lay down on the floor, and for the next half hour let his mind drift over the thousand things that buzzed in his head.

"Best thirty minutes of the week," he explained. "It's a time I can say, 'It's done,' and get my thoughts together. I take a nap."

He napped until 4:15, when offensive line coach Mark Loudermilk knocked and called out softly, "Okay, Coach."

Gillespie made his players do the same thing. Lights were cut off in the locker room as they spread out on the floor and benches until 4:30. Most listened to music through headphones plugged into cells that glowed green and blue in the blacked-out room and seemed to hover in midair, like a school of jellyfish.

Then the lights snapped back on and coaches lined up in front of the room to go through the night's assignments: punt team ("Don't screw it up, men," Lucas advised), punt return team, kickoff team, kickoff return team.

Players then returned from a quick walk-through in the gym to get ready for the buses' 6:15 departure for the stadium. They gathered all their equipment, applied more eye black, strung rosaries around their necks (Dashay strung two). With their heads still bobbing to their piped-in music, it was impossible to read their state of mind.

"You always wonder," Coach Al said. "Are they going to do what they're supposed to do? Or are they going to go crazy out there under the lights and get those big, wide eyes?"

◆

The locker room had emptied when Gillespie stepped into Loudermilk's office. He and Mark went back to Thomasville, Gillespie's first job.

Then Rodemaker dropped by; he was at Thomasville with them, too. Those were the days when they had to mix the paint and line the field themselves on Thursday nights.

"A three-hour job." Gillespie smiled. "You didn't leave until nine, if you really got after it."

Then they were assistants together at Peach. Gillespie and Rodemaker drove their pickups across the county every morning to see who could round up the most players missing that day from school.

"We'd make it a competition," Gillespie remembered. "I'd say, 'How many you get today?' and Alan would say, 'I got eight.' And I'd go, 'Aw, man, I only got *four*.' But we'd always go get them."

Now here they were again, in Valdosta. Not one of them would've guessed twenty years earlier that they'd be here to make this place whole again. Back then, the three best coaching jobs in the state were Georgia, Georgia Tech, and Valdosta, and Nick Hyder sure wasn't going anywhere.

Now the three of them, all in their forties, looked at each other in the windowless room's lousy light, bonded by everything they'd been through and everything still ahead. They almost looked like kids again.

"Been a long time since we've gone through one of these things together." Gillespie smiled.

Then he turned to head out. Called behind him, "Let's go."

◆

Two Valdosta squad cars flipped on their blue lights and sirens as they turned out of the school and led four yellow buses on a nonstop three-mile ride to the stadium.

Cars ahead pulled over to let them pass, and those headed the other way stopped, out of respect, like they would for a funeral procession. The buses snaked through several neighborhoods—some solidly working class, others ramshackle—as men and women and kids, alerted by the police sirens, rushed from their houses to wave or give a thumbs-up or yell out "Go Cats!" Some folks seemed surprised by their own excitement, as if this were a ritual they'd long ago stopped caring about.

Ten minutes later, the buses turned left on Ann Street and stopped under a stand of crepe myrtles. A roar went up; players peered out the windows to see hundreds of fans lined up on both sides of the sidewalk that led to the stadium's brick entrance.

Gillespie hoped the "Cat Walk" would become a kind of block-long red carpet stroll, minus the red carpet, that brought players and fans together. That's what Valdosta had always been about—town and team as mutual admiration society—and that's what had largely dissolved over the last decade.

Gillespie figured the first walk would draw a couple of dozen fans. He never expected this throng. As another coach looked out at the scene from his seat, he peeked down at his bare forearm. "Look," he said. "The hair is literally standing up."

Led by Gillespie, the Wildcats lugged their shoulder pads down the walkway like soldiers toting duffel bags through an airport. They slapped hands with kids and coots, parents and ex-'Cats. They moved along to Valdosta High's favored slow-striding soundtrack, "No Mo Play in G.A." by Pastor Troy and the Down South Georgia Boys, bleated out like an anthem by a tight contingent of Marchin' Cat band members.

They passed by a strip of grass in front of the superintendent's office where sweaty little kids in black-and-gold jerseys played football and wrestled with each other. Tailgaters in the stadium parking lot left their wheeled smokers and grilled meats to slap the newest 'Cats on the shoulder, wish them luck.

"We love you!" somebody sang out. "Y'all go get 'em now!"

Wildcat football once again looked like the biggest show in town.

🏈

The players marched through Bazemore-Hyder's arched gated entrance and passed beneath all twenty-three state and six national title banners, strung high under the stands from one end to the other. Nub put them up yesterday with a cherry picker.

The Wildcats shared the locker room with the Valdosta State Blazers, so the space was neutral and impersonal. No inspiring quotes from Vince Lombardi or Winston Churchill or Proverbs covered the walls, like they did in the locker room up at the high school.

So the players just dumped their gear and headed straight for the turf to walk around before warm-ups. Several knelt in prayer around the gold paw painted on the 50-yard line, where Hyder's open casket once sat. Others stayed inside the hip-hop world piped through their headphones.

Jay spotted some Brooks County players as they trickled from the visitors' locker room.

"They all know they trespassin' in the Valley," he called out, the wooden billboard behind him painted with a snarling cat that welcomed visitors, without a wink, to Death Valley.

Back inside, the locker room turned raucus. Players shouted chants, clapped in rhythm, exchanged intricate handshakes.

Swoll stayed prone on the concrete floor, a towel over his face, listening to music. When he finally got up, he tapped out a quick Facebook update:

"Last moments b4 my 1st last game so im going hard."

◆

Twenty minutes before kickoff, Gillespie stepped out of the coach's room and told his players to take a knee. Though the locker room had been rebuilt a few years ago, it stood on the same ground where Bazemore and Hyder and only a handful of other coaches had exhorted more than half a century of title-winning Wildcats. He was humbled by it, he embraced it, and he moved on from it.

"There is no other program in the country with the tradition Valdosta has," he told his players. "But men, tonight, you make your own history. You make your own legacy."

He went on like that for a little longer, but not much longer. He had a game to win tonight.

So his voice firmed up as he barked, "*And you lay their ass out!*"

Gillespie wasn't finished, though. When the shouting died down, he put in what he always put in: "Who's got my prayer?"

Coach Lucas stepped up. The room hushed.

"Thank you God for the opportunity to play this game, this wonderful game of football," he rasped. "Help us to play the game the way it's supposed to be played."

Following a collective "Amen," players opened their eyes, lifted heads, bunched up by the door.

Lucas wasn't finished.

Last thing he said: *"Now let's make that tin rattle!"*

A hundred delirious 'Cats jammed the dark tunnel and threw their helmets into the metal. Thunderclaps ricocheted off the cement floor, doubling and trebling the volume. Nub had rerigged the roof over the summer with chains and bolts so that it now was a series of separate panels, each of which flew into the air when it was banged, then crashed right back down. From the outside, the thing looked like it was about to blow clean off.

An end-zone speaker pumped out an apt accompaniment: a Dirty South ditty called "We Ready." Only the chorus was played (*"We ready!"*), but players knew the rest of the lyrics:

"The game's raw, boy, please believe it/ Keep your Bible with you 'cause you gonna be needin' Jesus."

Ryan closed his eyes and let the commotion pour over him like a cool, calming shower. The din created its own kind of serenity. Jay banged away like it was a historical reenactment, a furious tribute that mimed what his father and uncle and all those other gloried 'Cats did before their own epic battles.

For Dashay, the tunnel's pandemonium was a soothing unction that felt, he said, "like heaven."

"You got to be in the tunnel to feel it," he explained. "It's better than war. You're not scared, you're *thrilled*. It's like you're about to take a good ride—a good, good ride."

Even the ol' boy refs took the stadium's scene in with a kind of studied wonder, the bills of their caps rock-still as their eyes roved the full stands, the brick wall beneath the weathered scoreboard, that roof. They nodded at all the former 'Cats who stood together on the edges of the playing field and heckled the officials every Friday night—Valdosta's "sideline mafia."

"Gentlemen, let me tell you," one official confided to the four Wildcat captains before he escorted them to midfield for the coin toss. "Not everybody gets a chance to play football for Valdosta. Enjoy every minute of it."

The slightest smile creased Gillespie's face while he held his pounding troops back. For all his technocratic tendencies—the runelike playbook, the incessant film watching, the scripting of nearly every minute on the practice field—Gillespie, at heart, loved the visceral, smashmouth part of football best.

"It's a tough game," he liked to say, "for tough kids."

When the white helmets of the Trojans from Brooks County High, a tough little school in nearby Quitman, finally turned to peek at the bedlam, Gillespie cut his 'Cats loose. Dashay led the charge, the tin and "We Ready" and God knows what else echoing in his head.

For a lot of these Wildcats, including Dashay, the Friday night charge down the length of the field was more release than entrance. There was a kind of comfort in taking this carpeted, light-flooded stage, despite the pressure and violence ahead. The noise and the crowd's delirium—a crazy modern mash-up of hip-hop and country, of bling and overalls, echoing the bleachers' mix of races, cultures, ages, and sides of town— formed a protective bubble that allowed them to think more clearly and deeply than they'd been able to all week.

All the messy stuff at home and school, all the things they'd seen or done—gone.

Or transformed: When Reggie hit the turf, he talked aloud with his murdered cousin, like he was a teammate playing in the secondary beside him. Or he'd speak with a long-dead aunt who was the sunshine in Reggie's young life. Her killer nearly got away with it, until the cops dug up her casket and found the gun he'd used stuffed under the corpse.

"I got a lot of people who aren't here on my back," Reggie said. "On Friday night, they're living through me.

"On the field, it's my own world. It's a place where I can be myself," he went on. "I don't have to worry about anyone fussin'. My parents come to games and I see them smile and clap their hands and stand up— stuff like that doesn't happen at home. At home, there's always bills to pay. A tragedy. That's why I'm not just playing ball. It's more than a game. It's what I live for."

Tonight: no problem.

"Football," he said, "was never something I couldn't handle."

Malcolm found his separate peace on the playing field, too.

"For an athlete who loves to play the game, it happens more than you know," he said. "We're not just running around."

Seconds before kickoff, as the Trojans leaped around their coach and raised their arms toward their own fans crowded in the visitors' bleachers, the 'Cats circled Gillespie and took one more knee.

"Our Father . . ."

They then swagged out onto the field. The sky was low and gray—the threat of thunderstorms rolled in almost every evening this time of year—but by the time the referee blew his whistle a corner of setting sun peeked out and streaked the Spanish moss on the oaks just outside. The crowd rose up for the kickoff and then stayed that way as Dashay cradled the ball and slashed his way out to the Valdosta 41.

Ryan jogged out with the first play of the first snap of his varsity career, then did what he'd do most of the season: took a step back, turned to his right, hit Malcolm, and watched him fly for 14 yards. Next he did the other thing he'd do all year: tucked the ball into Swoll's hard belly and watched him grind out 6 yards.

"You're going to see some down-home South Georgia football," one booster near an end zone enthused. "Not like what you've seen here the past few years—least that's what I hope."

Then Ryan took a snap from the shotgun, looked left, and delivered a fastball to Dashay, who caught it near the line of scrimmage.

Dashay didn't hesitate. Standing on the Brooks County 46, at full speed a yard later, he already knew he would score—saw the line ahead he could take, assessed the only white jersey with an angle on him, and calculated that the dude didn't stand a chance. He ran until an official signaled that he didn't have to run anymore.

Just a couple of miles away, under a blanket with his radio, Odell started to bawl like a baby.

As he high-stepped across the end zone and toward his own sideline,

Dashay spread his arms to receive the town's adulation. Meanwhile he searched the crowd until he found his mother and grandmother, clapping, yelling out his name. His father stood and shouted a couple of rows away.

La La didn't come to many games. Usually she listened at home on the radio with her blind youngest daughter. When La La got excited, Dashia got excited. Then when Dashia heard an announcer say her brother's name, she'd beat on a wall or the floor and jump around the house. It was a big time.

Tonight La La was there to see Dashay run down the sideline just like she used to run when she lived over in Europe, a straight sprint on thick legs, measuring her speed by how fast everybody else fell behind her. She always loved that, the "outrunning everybody."

Now Dashay loved that, too. When he ran, he could almost watch himself—see himself running on the whole field, like it was projected in front of him on a scoreboard big screen.

Or as he put it, "I live in my own movie. I'm my own reality star."

◆

A school of only about 600 kids, Brooks County already looked out-manned. The Trojans fumbled on their next possession, and Valdosta went back to work. Ryan completed a couple of passes, took a late hit, and suddenly the 'Cats were on the Brooks County 5.

They stalled at the 1 but went for it on fourth and goal. Ryan slid the ball again to Dashay, this time at running back. A defender nearly tripped him in the backfield, but Dashay pulled his heavy leg away and went on through left tackle. There he hit a low wall of defenders in front of the end zone and stood straight up, hardly able to move, like he was wading through quicksand. So he just reached out and put the ball over the goal line. Still unable to move for a few moments after the score, he taunted a defender to come get him.

La La's boy.

◆

The Wildcats jogged into the locker room at halftime up 25–0.

"There's a different energy," said Stan Rome, who trailed the 'Cats inside and took a seat, like he'd do the rest of the year.

He pointed his cane toward Ryan, seated between Dashay and Malcolm, who'd scored on a 45-yard pass play.

"For a quarterback who never played varsity football," Stan said, "I thought he did good."

Gillespie disappeared into the coaches' room, stayed there until his players settled down, then came back out to talk. He wasn't unhappy—heck, he'd had a ball out there, even got the crowd roaring when he stormed the field and chewed out a ref who'd messed up the call on an onside kick—but he couldn't let these guys know that.

"You're a better football team than what you played, even though you're up 25–0," he said.

Tough and demanding as he was on them, though, Gillespie believed players played best when they enjoyed themselves. Football was a great game. He wanted them to know that.

"Let's go out and have two good drives and let everybody have a good time," he said. "Have some fun!"

The second half was over not long after it started. Ryan hit Malcolm with a quick screen at the Trojans 48; if the play had not been blown dead when he crossed the goal line, Brooks County might still be chasing him. Zach then hit a field goal to make it 35–0. Reserves played the rest of the game with a running clock.

"I haven't seen this in years," said Berke Holtzclaw, who played quarterback on Valdosta's 1984 national championship team and now quarterbacked the sideline mafia. "Some of this I ain't never seen. This is the first game of the year, and there's no telling what we'll see if they get better every game."

The locker room was pandemonium—except for a subdued Alex, who still looked rocked from having lost the quarterback job. He played the fourth quarter tonight, meaningless minutes.

"I feel all right," he said. "It's hard to let go of something you worked so hard for."

Then Gillespie walked in. Swoll stepped right up to him, surrounded by the rest of the team. He held out the game ball and then handed it to his new coach.

"It's a new generation," Swoll proclaimed.

Gillespie stood there stunned. He took a deep breath as his eyes roamed the room. He then raised the football high so that everybody could see it.

"I promise you," he told them all, "this is the first one ever presented to me by a team. This one will have a place in my heart."

He paused, collected himself.

"It's the beginning."

●

Players streamed out of the locker room and headed toward the buses now parked across from Drexel Park. They were swarmed before they got through the gates by family, friends, girlfriends, girls.

Standing beyond the gates, beneath a streetlight near the idling buses, Dashay's girlfriend waited impatiently with their seven-week-old daughter cradled in her arms.

Despite her boyfriend's two touchdowns tonight, Shan wasn't happy. She'd waited there for what seemed to her like forever. When Dashay finally appeared—beaming, acknowledging compliments from everybody he passed—she dropped tiny Kaydence into his hands and gave him a cold stare.

Dashay kissed his little girl, bounced her in the air.

A stunning junior with college ambitions, Shan just stood there, all SMH—shake my head.

"Basically, he was still doing the same old stuff," she'd say later of the dynamic that night. "Even at the hospital when I had the baby we were mad at each other. He cut the cord, but at the end of the day he got another girl at the hospital to pick him up. Same old Dashay.

"After the game, I thought he was just trying to be slick. He told me to come to the game, that he'd be mad if I didn't. Then he came out and was talking to some girl he wasn't supposed to be talking to anymore. And I was like, 'Really?' He was walking superfast, trying to be sneaky. He didn't want the other girls to see him with me and the baby. He wanted to keep his image until he got back there and it was just me and him and his teammates.

"I don't know what was going through my head. He told me he loved me, asked me if I would do something for him—asked me to have a baby. And I did. Why? Because we had like this little fairy tale planned out. I was just a little sixteen-year-old in love, willing to do anything for him. And I felt he would do anything for me."

The team had boarded the buses. Dashay still stood under the street-light in the warm, humid air, playing with his baby girl. Finally, Coach Rodemaker boomed out for Dashay to *come on*.

He handed Kaydence back to her mother, jogged up to the bus, and disappeared.

Gillespie rode in an assistant's pickup back to the school. He glanced at the game in his office as it was copied onto a disc; he'd drive ninety miles to Cordele in the morning to exchange film with next week's opponent.

Claudette and Kennedy were already back at the house, along with a couple of coaches, a few friends, and Rance's mother, who'd driven down from North Georgia. They were ready to celebrate Rance's maiden victory at Valdosta High. Only 199 more and those gravesites David Waller offered were theirs.

Gillespie left the office just after midnight. The sky was clear and black, with stars crowded near a yellowed wedge of moon.

"Feels good," he said of the win as he crossed the emptied parking lot.

Before he slipped into his car—the Saturn that still had three months left on its lease—Gillespie blew out what seemed like the first relaxed breath he'd taken since he'd arrived nine months earlier.

"When you win and play well, there's nothing like it for those couple hours after a game," he said. "It's an adrenaline rush. It's why you do it. It's addictive."

On the drive home he passed near the Waffle House, already filled to standing with boosters, cheerleaders, and players, some of whom waited with their girlfriends in the parking lot for a booth to open. It would stay crowded like that for a while, a Valdosta tradition.

Gillespie pulled into his driveway a few minutes later. Everybody was crammed in the Gillespies' kitchen. "I don't know why we always end up in here," Claudette said, but she was clearly pleased. She loved these moments when Rance was relaxed and could just enjoy himself with friends, the talk easy and loose and filled with laughs. It was addictive, too.

They all toasted the night: lifted cold beer, a little wine. Rodemaker hauled in a couple of family-sized bags of pork rinds and deep-fried onion rings. He ate them by the handful while he tried to remember the name of a back-road barbecue shack, in some distant county where he and Rance once coached, that served goat.

14

Hero Worship

or Can I Google You?

O f all the clans that make up the breakaway republic of Valdosta High—ballers, stoners, nerds, born-agains, skaters, ROTCs, thugs, 'hos, cheerleaders—it's no surprise that none rank higher than football players.

"In Greek mythology, there's Mount Olympus," deconstructed Randy Cook, the defensive back who ran all those after-practice gassers to channel the school's historic lineage. "Football here is Mount Olympus. We are the gods. The quarterback, he's Zeus."

It's not brag if it's fact, and it's been a fact at Valdosta forever. Times have changed, but that legacy hasn't. Back in the '50s and '60s, players got a hero's escort after games from their girlfriends. Now players' phones fill with texts from girls who want to hook up. Football players are still the kids in the hall with the most swag, the most idolatry.

The most sex appeal.

The hero worship seeped down from the high school through the entire system. Elementary school principals invited a half-dozen players each Friday to talk or read to their students. The Wildcats were many of these kids' profoundest role models. They rushed and squealed when the Wildcats arrived as if they'd just leaped off a TV screen. Boling called the high school players in Valdosta "the Michael Jordans and Drew Breeses of our schools."

One Friday, though, inside an elementary school gym, a black fourth-grade boy walked up to kicker Zach Wang and asked him, "You the quarterback?" Given that Wang was the only white Wildcat there that day, and that there were only two white starters on the team, including the quarterback (the other was an offensive lineman), it wasn't a bad guess.

Yet not that long ago, every kid in Valdosta knew for sure the starting quarterback.

Zeus.

"I could name the players on any roster for Valdosta from '78 or '79 through when I played," said Ben Hogan, the Wildcats quarterback in 1988 who went on to play at South Carolina and now was the team doctor. "Watching those guys as a kid, I'd watch how they handled themselves, how they spoke to teammates. They molded you. You thought, 'When I'm in that position, that's how I'll handle it.'

"Valdosta was this city's pro football team. The rest of the school took its cue from us. But you also lived in a fishbowl. There were kids who didn't like that pressure, but it was part of the job description. You were the image of the school in this city, and you were the image of this city to an entire nation. That's a lot of pressure on sixteen- and seventeen-year-old kids."

Then Hyder died, three coaches who followed left or were kicked out, and now fourth-grade boys asked the placekicker if he was the quarterback.

"As great as that tradition was, it's amazing how quickly it gets dissipated," Hogan said. "It takes about four years for guys to come up in elementary school and middle school who suddenly don't recognize the guys in high school.

"We looked up to Stan Rome and John Bond and Pernell Bee. Who are these kids looking up to? Who are these kids going to say about, 'Remember that Friday night when . . . ?'"

❖

When Alex transferred to Valdosta from Ware County last spring, Malcolm warned him to be careful, that girls would chase him just because he played football, that they had "superstar fever."

Different strains of that condition exist at most high schools, of course, but at Valdosta, it was epidemic.

"Everybody knows everybody here's going somewhere," explained Raven Richard, one of the three junior girls who filmed Wildcat practices and games for the coaches. "If I can Google you, chances are you're going somewhere."

Superstar fever broke out this season in the first half of the first game. Moments after Malcolm caught a 45-yard touchdown pass, the phone he left back in his locker vibrated with texts from girls who wanted to see him (teammates razzed Tampa as "the King of the Texts"). His wasn't the only one. Cell phones hummed like a swarm of bees in the 'Cats' empty locker room throughout the Brooks County game. Some players checked their messages at the half.

"You score a touchdown on Friday night, you're going to have a new number in your phone—you're going to have about four of them," Malcolm said. "It's all about football here. You do something on the field, they will know it and they will come."

Some players, like Malcolm, handled it coolly. Others, not so much. Some players would become fathers in the months following the season.

"You don't know how a girl's mind works. You just have to be careful and watch out," Malcolm said. "A girl that texts you after the game because you scored a touchdown is not one you need to talk to. They text because they want sex. They text, 'Come to my house.' I just don't text them back. They get it."

It wasn't as easy as Malcolm made it sound, of course.

"Telling them no is the hardest part," he conceded. "The ones that look good—it's just hard. It's hard to tell a good-looking girl no."

He smiled his just-chillin' smile. "Know what I mean?"

●

Harder still: dating a Wildcat.

Tasha Williams was pretty and sweet and a year younger than Malcolm. She wasn't interested in Malcolm because she could Google him. When they met in Spanish class the year before, she wasn't interested in him all.

"I thought he was cocky," she said. "After practice one day, he was with Alex in a truck, telling Alex's dad, 'That's my girlfriend.' And I'm like, 'No I'm not.'"

Over the summer, though, she did the one thing girls in Valdosta apparently couldn't stop themselves from doing: texted Malcolm. She was headed to Wild Adventures, the local amusement park, and asked him if he wanted to go. They talked a lot after that, became friends, hung out.

Texted.

By the Ware scrimmage, they were together. Dating mainly meant hanging out more. They saw each other a lot at practice because Tasha was one of the trio of girls who filmed the Wildcats practices and games for Gillespie. With practices ending late and Malcolm beat, weeknights were pretty low-key. Tasha stayed home a lot on weekends, too; her mother underwent chemo treatments for cancer.

Tasha had dated football players before and didn't think this would be much different. She'd never dated a football player of Malcolm's stature. It *was* different.

Way different.

"I didn't even look at him like he was a football player," she said. "Everybody calls him Tampa. I call him Malcolm. Dating Malcolm was perfectly fine. Dating Tampa was totally different."

Dating Malcolm was between her and him. Dating Tampa was between her, him, and, it seemed, every other girl in Valdosta.

"Every other day," Tasha said, "someone would come up to me and say, 'So-and-so is talking with Tampa!' Or 'I saw so-and-so with Tampa.' Sometimes I feel like . . .'"

Sometimes she didn't really know what she felt like.

"I try to trust him. But it's hard when people tell you the same story. In the back of your head, you wonder."

She'd talk about it with her closest friends. She'd call crying in the middle of the night. If being Malcolm's girlfriend was a full-time job, so was being the girlfriend of Malcolm's girlfriend.

"I just have the phone in my ear, saying, 'Yeah, girl. Yeah, girl,'" said Raven of Tasha's 3:00 A.M. calls. "I *hate* being woken up."

Raven also understood. While there was a certain prestige to being with a football player at Valdosta High, there was a price attached, too.

"It's pretty hard—all the gossip, all the groupies. There's only so much you can take," Raven said. "Most girls just see dollar signs."

She added that the players didn't help, that they weren't the most sympathetic audience. Why would they be?

"On top of being boys, football players are also the cheating-around type," she said. "They're on top of the chain of being the epitome of a guy."

The Wildcat at the top of that chain?

Raven didn't hesitate.

"Dashay," she said. "He's the straight epitome of being a guy."

She rolled her eyes.

"He is a bad boy."

Being Dashay's girlfriend was a whole other kettle of crazy.

"Everybody wanna be pregnant from HIM all of a sudden like he 50 Cent and it's gon make Dem a millionaire!" Shan posted one late night on Facebook, more for her haters than for her friends. "I swear its like yall pray about it at nite lol! Having his baby won't make him love you sorry! I SWEAR I NEVER MET SO MANY KRAZY HOES TIL I KAME TO VALDOSTA! SMH."

Shan and Dashay met during the brief time Shan attended Valdosta High. She had a class with him. History, she thinks. They didn't really talk much, but when Dashay's birthday rolled around she . . . texted him. She didn't know much about Dashay back then—didn't know he played football, didn't know his bad-boy rep—but soon they were talking all the time. Then Dashay asked her to be his girlfriend.

"The only thing I knew about him was I knew the way he acted with me, his personality," she said. "He can be really sweet."

Shan saw a side of Dashay that a lot of teachers, administrators, and even coaches didn't often see. She saw the porcupine beneath the quills. She saw what she called "the real him. The core of who he is."

"I know he's deeper than football, that there's more behind him than that,' she said. "The way he says stuff to me—it isn't romantic, like out of a movie or anything. But I understand it, the way he's trying to make me feel.

"I can always be myself," she said. "Even on my worst days, he says, 'I love you. You're beautiful.' On the days other people don't want to be around me, he does. He accepts me for what I am."

The drama started immediately. It tailed her across town when she transferred to Lowndes. Her second day there a girl she didn't know came right up to her, said she'd gone to Valdosta, too, told Shan all the people she knew there: so-and-so and so-and-so and . . . oh yeah, Dashay.

"She said, 'Yeah, we talk. He wanted me to come over. Wanted me to see him.' I said, *'Really?'*"

Shan sighed. "It was always something or other."

The drama only escalated after Shan got pregnant.

"A lot of girls called my phone with blocked numbers and threatened me," she said. "They'd say, 'I heard you're pregnant. If it's true, I'm beating that baby out of you!' I never worried about it. I just figured it was some stupid girls."

Shan did announce her feelings where they'd get the widest play: on Facebook.

"Just realized a lot of females in my friend list I don't even knw," she tapped out in one status update. "I guess shay's groupies become my groupies. SMFH."

"Chilling at his house goin thru his phone lol SHHHHHH!!! Later Facebook."

"Did not know there was a football wives show lol yes I'm gonna watch it ;)."

"Boy I hate hoes."

15

Quarterbacks and Comebacks

or Turn It Up a Little Higher

The town buzzed for a week after the 'Cats' opening-night victory. Boosters fell over themselves to thank and praise Gillespie during his first Monday night game-film review in the school's performing arts center. Fans packed the long tables inside the Smokin' Pig's back room for Wednesday night's inaugural radio show.

This renewed euphoria lasted two weeks, until the second quarter of the third game. That's when fans called for the quarterback's head.

It's also when race popped up, as it inevitably does in the Deep South—as it inevitably does all over Obama's America—itchy to become the team's undermining twelfth man.

Ryan's play had been sketchy even in Valdosta's second win, a 36–0 flaying of an overmatched Hardaway team that traveled, like a journeyman club fighter, 175 miles down from Columbus, Georgia, to pick up its $8,000 guaranteed payout.

Ryan completed fewer than half his pass attempts in that rout, and while he threw for 2 touchdowns—both screens, including one that Dashay danced with for 56 untouched yards—he was also picked off twice and missed a stable of wide-open receivers. Gillespie was concerned enough that he ordered Ryan to keep winging it in the third quarter, with the 'Cats already up 29–0, just to get him more passing reps. The offense wasn't instinctive yet to Ryan; his movements weren't yet in sync with the thoughts rolling in his head. He hadn't achieved that South Georgia Zen.

Ryan was a green senior and needed all the seasoning he could get before facing Valdosta's next opponent: the Lincoln Trojans, a perennial power from Tallahassee and the eighth-ranked team in Florida. Big and bad and fast, Lincoln looked like it could match the Wildcats athlete for athlete, swag for swag.

Players knew that the stakes were high. If you grew up in Valdosta, the stakes were always high.

"We'll finally see what we're made of," said senior kicker Zach Wang, who took everything in stride and so far hadn't missed a field goal or extra point attempt. Zach was determined to erase any memories of last year's crucial misses. His golden hair seemed to vary from week to week, from short to shaggy. Before this week's game it was buzzed down into a kind of low-riding, military-style Mohawk.

Wang . . .

Gillespie also believed Lincoln would be a significant measuring stick. That's one reason he was patient with his inexperienced quarterback—far more patient, it became clearer by the game, than a lot of fans.

Mostly black fans.

Dashay's fans.

"People were calling me at the game, asking me, 'What Dashay did?'" said Matt Washington, Dashay's ebullient, in-and-out father, noting that many of those calls came from the late-night patrons at Ace of Fades, the barbershop down on Highway 84 where he now worked cleaning up.

Dashay's uncle Bones added, "For a lot of people, Dashay is the highlight of the game. If he isn't going to be quarterback, they don't go."

Quarterback remains the one position on a football field where race still creeps into the conversation. It used to be a loud conversation in Valdosta. David Waller marks his acceptance of the Wildcats' first black play caller as a kind of final step in his own racial enlightenment (black coach might still be the last one). Up until the late '80s, the notion of a black quarterback here was still as crazy as the notion of a black . . . president.

Never happen.

"When we finally integrated and won a national championship, I thought, 'This isn't so bad,'" Waller said. "I evolved into it. But always in the back of my mind I thought, 'We're integrated and that's fine, but certainly we'll never have a black quarterback.' I couldn't see that. It just wouldn't work."

Then, in 1989, the regular, white quarterback broke his leg the first day of camp and Hyder moved an African American wide receiver under center. The Wildcats won consecutive state crowns.

"And I began to love Alton Hitson," Waller said of the black starter. "He was such a good kid. Coach Hyder taught me more about black and white than anybody. We're all brothers in battle."

Yet after a succession of black quarterbacks followed Hitson, Hyder still sensed boosters' discomfort.

"Some of the people do not like the fact that our quarterback is black—that one position," he told an out-of-town reporter in 1994, to the dismay of local whites.

The noise that surrounded Dashay, however, was more complicated than just black-or-white. As with Michael Vick, with whom Dashay had been compared since middle school, race now seemed mixed with culture, class, identity.

His earrings, tattoos, on-field posturing, and off-field rumbles reflected for many whites a thug lifestyle they associated with the rise in gang activity and the spike in the previous year's murder rate.

In their minds, you couldn't walk down some Valdosta streets anymore without the sight of grade-schoolers crotch-grabbing like rappers or the scent of high school kids puffing on a Black & Mild, the cigar of choice when it came to subbing out tobacco with weed.

Dashay so encapsulated those images during the previous season that an embattled Tomberlin said he was pressured by the school board to replace him at quarterback with the son of a white board member. Tomberlin said he refused. He believed it contributed to his sacking.

Yet for many African Americans, Dashay's chaotic upbringing and dazzling talent simply made him an example of just the kind of kid football could rescue. Half the town seemed invested in aiding Dashay: coaches, teachers, boosters, the local chapter of 100 Black Men.

"It's the type of story people like to hear. He made it through so much," explained his girlfriend Shan. "They have so many high expectations for him."

Still, Dashay tried everyone's patience.

"It was pressure for him and he didn't want to disappoint anybody," Shan said, "but it also gave him a big head, as far as girls and getting in trouble at school."

Gillespie knew all about Dashay's polarizing effect in the community—and didn't care. He had games to win. He also had Stan Rome on his side. Stan thought Ryan would eventually develop under Gillespie's touch. That support could help keep a quarterback controversy from igniting into something thornier.

To Gillespie, the football nerd, the issue was simple: Dashay had missed too much preseason work to get a handle on the new offense, and his off-field résumé of suspensions and borderline eligibility made him too big a risk to count on for an entire season.

Gillespie did work up a kind of "wildcat" package that featured Dashay in the shotgun and exploited his speed, power, and elusiveness. Even so, this team wasn't going to win without somebody getting the ball out in space to its other home-run hitters: Malcolm, Jay, and, yes, Dashay.

Gillespie believed Ryan was the guy who could do that best. He'd just have to coach him up.

"He's limited in some areas," Gillespie allowed during a quiet hour in his office before the Lincoln game. "He's a tough kid. He's intelligent. He's competitive. He wants to do well and it bothers him when he doesn't.

"But right now it's too much to ask him to be the guy we lean on. He could lead us to a big win if he gets the ball to the right people, makes good decisions and solid plays. That would be a huge stride for him."

Like a gambler playing the long game, Gillespie knew better than to get greedy. The key now was asset management. He'd call on Ryan to give him more as the season rolled on. Then when he really needed it, he'd ask Ryan to go all in.

Meanwhile, he just wanted to buy the kid time.

"The next progression for him is to step up and make significant plays that lead us to a big win," Gillespie went on. "Maybe he'll go the whole year where he won't do that. But he got twenty-nine varsity reps in that last game. It's interesting to see him struggle. It ain't easy when a coach says you're going to throw on every down. He threw a pick, but then he moved them downfield and made good decisions.

"We want to put him in a position to be a better player in week twelve. He's got to have opportunities to make mistakes, and thank God we were in a position last week where he could make those mistakes."

Gillespie stared down at his play sheet for Lincoln.

"He just better not make those mistakes tonight."

●

Ryan's mistakes against Lincoln came early and often. The Wildcats' first drive sputtered after a bad snap and a sack. Lincoln, big and bad and fast as advertised, then took the ball right in for a score, the first points given up by the Wildcat defense this season.

On the 'Cats' next possession, Ryan overthrew a wide-open Malcolm and the 'Cats were forced to punt. The defense held, then went out again and recovered a fumble on the Lincoln 17. Gillespie played it close to the vest and had Ryan hand the ball twice to Swoll, who on the second carry bounced off a defender at the 1-yard line—that defender might still be on the grass—and tied the game.

In the second quarter, Ryan threw the ball to the wrong guy—the wrong team—but the defense kept Lincoln to a field goal. Yet when Ryan came back out and dropped two more snaps, the already restless crowd began to grumble. Then boo. Then, from the first few rows behind the Wildcat bench, to chant.

"We want Dash-ay! We want Dash-ay!"

The always emotional James Eunice, his model-handsome white face smeared menacingly with eye black, became furious on the sideline. He tore off his helmet and yelled up at the crowd to stop chanting and start supporting the quarterback on the field.

Then, just before the end of the half, Lincoln blocked a punt and ran it in for another score. The chants swelled into a loud, nasty chorus as the 'Cats jogged back up the tunnel, trailing 17–7.

It was ugly. Ryan had completed a measly 4 of 17 passes, along with that interception. His mother, father, and older brother sat together in the stands and took deep, shell-shocked breaths.

Gillespie speed-walked straight into the coaches' room. The white-washed walls and mopped cement floor made the place seem better suited for an autopsy. As he stood in the middle of his assistants, three words dropped from his mouth.

"We. Are. Screwed."

Coach Pruitt, who had a bird's-eye view from the press box, expanded on Gillespie's sentiments.

"He's just spastic back there," he said of Ryan. "He has more time than he thinks. He's just freakin' out."

Gillespie looked up and down his play sheet. Pruitt, who played quarterback at Valdosta State, told him that Lincoln's defense wasn't doing anything the Valdosta coaches hadn't expected them to do. Ryan just couldn't get his receivers the damn ball. Jay and Malcolm had just one catch each.

"The only other option," Pruitt offered, "is to run the ball, run the ball, run the ball."

Gillespie pushed the door open and strode back out into the locker room. The players looked like they weren't sure what they should think. They knew they were the better team, yet here they were down by 10. They braced for a Gillespie tirade: That's what football coaches did when you were down by two scores at the half.

In Title Town.

Gillespie knew these kids weren't losing for lack of effort, though. In fact, he thought they might be trying too hard.

"Listen," he told them, "relax. You're two scores down, but I guarantee you they're going to give you an opportunity to get back in this. Nobody works harder than you."

He turned to Ryan. The room quieted. Nobody had to tell anybody what a horseshit half Ryan had, but this mostly black team was behind their "white black dude," as Reggie had dubbed him.

Ryan's biggest backer: Dashay.

"They need to quit criticizing him," Dashay said. "People still saying this slick stuff about me, my friends keep saying, 'You need to go back to quarterback.' But we had to get Ryan in the picture. He has the talent.

He's good enough for whatever it takes. If he has to take a lick, he'll do it. Ryan's just . . . Ryan."

Even Alex had put aside his pouty ways when the booing started and shouted out encouragement from the sideline. "Way to be smart out there, one-two!" he yelled after Ryan, number 12, threw a ball away before a Lincoln monster could sack him.

Gillespie's tone to Ryan was calm, clear, and straightforward, like he was giving him directions to his house. Resting on one knee, with sweat rolling down his face and following his bright pink scars, Ryan looked straight up at his coach, like he really wanted to hear those directions.

"Ryan, you got to make a play or two for us, okay?" Gillespie said. "It's real easy. Relax, pop it out there, and let them make some plays."

Armed with that stupid-simple wisdom, the 'Cats trotted back down the dark tunnel and out onto the field, face-to-face again with their ever loyal but always ready to hang you fans.

The defense struck first.

Jonathan Hester, the 'Cats' heady junior linebacker, began the second half with a relaxed, intuitive bang: picked off a tipped Lincoln pass and rambled 32 complicated yards through the middle of the field and down the sideline until finally he scored. Valdosta was back to within a field goal.

The crowd's high-fiving frenzy lasted exactly 14 play-clock seconds. Lincoln returned Wang's ensuing kickoff 82 yards to put the Trojans back up again by 10, 24–14.

"They're playing a real good football team," Stan observed.

He'd moved from the locker room to the end zone to his Escalade in the parking lot, where he listened in the dark on the radio. He couldn't stand still during these games; he'd hardly been able to watch a full game since Jay was in middle school.

"We got our expectations, but I don't know if they're realistic," he went on, in damage control mode. "We got a new coach, a new offense— we're trying to do a lot of things we haven't done in the last few years."

As for Ryan, Stan said, "When they've gotten open, he's missed bad. The only thing that can cure that is experience."

With that humiliating first half behind him, the second half's initial back-and-forth chaos, in some weird way, seemed to settle Ryan. It was just ball now, not the eighth-ranked team from Florida playing the most storied program in Georgia in front of a big crowd under the same high-performance, daylight-mimicking stadium lights used at Daytona International Speedway.

All of a sudden, it was just say-hike, throw-it-to-the-right-guy football.

Ryan had heard the boos and chants for Dashay as he jogged off the field and into the locker room. They mostly amused him. Hell, even he thought Dashay should be the quarterback.

"I think Dashay's better than me," he said. "I'm in it for the team, so, like, you might as well let him play. I could care less who gets mad, who thinks it's a wrong decision."

Coach left him in, though, told him to relax, let his teammates make plays. So Ryan did. Malcolm turned a short pass into a long TD—brought back because of a holding penalty. A few plays later, on a fourth and 1 from their own 48, Ryan slipped the ball to Swoll and watched him get one more yard than he needed.

It wasn't a lot, but it was progress.

Ryan remembered one other thing Gillespie told him in the locker room: Gotta make a play or two yourself. It sounded easy, the way he'd said it. So next time Ryan stood back in the pocket, the game suddenly did what games had always done for Ryan: slowed down.

An aroused Lincoln mob of old-gold helmets and black pants closed in on him, but this time Ryan calmly waited until he spotted Wesley Bee 20 yards down the middle before he tossed the ball loose and easy—like it was just the two of them out there, having a catch in Ryan's backyard. A couple of plays later, Ryan loitered in the pocket again while Malcolm separated himself by a half step from a spidery defensive back. He then snapped a low dart just far enough out ahead that Malcolm could dive and tumble and cradle it in the end zone.

"He ain't a quitter. He never gives up," Malcolm said of the quarterback—*his* quarterback. "He's not rattled by stuff that happens in games. When he threw that interception, I never saw it in his eyes in the huddle, that he was worried about throwing the next pass."

Malcolm then gave Ryan the definitive Malcolm compliment. "I trust him."

●

As usual, Malcolm's trust was well placed.

Ryan followed his 31-yard touchdown toss with sure, efficient patience. He just went along with the game. He threw seven more passes and completed almost all of them. More than that, he took what the game gave him. That meant turning around and then handing the ball like a fat graduation envelope to Swoll.

Swoll did the rest. Running with heart and even a little sadism, he bumped and bruised and galloped his way for almost 100 yards. He covered most of that ground when it counted most and scored three times, including the last of Valdosta's four second-half touchdowns.

Swoll often lamented that folks didn't consider you a real Wildcat unless you were a Bazemore or Hyder Wildcat. It was his generation's burden. But as he scratched and clawed and stiff-armed his way for every yard against Lincoln, he looked like a direct descendant of those old don't-mess-with-me 'Cats.

"I told him," Coach Loudermilk said afterward, "'Son, you can be in my foxhole anytime.'"

Ryan, meanwhile, clearly came of age—and so, by extension, did his team. There wasn't another boo, hoot, or chant for Dashay the rest of the game. When senior defensive end Carlton Harrell finally threw the Lincoln quarterback into the turf to end the night, the crowd rose, black and white, and stood together to cheer what they all valued more than anything else here: a team that never, never quit.

Final: Valdosta 35, Lincoln 31.

"They did something coaches can't coach," said Jack Rudolph, seated in the stadium's next-to-last row with a handful of the other coaches who'd helped create the legacy this team was trying to live up to. "They came back from a double-digit deficit twice and won the ball game."

Rudolph added of the new coach, "He's here to be the Valdosta coach for a while."

Maybe these were the first Wildcats that folks someday would look back on and proudly call Gillespie 'Cats.

A forkful of moon still hung overhead. Fans were hoarse and rumpled. A drained Claudette rushed onto the field with Kennedy, who wrapped herself around her father's thighs. Every win was different, but this one was a doozy.

"I ate a whole pack of Starbursts in two minutes," Claudette said of the nerve-racking ending. "Thought I was going to throw up."

Rance stood near the west end zone, accepting handshakes from Cason and Waller and just about every other Valdostan who'd waited too long for a win like this—a win that seemed to say there might be life in the old stuck-in-the-past program yet.

The crowd's reaction to Ryan still made him mad. "That booing, that was *ridiculous* for a high school," he said. "I'm about tired of hearing 'Dashay for quarterback.'"

Yet overall he was pleased. The kids showed him something tonight.

"It's a big shot in the arm for us," Gillespie said. "It's a big step in getting our swagger back."

A week later, that swag ran amok. Playing at home again against the Pirates from coastal Brunswick, two hours east, Gillespie's halftime words could not have been more opposite of those he delivered just seven days earlier.

"Listen," he told his huffing and puffing charges, who'd done nothing but run up and down the field for two quarters, "we *gotta* keep scoring."

Already they'd scored three touchdowns; Ryan looked like he'd started at quarterback his whole life. The only problem so far: Brunswick had scored four touchdowns, or as many as the 'Cats had given up the previous three games.

It was a track meet, with Valdosta only down 24–22 after Brunswick botched all four of its 2-point conversions. In the locker room, Gillespie devised more schemes to throw the ball to Malcolm ("There's about fourteen ways to get you loose"), to Jay ("Can you lose nineteen? You're gonna have to"), to everybody.

Except Dashay, who limped off in the first quarter with a high ankle sprain. He'd likely be out until the Lowndes game, three weeks from now.

"Kid did it on purpose. Went right for my leg," Dashay said of the hit he took on a kickoff return. "Could see it in his eyes."

The 'Cats grabbed their helmets when Gillespie finished, ready to run until the sun came up if they had to. As they headed toward the door, Stan jumped up from his seat and lurched toward junior receiver Tyran Watkins.

Watkins was a raw, talented, personable kid with a rough, iffy background. He grew up around Fort Lauderdale; his father, he said, had been in prison since he was nine. Watkins said he preferred robbery and burglary to football, until he discovered that he was a lot better at football. He moved to Valdosta with his mother in the eighth grade. Football now gave him purpose and drive. He hoped someday it might reward him with a better life.

Watkins missed two balls in the first half, both of them tough, in-traffic throws that nobody could expect him to catch.

Except Stan.

Stan straightened as much as he could with the help of his cane to get eye-to-eye with the 6'4" Watkins.

"You gotta pull that shit *down*," Stan told him, man to man—street kid to street kid. "You can't hold it up there—you have to snatch it down!"

Tyran stood still and straight. Didn't say a word. He knew he should've caught those balls—that Stan would've caught those balls—but he got anxious when he saw them spinning his way. He didn't see himself yet as one of the team's big playmakers, like Jay or Malcolm.

Now, Mr. Stan told him, he was.

"Just picture yourself making those plays," Stan went on, his tone almost therapeutic. "Picture yourself making great plays . . ."

●

The second half turned more insane even than the madcap first one.

Valdosta struck right away: a floater to Malcolm, who juked, stuttered, jitterbugged, and sprinted past every electric blue helmet and pair of caution-light yellow pants worn by the Brunswick side for a 26-yard touchdown. Malcolm scored again less than two minutes later, on a 56-yard pass.

Valdosta's fans breathed easier; some flipped through their game programs before the next kickoff to search for a cat's paw on the ad for Cass Burch's car dealership ("We stack 'em deep, sell 'em cheap. Drive it like you stole it!"). Winner got a dinner for two at the Pig.

But Brunswick quarterback Chris Anderson was having the game of his life. Small but canny and elusive, he played like a brother from another planet. He sidestepped Wildcat defenders like a teasing matador and hit any receiver who worked himself open.

The Pirates soon scored again.

Then again.

"Unconscious," Gillespie muttered of Anderson on the sideline.

Before the third quarter closed, Brunswick was back on top, 40–35.

Jack Rudolph turned to his old coaching confederacy of graying heads seated at the top of the stands and announced, "42–40. That's what the final score's going to be."

He revised that prediction less than two minutes later, after Reggie scored on a 95-yard kickoff return and Brunswick matched it with another TD. Suddenly it was 48–41, visitors still on top. Ryan then found Jay in the end zone to even it back up.

On it went, like a repeating decimal. The crowd applauded as if on automatic pilot. The cheerleaders seemed to run out of cheers.

"It's like the same thing happening over and over again," said Morgan Long of the game's *Groundhog Day* redundancy. Her bright blond hair was streaked with sweat. "It's like being at a basketball game."

The radio announcers in the press box were losing it, too.

"I ran out of room on my notebook to write this stuff down," Bobby Scott told his listeners after Jay's score.

Finally, Valdosta appeared to put the game away. Jay pulled in a 30-yard strike from Ryan to set up another score and put the 'Cats up by 6 with barely a minute left. Gillespie ordered a 2-pointer; Brunswick hadn't tried to kick an extra point all night.

Ryan stepped back, waited half a beat. He then threw low and slightly behind a Wildcat receiver slanting close across the middle.

Tyran stopped dead, crouched, and, with a defender flying in front of his face, plucked the ball with both hands just inches off the turf.

Assist: Mr. Stan.

●

Any other night, that would've ended it, but tonight was unlike any night anybody had ever seen in Valdosta.

So when the Pirates water-bugged their way down the field to score with 10 seconds left and throw the game into overtime, tied 56–56, Bobby Scott uttered a single word to his partner in the radio booth: *"Duuude . . ."*

In overtime, starting on the Brunswick 15, the Wildcats got the ball first and put it across on their second play, Jay pulling down a sweet toss from Ryan in the right corner of the end zone. As if to illustrate just how surreal the night had gotten, Ryan then scored the 2-point conversion himself, running a bootleg 3 yards around the right end in about the same time it took Malcolm to cover 20—but still making it in untouched.

A new chant rolled down from the student section. *"RY-an WHIL-den! RY-an WHIL-den!"*

Now it was Brunswick's turn. Their quarterback had already amassed on this hallowed field an unholy 539 yards—344 passing, 195 rushing. He'd passed for 4 touchdowns and run for 2 more. Gillespie would later call it the best performance by a high school quarterback he'd ever seen.

So nobody was surprised, least of all Valdosta's shredded defense, when the Pirates scored yet again, the game's eighteenth touchdown.

This could go on all night—a *Groundhog Day* marathon.

The Pirates lined up for their 2-point conversion, just like they had *eight times before.*

Enough times, anyway, that linebacker Justin Williams really did feel like he'd seen this movie already and that he knew exactly what Mr. Unconscious would do next. The moment the ball was snapped, he shot the gap on the left side like he'd called the play himself and mugged Anderson in the backfield.

Game over, just like that: 64–62.

Most points ever scored in a Georgia High School Association regular season game.

●

Fans looked as dazed as they were delirious, as if they'd just sat through a movie with too many car chases, too many shootouts, too many exploding helicopters—football produced by Jerry Bruckheimer.

Claudette was so ecstatic she hardly knew what to do. She glanced at the tunnel, wanting to bang the tin.

"Can I?" she asked Rance. "Or is that sacrilegious?"

Gillespie just grinned. His initial reaction after the game, "I'm worn out."

Rodemaker, the defensive coordinator, said he wouldn't get over this game for as long as he lived. "The Lord put this in front of us for a reason. I just got to figure out the reason," he said late that night inside his office at the school, sighing, running his hands through his thinning hair, thinking mostly un-Godly thoughts.

Another coach read aloud to him a text that just came in from a mutual friend: "Tell Alan to put down the gun."

Yet when Gillespie gathered his Wildcats around him in the end zone after the two teams had lined up and congratulated each on their shared, mind-blowing experience, he emphasized the positive.

"Hey, listen," he told them. "You keep finding a way to win—that's the important thing. Defensively, we got to get better. But listen, men, there ain't no quit in us. You do that every week and you're going to be smiling at the end of the year."

The players still had enough in the tank to erupt into a rousing cheer, then bow their heads in prayer. Then they circled Jay and bounced up and down as he led them in a minutes-long call and response.

Jay, who ushered at his church on the first and fourth Sundays of every month, sang in a choir until he hit "the age where my voice stopped sounding as good as I thought it did."

His deep booming vocals were just fine for a shout-out like this.

"Turn me up a little—"

"*Higher!*"

"Just a little—"

"*Higher!*"

On they went. Gillespie headed out. The scoreboard's yellow bulbs still burned above his head: 64–62. Inside the absurdity of those numbers, he found some solace. He now had a quarterback, or at least as much of a quarterback as he'd have this season. Maybe even as much as he needed. Ryan threw for 335 yards and 4 touchdowns—2 to Malcolm, 2 to Jay. Couldn't draw it up better. Ryan also figured out where to go when the going got tough; Malcolm's five catches averaged 40 yards each.

"Twelve showed balls of steel," Gillespie said of the kid he'd stuck with.

He went on about Ryan later that night in his own office while he performed the South Georgia version of multitasking: ate a chocolate cake with his fingers that the cheerleaders' sponsor baked for all the coaches; spit tobacco juice into an empty water bottle; and watched a replay of the game.

"It was a contest of wills between those two quarterbacks," he said. "It came down to which team was going to succumb to the pressure, and he never did. It would've been easy to get tight and give in to those emotions. But he didn't. That's big. That's what you want in a quarterback."

The silent movie on his wall flashed to the halftime scoreboard: 24–22.

Gillespie stopped, then added another task to the night's multitasking: sarcasm. "Both teams only score forty more points apiece."

Later, after most of the coaches had cleared out and the game film was copied—Gillespie had to be in Dawson, 120 miles northwest, at 8:30 A.M. to swap film with next week's opponent—Valdosta's fourth coach in nine seasons was asked about the razor-fine line between winning and losing, and the danger of riding that line in this town.

Say the Brunswick quarterback had eluded the Wildcats' grasp on the game's last play, like he'd done all night. Say he'd made that 2-point conversion. Say the Pirates went on to win the game in double or triple overtime—anything was possible after a while.

Say all that happened: The mood inside the Waffle House tonight and Bynum's Diner in the morning and on the radio Monday—would be very different. Instead of celebrating one of the damnedest Friday nights they'd ever seen, fans and boosters might be calling for the head of the coach whose team had just allowed more points than any other Valdosta team in history.

The previous record was 57 points, put up against the Wildcats last year by Lowndes. It took Valdosta's powers that be four days to fire the coach after that one.

Gillespie smiled at the hypothetical—almost a devilish smile. Same smile he flashed when the search committee interviewed him and came away believing that this was a guy who was not only unafraid of coaching in Valdosta but who relished the challenge.

Gillespie knew the pact all coaches signed with the forces of good and bad. Win: It's all good. Lose: You're hunting the state all winter for another paycheck.

"I know," Gillespie answered, when asked about that dangerously thin, fatally sharp line, still smiling. "That's what I love about it."

16

Saturday Night Lights

or Bumpin' with the Principal

It wasn't their parents' homecoming dance.

Just feet from the consecrated linoleum where Nick Hyder dropped from a heart attack, a white kid with a circular-saw Mohawk bobbed his head beside a black kid with VHS mowed into his hair. Dress ranged from formal to funky to forget-about-it. Boys wore suits and pressed shirts and sport coats with ties and khakis, or untucked polos with jeans and sneakers. Girls wore sky-high heels and short-short satiny dresses, or cotton dresses only a little less short, or slacks with flats.

Some kids wore sunglasses. Others wore backward baseball caps. James Eunice, the senior backup receiver who'd get his first start next week on special teams, wore a white suit and white sunglasses. Later, he put on a baseball cap and wrapped his tie around it.

Eunice gazed around the cafeteria, then gave an upperclassman's obligatory assessment of any school-sanctioned event.

"Lame," he said.

The sprawling, overlit room—the principal ordered the lights on—looked pretty much like it looked at lunch every weekday afternoon, except for some black-and-yellow balloon arbors and a DJ booth back by the Powerade machine. Missing: the mystery scents that usually wafted from the kitchen.

It was a Saturday night. The Wildcats had won the evening before with a businesslike shutout of Robert E. Lee, a luckless squad from Montgomery, Alabama. It was the second leg of what could be called the Civil War vs. Civil Rights portion of Valdosta's schedule. They'd already beaten Lincoln and Lee. Next week: Martin Luther King Jr. in Atlanta.

"Only in the South," one Wildcat coach noted dryly of the scheduling quirk.

Cheered as larger-than-life idols just a night earlier—folks rushed up just to touch them during the Cat Walk—the players now looked more to scale out of uniform and on the same floor with their peers.

Ryan showed up alone and without a ticket—students had to buy them in advance—and was turned away at the door. Ryan being Ryan, he didn't say a word. The starting freaking quarterback for Valdosta High School barred from the homecoming dance and he simply spun around, paused when a girl asked to have her picture taken with him on her phone, then ambled back to his pickup and drove off under a butterball harvest moon.

Minutes later, Alex arrived, both ticket and girlfriend in hand.

Crowned homecoming king Friday night, Malcolm mostly just watched the action now from a far wall, looking smart in a purple shirt, black pants, black shoes, and sweater vest. Other teammates hung out beside him: Reggie, Jay, Justin, Hester. Swoll limped in on his bum ankle.

Absent tonight: Jermaine Holmes, aka Freak. The Freak worked Saturdays at Arby's, across town. He was decked out in a different kind of uniform over there: red shirt, red Arby's visor, clear plastic gloves.

Wildcat names dominated the "Senior Picks" listed on a paper sign taped to a cafeteria pillar. Best Bromance: Wesley Bee and Malcolm Mitchell. Class Clown: Wesley Bee. Most Athletic: Malcolm Mitchell. Most Likely to Succeed: Jay Rome.

Yet standing off to the side together, the players as a group looked almost isolated by their athleticism, their camaraderie, their long season's singular, all-in experience. Most kids in the room had no idea what they'd be doing next week. These players knew *exactly* what they would be doing, not just next week but the week after that—and knew it down to fifteen-minute intervals. In that sense, at least, they stood apart in their excellence and their focus, like violin virtuosos who could go up and get a ball in traffic, or math nerds who could deliver a big hit.

The other students liked them, even revered them, certainly wanted to hang with them, but few really understood them.

As one coach told the players during camp as they ate dinner one late night in this very room: "If this was easy, we'd have five hundred kids on air mattresses in that gym tonight. We don't. You're the select few."

Not many students danced at first. With the principal and a handful of his assistants strolling the perimeter, it looked more like a fifth-grade field trip than a Saturday night dance at big, bad Valdosta High. A mild chant soon went up: "Kill the lights! Kill the lights!"

Out in the parking lot, a bored girl spoke absently into a cell. "I'm here," she sighed. "It's too early to go in."

Then the lights blinked off and the kids cheered.

"Finally," sighed Ed, the big, curly-haired DJ.

Ed, who graduated from Lowndes twenty years ago, knew just what to do next: punched some buttons on his machine to blare the dance-craze hit of the moment, "Teach Me How to Dougie." Students rushed the dance floor—that is, the center of the cafeteria—and each gave the song's lyrics his or her own bump-and-grind interpretation.

"All I need is a beat that's super bumpin/ And for you, you, and you to back it up and dump it!"

Gary Boling, the aw-shucks prison warden of a principal, looked stricken. His assistant principals scanned the crowd for dirty dancers and yelled "Hands up!" every time they spotted one.

"I'm the evil witch tonight," one beleaguered-looking female assistant said. "Worst job in the world: chaperoning dances."

The floor quickly turned into a hands-up, back-to-front, front-to-back scrum. Kids bunched together as close as they could get without actually touching. Some snuck in a dirty dance while hidden in the middle, but most just did their thing, whatever that thing was, side by side, black by white, at once shockingly sexual and coolly apart—a kind of 3-D version of Facebook and Twitter intimacy.

"These kids get a bad rap, but they're just the same as the kids at the other school," Ed said of the difference between the mostly black students at Valdosta and the mostly white students at Lowndes, where he also DJ'ed. "They just want to get through their four years and get on with life."

At Lowndes, administrators made him sign a contract that specified what he could and couldn't play. Here, he waited for cues.

So he slipped on "Walk It Out" by Unk, "Right Round" by Flo Rida with Ke$ha, "Ms. New Booty" by Bubba Sparxxx (*"Girl I don't need you but chu need me/ Take it off, let it flop, shake it freely"*).

Dirty dancing broke out all over the room. Girls lined up by the Powerade machine to back into a player; he took pictures of each one with his cell. Other players—Jay with a glow stick in his mouth, Zach Wang in outsized sunglasses—danced with their arms high at the edge of the floor. The kids were finally having a ball.

Boling looked like he was about to stroke out. He strode over to Ed's booth. "Not this," he shouted.

"It's getting a little crazy out there. There's too much dirty dancing, and the principal doesn't like it," Ed allowed as Boling slipped off to snuff another outbreak of bad stuff. "He's the one who pays me, so I have to do what he says."

Ed punched up Jay-Z's slow-it-down "Forever Young." Things cooled, but the students never danced as couples. "It's weird," Ed said. "Even the slow songs, they don't pair up."

Most of the players looked content just to hang and watch. Some still smarted from Friday night. Linebacker Jonathan Hester could hardly turn his neck, a memento from a blind-side block.

"I gotta take a hit to give a hit," he philosophized. "I gotta know how it feels when I give a hit. My daddy played one year in the pros. He knows. He's the one who told me, 'You gotta take a hit to give a hit.'"

Dashay took an opposite approach. Nursing his high ankle sprain, he leapt into the middle of the floor.

Song that got him there: Rihanna's "Rude Boy."

●

Like most everyone else, linebacker Justin Williams came solo—these dances were more like flash mobs than date nights—but still checked texts from his longtime girlfriend. She'd graduated last year and now went to Valdosta State. Her latest text: "I wanted to go with you."

"When I brought it up before, she said she'd just be bored here," Justin said, shaking his head.

Girls were still a lot harder to read than offenses. Next day, Justin's Facebook status changed from "in a relationship" to "single."

Kids came up to Ed's booth and begged him to pick it up. A roar greeted Eminem's *"Love the Way You Lie,"* a rappy torch song that mixed teen angst with "huffin' paint," "a steel knife in my windpipe," and aiming a fist "at the drywall"—inner-city poetics that played as well in South Georgia as they did in Detroit.

Another roar went up for Bone Crusher's "I Ain't Never Scared." They reacted as if it were their anthem—their "Born to Run." Their mouths stretched wide as they hollered out the chorus ("I ain't *never* scared!"), first like a plea, then a mantra, then a repudiation of all the things that they faced every damn day—from missing parents and dead cousins and crying babies to too much homework and parents who didn't understand and boy problems.

The cat-and-mouse between students and Boling continued all night. Then the lights blinked back on. It was late. Sweating through his shirt, Ed wound it down by tapping Ne-Yo's near-falsetto *"So Sick."* For the first time this evening, kids danced in each other's arms. R&B hadn't lost its touch.

Ed's explanation for the sudden intimacy: "They know they ain't got much time left."

A few songs later, he leaned into his mike. "Thanks, y'all," he said. "Y'all drive safe."

Kids shuffled out the doors, sweaty, bitching about the lights being on half the night, looking for rides, looking for something to do next. The chaperones looked like they'd just been paroled.

Ed watched the room clear, the floor littered with empty water bottles, spent glow sticks, busted balloons, and candy wrappers. Through segregation, integration, white flight, the Age of Obama's postracial whatever—it all looked pretty much the same.

Ed packed up.

"The high school experience hasn't changed in fifty years," he said.

17

The Content of Their Character

or MLK in the ATL

Martin Luther King was in the house.

"The hell you lookin' at, nigga?"

Stony silence.

"I *said*," a long, ropy kid from Martin Luther King Jr. High repeated, his dark face and Cheshire cat smile half hidden deep inside a silver helmet, "'what the hell you *lookin'* at, nigga?'"

The freakishly talented MLK Lions entered their drab concrete stadium to play unbeaten Valdosta with the supersized swag of a hip-hop video. It was a cold, clear Saturday night in Clarkston, Georgia, a sketchy suburb on Atlanta's raggedy eastern edge, and the culture clash between the two teams on this first Saturday of October couldn't have been more combustible:

Down South Georgia Boys vs. the ATL.

The 'Cats rolled up to Atlanta the way they always rolled. Four yellow buses pulled out of the school parking lot around noon, then followed their screaming two-car police escort up I-75 for almost 250 miles. They stopped in Macon for a pregame buffet, courtesy of the Touchdown Club, then arrived at 15,000-seat Hallford Stadium late in the afternoon, the sun still spinning low in a cloudless aqua sky.

Players unloaded their gear and stretched their legs on the field's big green carpet, then filed into rows of empty bleachers as quietly as if they were stepping into a Sunday church service. The Valdosta State sports chaplain who usually gave the pregame devotional didn't make the trip, so Coach Loudermilk—who baptized four of his players during his last head coaching job—stepped up.

Bible in hand, ball cap riding high on his forehead, Loudermilk quoted first from this chapter, then from that one. He rambled on for a while like a sermonizer in search of his sermon. He talked about how the gate to hell was wide and the gate to heaven was narrow. He talked about playing with a purpose. He told them to give it their all, to show out to the best of their ability, to play like champions.

All that stuff.

Then he read aloud from Corinthians 9:24.

"Do you not know that in a race all the runners run, but only one gets the prize? Run in such a way as to get the prize."

Loudermilk interpreted the verse for his quizzical-looking players. He told them it was important that they compete hard, that they display self-discipline, that they make sacrifices and stay focused and dismiss distractions to keep their eyes on the prize, whether that prize was on the field or in the classroom or at home.

A few players shifted on the hard seats. Most had slept during the long ride up—one watched all of *Robin Hood 3* on his iPhone—but some now looked like they were about to nod off again.

So Loudermilk called an audible. He brought up a taunting rap song called "Meet Me @ the 50" that an Atlanta hip-hop artist named Skinny-C, whose nephew played for MLK, had posted earlier in the week on the team's Web site. While it didn't mention the Wildcats specifically—"I just happened to put it up that week," Skinny-C explained later—it still was interpreted as a personal dis and became part of Valdosta's game-week chatter on the radio, around tables at the Smokin' Pig, inside the locker room.

Now, at its mention by Loudermilk, a row of hanging heads suddenly popped up.

"I hope Coach doesn't mind and that the Lord forgives me," Loudermilk then went on, shooting a quick glance at Gillespie, who stood impassively off to the side, "but they have that song. So the last thing I want to say is this: *I want you to destroy their asses! I want you to take those suckers apart!*"

He had their attention now—this was a biblical interpretation to which they all could relate. Grins broke across faces. Several players rose up.

Loudermilk then asked for the forgiveness of his personal Lord and Savior one last time.

"They want some," he called out, his words ricocheting around the deserted stadium, *"they're gonna get some!"*

Players erupted: leaped up, hollered, pounded on each other's pad-less shoulders.

Before they all poured out of the stands and into the locker room to get dressed, Loudermilk had one more thing he needed to say. He had to finish the way a Wildcat always finished.

"All right," he said, "who's got my prayer?"

◗

The MLK buses rolled up behind the stadium about ninety minutes before the 7:30 p.m. kickoff. Players in maroon-and-white jerseys stepped out coolly and spilled onto the field just as the 'Cats had started their initial warm-ups. The MLK players looked like they'd walked through the door of their own home to find intruders ransacking the living room.

Some stopped and shook their heads. Others circled around, like they were cutting off escape routes. A few pointed, bobbed their heads, broke into up-to-no-good grins. The deep thumping of a rap song was already booming from inside their low brick locker room, which adjoined the Valdosta locker room in the stadium's shaded south end zone.

Dashay stood near a line of finger-wagging MLK players and stared right back.

"What?" he said to one of them.

It wasn't a damn question.

Soon, almost two hundred ready-to-throw-down teenagers were massed at one end of the field, most within a few feet of each other. Both sides inched their way closer, a kind of choreographed pre-rumble scene straight out of *West Side Story,* as reinterpreted by the ATL's own Andre 3000.

"I saw us out there and then them coming in, and I knew we were in a place we shouldn't be," Coach Al said. "You could feel it."

MLK players chuckled and called out taunts about how South Georgia was nowhere, how the Wildcats were in the ATL now, how it was going to be one long damn ride back to Valdosta or wherever the hell they were from.

Backs bowed up. Coach Taz thought it worked to the 'Cats' advantage. "We have a handful that would've liked to go off in that direction," he observed, "and it fired them up."

Other Wildcats were stunned at first. For all the posturing and theatrics that players displayed in South Georgia, there was still a certain sporting decorum that few violated, unlike this open, clearly encouraged act of barely controlled mayhem-inciting.

Reggie's eyes burned and even started to tear up as he watched and listened, so ready was he to *go,* so aroused were his instincts, yet so programmed was he now to hold back, to remember the mission and to, well, "run in such a way as to get the prize."

Damn.

The Valdosta coaches saw what was going on and rushed in.

"Don't even look at 'em," Coach Al barked.

"It's Atlanta city kids—it's all they know," Coach Pruitt threw in. "I guarantee you they'd beat us in a rapping contest."

The Wildcats quickly drifted away and went about their own preparations, all the while keeping one eye on the other end of the field, where the Lions still stared, pointed, grinned.

"Them boys over there starin' at us, they don't know I'm takin' numbers," said a slow-simmering Justin Williams.

"We gotta shut them boys up fo' real," Terry Allen, the outsized defensive lineman, put in, then added as Ryan walked by, "Hey, Ryan. Shut them boys up tonight!"

Standing with his arms folded near midfield, Coach Rodemaker blocked out all the noise and posturing to do what he always did during warm-ups: get a bead on his opponents' athleticism. It was one thing to see teams on film, another to finally watch them live. MLK had scored more than 40 points in every game it played, including its only loss, a 44–41 shootout. Record-setting junior quarterback Jonquel Dawson had a whole fleet of gazelle-like four-star receivers, including senior Demarco Robinson and a talented tall drink of water Georgia already had its eye on, named Blake Tibbs.

Rodemaker just stared.

"They're beautiful," he finally observed without taking his gaze off the Lions as they eased through their passing drills. "They look the part. Every position, they look the part."

One of the MLK gazelles pulled in an overthrown pass with the one-handed casualness of a handshake.

Rodemaker added, his eyes still locked downfield, "This'll be our toughest test so far—by far. We just got to start well. The two close games we've had we created every bit of it by letting the other guys get excited.

"We need to get three or four three-and-outs, run some clock, get a nice drive," he went on, his eyes never leaving the MLK end of the field. "We don't even need to score right away. We just need a good start. With fifteen-, sixteen-, seventeen-year-old kids, that's half the battle.

"But you don't want to sell that too much to your kids," he added, explaining the pretzel logic coaches sometimes had to use to untwist adolescent psyches. "Because if you don't start fast, they'll panic."

●

MLK looked . . . *fresh*. The program was neither emboldened nor bound by its own history; unlike Valdosta, it hardly had one.

The virtually all-black school of fewer than 1,800 students had opened in a modern campus less than a decade earlier and wasn't a complete 9-through-12 high school until 2003; Valdosta had won almost eight hundred games by then. MLK didn't even have its own stadium, sharing this cold, impersonal, forty-year-old structure five miles north of campus with Stephenson High, another ultra-talented, predominantly black DeKalb County school.

MLK sits in Lithonia, a suburb whose population had swelled the last two decades with the largely middle-class African American spillover from Atlanta, the South's unquestioned chocolate mecca. Underscoring that point was Lithonia's New Birth Missionary Baptist megachurch, whose 25,000-member congregation was led by controversial televangelist Eddie Long.

The past few years, the church had hosted two nationally publicized, era-spanning funeral services: one for Coretta Scott King, widow of the high school's iconic namesake; and the other for Lisa "Left Eye" Lopes, singer for the Atlanta-based R&B girl group TLC, notorious for once torching the mansion of Andre Rison, her then NFL-playing boyfriend.

Coretta to Left Eye—that about covered it.

Under Corey Jarvis, who'd interviewed for the Valdosta job that Gillespie got, the football program developed almost instantly into an annual playoff contender—it won almost fifty games in Jarvis's five seasons—though it never advanced quite as far as its talent promised. New coach Michael Carson appeared to have continued the program's winning ways, while amping up its already formidable street swag.

Given its location, relative youth, and influences, MLK's DNA was more Dirty South than New South. To get the kind of respect that they desperately craved, the Lions first had to vanquish the Old South.

That was Valdosta.

Even though few of the young Lions players knew the specifics of the Wildcats' storied past, they did know there was a singular aura associated with this little place way, way down state. Like the rest of Valdosta's opponents, they'd pointed toward this game since the first day of summer camp.

"Any time a team sees Valdosta on the schedule," Reggie said with a shrug, "they go black."

So MLK's brazen, over-the-top entrance this Saturday night was their way—the ATL way—of announcing that this part of the South's past was indeed *past,* and that business on the field would now be conducted very differently.

Coach Carson explained, "These kids playing football today, they're talking trash at every level. Not to be offensive to other guys but, to me, it's really a level of confidence a kid has in his ability to play the game of football.

"Our kids are just trying to show their opponent that they're not inferior," he continued. "If they don't want to play us, don't come in. With Valdosta coming up here, bringing that history, it was like they were saying, 'We're Valdosta, you're MLK and you don't stand a chance.'

"Look," Carson added, "we had Valdosta coming to town and everybody was like, 'Wow.' It definitely made for a situation where you knew this was the game to be at."

Gillespie stormed into the Wildcats' cramped locker room—some 'Cats dressed next to urinals—furious with what he'd just witnessed.

Players quieted instantly, bunched up pad-to-pad, and took a knee around him. They'd never seen his eyes burn like that, his eyebrows get that arrow-sharp.

He got straight to it.

"Men," he began, "if you can't get ready to play a bunch of shit asses like that, then your frickin' wood's wet."

From there, he barely stopped for air.

"Do not, *do not,* get into a mouth game with them," he continued. "Because, men, that is no class. You conduct yourself like a champion—the champion you are, the Valdosta football player you are. You play like a Wildcat tonight! You do not—*do not!*—lower yourself to that bullshit. Because that's what it is. That's all it is. A bunch of trash mouth and it pisses me off."

Players stared ahead wide-eyed. They'd bought into this new guy so far because he seemed to have bought into them. Now it was clear that he was asking for something much more.

"Hearing that come out of Coach G, we were ready for war," Reggie said later. "Because *he* was ready for war."

Before Gillespie continued with his nonstop screed, he tugged on the reins a bit. He didn't want anybody going out on the field and throwing punches. He didn't need anybody suspended for next week's game—the Lowndes game.

"You jump on their ass when they start it with you, you lose," he told them. "You lose next week. So be smart."

Smart, Gillespie then made clear, did not mean soft.

It meant the opposite of soft.

"If it don't get your juices going just a little bit and make you want to knock the shit out of one of them, then there's something ain't right with you inside," Gillespie told them, his voice rising. "Because by God I'm pissed off. I'd like to walk up and knock the damn coach in the mouth for letting it happen."

His troops weren't wide-eyed anymore. They were wild-eyed. They sprang up off their knees. Cheered every rough word Gillespie uttered.

"You do your talkin' with that hat! Don't you run your mouth—you knock the piss out of them! When we kick it off, and then when there's one second left and they got that one desperation play left, you knock the hell out of them again! For forty-eight minutes!"

Players were ready to rush the door—hell, ready to tear the door off its hinges, toss it aside, eat through it if they had to—but Gillespie wasn't quite finished.

"And when you got your foot on their throats," added the skinny little white dude from the cool blue mountains of North Georgia, who once launched himself into every scout team pile like a national championship was at stake, "don't you let up . . ."

Breath.

"You snap their damn necks tonight!"

●

The Wildcats bolted onto the field, their own swag now sky-high.

They were booed and taunted by a decent enough crowd on the home side, but the cavernous stands swallowed up the couple of thousand Lion faithful and made the steep bleachers behind the MLK bench look only half full. Without the spirited MLK band, it would've looked a lot worse.

Across the field, as the Wildcats stormed out of their locker room, the more than a thousand Valdosta fans who'd made the four-hour trip up from South Georgia rose as one utterly integrated black-and-white wall and drowned out whatever racket was being made on the other side.

Then . . .

Then those sky-high teenaged Wildcats did the one thing that Coach Rodemaker declared they could not afford to do: got behind by two touchdowns before eight minutes had even clicked by in the first quarter.

It looked more like a no-huddle drive-by than a football game. As the Marchin' Cats bleated their stirring Pastor Troy anthem from the rows behind the Valdosta bench, MLK's Demarco Robinson took a screaming opening kickoff right up the middle for a high-stepping 93-yard touchdown. Time elapsed: 14 seconds.

Not long after that, Ryan threw an interception near midfield. MLK scored again—an arching 18-yard pass to Robinson, who stretched his full, elastic length to tip it with one hand, then snag it in a far corner of the end zone, thank you very much.

The MLK side went Dirty South wild.

Valdosta fans, meanwhile, sat on their cold, hard seats almost unnaturally still, their faces set like stone, not even exchanging glances with each other, as if that would acknowledge the carnage they'd just seen. They simply stared out toward the field, lost in their own never-quit, but-this-doesn't-look-good thoughts. Ryan's parents huddled together closer.

"We just got to settle down," Berke Holtzclaw said as he paced the edge of the field with the rest of the Wildcats' traveling sideline mafia. "Somebody's got to step up."

"We better get a break," added Derek Shaw, a fellow 'Cat mafioso. "If we get a break, we'll be all right. But we can't let them get up more than this."

Then . . .

After MLK stuffed the Wildcat offense, senior Tyler Yelito launched a punt from the 50 that settled on the Lions' 4-yard line. Two plays later, with four minutes already gone in the second quarter, linebacker Justin Williams—who'd been taking numbers before the game—jumped an MLK receiver in the end zone for a safety.

"That," a rejuvenated Shaw announced, "was the break we needed!"

It was. The Wildcats got the ball right back, and Ryan immediately let fly with a 45-yard toss down the left side to a wide-open Wesley Bee, whose string-bean frame wasn't wrestled down until he reached the MLK 7. Before most of the Valdosta crowd could even sit back down, Ryan lofted another pass, this time to Jay Rome, who reached over his head with one big paw, a Lion defender draped around him like a spare belt, and pulled down Ryan's too-high pass like he was plucking a ripe peach.

Touchdown.

14–9.

It now seemed as if one end of the field had been jacked up on hydraulic lifts so that everything ran down toward the Valdosta side. Justin Williams, playing with a cool abandon, intercepted a pass on MLK's next possession, and Ryan "just-throw-it-to-the-right-guy" Whilden threw a sizzler over the middle to Malcolm, who did the rest on his own: dodged two tacklers, ignored another like a stray dog nipping at him from behind, and took it 54 yards to the house.

With three minutes left in the half, the 'Cats were now up by a point.

Holtzclaw—the Claw—exhaled on the sideline. "Told you these guys just take a while."

On the first play of the Lions' next possession, Valdosta's Carlton Harrell stripped the ball from the MLK quarterback, and the 'Cats pounced on it at the home team's 18. Gillespie punched the air with both fists. His players were doing just what he'd asked them to do: talking with their hats.

MLK? Not so much.

The Wildcats made their loudest noise with less than a minute left in the half. With a fourth and 1 from the MLK 9, they went for it.

The call was for Reggie to go up the gut. In the huddle, Reggie, who was playing running back because Dashay and Swoll both had tender ankles, used the line that Gillespie used back in the locker room: "Put a hat on somebody!" Jay told Reggie what he'd been telling him all game: "Just follow my ass!"

The offensive line then shoved their yellow hats deep into the MLK defense, and Reggie followed Jay's ass to a first down.

Three plays later, with only twenty seconds left, the 'Cats faced virtually the same situation: fourth and goal from the 3. MLK called time-out as Zach Wang set up to kick a field goal. Gillespie suddenly changed his mind and sent Ryan back out with the offense.

"If they stop it," Gillespie told his assistants through his headset, "they stop it. We need to go for a touchdown."

With four receivers split wide, Ryan took the snap and calmly dumped the ball right in front of him, to a slightly gimpy, all-alone Swoll, who trotted into the end zone on his sore ankle untouched.

Having scored 22 unanswered points, Valdosta raced off the field with an 8-point lead.

Gillespie strode into the packed cell of a locker room in a kind of elevated state, having gone into a scary battle and returned just fine. He was at once exuberant and collected. No detail was too small, no picture too big. He seemed to see it all right now.

"Jay Rome," he called out, "get that blood off your pants. They'll take you out for that."

He stepped in front of a whiteboard, marker in hand.

To Jay again: "I need to do a better job getting the ball to you. I need to get the ball to you in the flat."

He scanned the players and coaches around him. He believed in the give-and-take of fellow warriors. Every moment was a teachable moment.

He could've been standing in front of a history class right now—a history class filled with students in full pads, bloodstains on their pants, about to face off for another 24 minutes against MLK.

An unfamiliar face—tall black guy, early thirties—nodded his head and smiled slightly in one corner of the room, not far from where Stan Rome leaned on his cane.

"I need honest opinions," Gillespie said to his players. "We got to get the ball to that guy"—he drew a circle on the board—"and let him run."

They talked it out. A play emerged.

He turned next to the fullback, Jarvis Roberts. Gillespie fell in love with Jarvis the first day he laid eyes on him. He was big and strong and tough as a nest of snakes. Knew the game, too—uncle was a Wildcat. Asked once to describe Jarvis, Gillespie simply called him "a football player," the highest accolade a coach can utter.

Not tonight.

"Jarvis, you're getting outplayed," he told him bluntly, his voice firm but even, nothing personal in it, except for the implicit challenge. "You got to be a man and body your ass up."

He didn't linger. Made his point and moved on. Jarvis nodded. Took it like a man.

Next, he broke down an elaborate blocking scheme for the offensive line. He scribbled on the board. He scribbled some more. It started to look like a Jackson Pollock drip painting. He tried to explain it. Then explained it some more.

"You with me on that?" he finally asked the puzzled faces bunched around him.

The linemen looked back at him like their heads hurt.

Gillespie shook his own head—at himself.

"I did a piss-poor job explaining that to you," he said and erased everything he'd just drawn.

Maybe he was loving this a little too much.

He got a signal for the end of halftime. The players stood, huddled.

"We got to take this drive down the field and put points on the board," he told them. Then he led them out the door.

On the way out he stopped and put a hand on the shoulder of the tall black guy who'd been standing in the corner. The two talked for a minute, laughed, embraced.

"One of my sons," Gillespie said before he ran off.

Regan Torbert played quarterback for Peach County when Gillespie was the team's offensive coordinator. He was a poor kid from Fort Valley who got a football scholarship to the University of Georgia. Football didn't pan out for him at UGA, but he now worked as a service manager for a health care company in a northern Atlanta suburb, where he lived with his wife and young daughter.

He drove to the game just to see Gillespie. He'd drive anywhere to see Gillespie.

"He put me in college," Torbert said. "That's what he did for me. He made sure I took the right classes. He made me be the best I could be, on and off the field. He personally came to pick me up when I couldn't make it to school. He cares. I can honestly say he cares about his players."

Torbert looked down the sideline, where Gillespie slipped on a pair of headphones as the second half was about to start.

"I owe everything to him," he said.

Then Torbert pointed one finger at the scoreboard: 22–14, visitors. Said he wasn't surprised.

"Give him another couple years," he said. "They're excited about him down there now? You wait . . ."

●

The second half became all epilogue to the culture clash that, for all intents and purposes, ended with the Wildcats' first possession.

Malcolm pulled in another soft bomb from Ryan, and his second touchdown of the game gave the Wildcats 29 unanswered points. Was there something about a rap song? Though MLK scored twice more—their receivers really were beautiful—the final outcome was never in any doubt.

"They 'bout look like they're going to give up," Ryan said when he jogged off the field after his toss to Malcolm.

He then threw another touchdown pass to Jay, and Dashay tested his high ankle sprain by running untouched for a score from the 7. Ryan oversaw it all with a career-high 343 yards and 5 TD passes. His critics were silent—at least for one more week.

With less than a minute left and the 'Cats up 43–28, the MLK band paid tribute: broke into a loud, brassy rendition of Usher's "Oh My

Gosh." It was their grudging salute to the visiting boys from way, way down south.

"Oh, oh, oh, oh, oh, oh, oh, oh, oh, oh, oh, oh, oh, oh, oh, oh, Ohhh myyy gosh . . ."

The Valdosta players sang along and bobbed their heads to the beat as they counted down the last seconds from the sideline. Dashay jumped up on the back of a bench, then waved his yellow helmet for the Valdosta fans who'd gathered behind it and chanted, "Six-and-oh! Six-and-oh! Six-and-oh!"

The night's real warrior was Reggie. With his eyes still stinging from MLK's pregame theatrics, his heart thumping from Gillespie's call to arms—and his dreads seeming to lengthen by the minute—Reggie played every snap on defense and 39 snaps on offense, galloping for more than 100 yards on 18 carries.

He knew his gunned-down cousin was smiling down tonight on the bright lights of Atlanta.

Reggie could've played all night.

"I still wanted to play on kickoffs," Reggie said after the game, his dark eyes wide, wide open.

The Down South Georgia Boys and the ATL then lined up in the middle of the field to shake hands. Loud arguments broke out among some MLK coaches behind the locker room.

"Whew," Gillespie whistled after he walked away from the line, his own eyes about as wide as Reggie's. "I thought they were going to kill me."

Claudette and Kennedy rushed to midfield to hug him. When somebody announced that Ryan had thrown for more than 300 yards for the second time this season, Gillespie turned toward his old Peach County quarterback, standing nearby, and allowed, "Credit that to Regan Torbert. Every time I looked back, he was giving Ryan advice."

Torbert beamed.

Gillespie did, too: The Wildcats were now 6-0 for the first time since 2001—or, in Valdosta time, since three coaches ago.

Players circled him and chanted *"Coach G! Coach G! Coach G!"* until he finally quieted them down.

"Hey, you keep finding a different way to win every week," he told them, then looked around at their rapt, sweaty faces. He'd asked them to go to war tonight and by God they had.

So he threw them a bone.

"This might not be the most . . . *class*-ful thing I ever said," he finished, "but I guess now they gotta write one more verse to their song!"

The cheers that followed rang in the 'Cats' ears that dark, late night all the way back to Valdosta.

18

Thugs vs. Plowboys

or Winnersville, Baby!

Lowndes game.

For the state championship.

Of Valdosta.

"It's a whole other kind of week," said Reggie, tugging a helmet over his heavy mat of dreads before practice. "Biggest game of my life. Ten years down the line I want to be able to say I beat Lowndes as a senior.

"I guarantee you," he added, "whoever loses, they're gonna cry."

It was the second week of October. The sky was still cloudless and bright blue, the sun still unrelenting. Dragonflies still ran their low strafing missions over the grass. The air had dried and cooled a bit, though, so that what would feel like an early-summer afternoon anywhere else, here it finally felt a little like fall.

Reggie stood beside a goalpost, in the end zone closest to the high school. A trail of teammates jogged out from the locker room, most of their yellow helmets already on. The only sound was their cleats, clacking on the sidewalk until they hit the grass.

"I see somebody not focused," Reggie said, watching the line closely, "I'll slap the spit out of them. It's time to do it. No more talk. No more playing around.

"Last year was more than embarrassing—it was to the point where it wasn't even necessary to cry," Reggie went on. "But it's a whole new ball game this year. We got a new coach, a new swag, a new heart.

"The big difference between this year's seniors and last year's: the want-to," he said. "Period. I never been around a hungrier group of seniors. We hang around together Monday through Sunday. We hug each other. We kiss each other."

Gillespie's head stood out amid the helmets. He walked straight to the field, baseball cap low, whistle in a corner of his mouth.

Reggie nodded in his direction. "Our confidence is one hundred times higher because of him. Our belief in ourselves is one hundred times higher because we believe in him. Last year, it was shaky. If it was the same as last year, we'd be 3-3 or 2-4 right now. We wouldn't be undefeated.

"I love him," Reggie said, smiling through his wispy free-range goatee as he watched Gillespie bark at somebody whose helmet was off when he hit the grass, then tell some other slow-shuffling player to *move it! move it! move it!* "He wishes he had four years with us, and that's just how we feel—we wish we had four years with him.

"It's more than a job for him and these coaches," Reggie added before he stepped over the green rectangle's white line and became a whole other character. "They go the extra mile. They were here the other night till 12:30. I heard about it and I thanked one of the coaches. Know what he said? 'Don't thank me. We're supposed to do that.'"

Gillespie blew his whistle. Players circled up. Pounded their thigh pads.

Boomph!

Boomph!

Boomph boomph boomph boomph!

Ready.

Lowndes County High opened in 1959 with 671 students. Its football team didn't play Valdosta until 1968. It lost its first nine games to the Wildcats by a combined score of 278–26.

The Vikings finally broke through in 1977 when Joe Wilson, a former Wildcat and assistant both to Bazemore and Hyder, jumped across town to become head coach. He led Lowndes to its first state title in 1980.

Lowndes won state again in 1999 but didn't leapfrog Valdosta as the town's recurring power until the arrival three years later of Randy McPherson, a bearish, mumbling, stuff-'em and run-it-down-their-throats kind of guy from nearby Madison, Florida.

McPherson wore a rut in the blacktop that ran the thirty miles between Madison and Valdosta during his eighteen years in Florida. He audited Wildcat practices like a continuing ed student and soaked up everything he could of the program's standard-setting defense.

"Looks kind of dumb now," Jack Rudolph, Valdosta's principal defensive architect, said of those early tutorials. "If I knew where he was going to wind up, I wouldn't have shared anything."

The tutoring ended the minute McPherson landed at Lowndes.

"When I got here," he deadpanned in his deep, deliberate delivery, "there weren't no more free clinics."

He didn't need them. With demographics now in his favor both in numbers and selectivity—"You see a 6' 230-pound white kid," one Valdosta coach said of the exodus of offensive linemen to the county school, "let me know"—McPherson paired a Wing-T offense with a punishing, Valdosta-style defense to win eighty-seven games and three state titles in his first eight years.

More importantly in this town, he beat Valdosta six straight times. Expectations to win every game moved to the other side of town. Lowndes rewarded McPherson the South Georgia way: $112,000 in salary, according to the state's department of audits and accounts, one of the highest in the state, as well as a truck.

"We have had some success against them," he allowed one afternoon inside his office at the Vikings' gleaming football complex, with its separate viewing room for game film and bright, modern weight room. By contrast, Gillespie projected film on his office whiteboard until he got a maintenance man to screw a roll-up screen in front of it.

"I knew if I didn't have success against them, I wasn't going to be here long," McPherson went on. "As a coach here, you have to accept that. The pressure to beat Valdosta started the first time Lowndes beat them. That's just the way it is."

Valdosta fans mock McPherson, with his hulking frame and low, slow-talking ways, as "Sling Blade." He mocked them back with his success. He was a nagging reminder of their flawed coaching decisions.

Lowndes entered the Valdosta game with a 5-1 record, their lone, one-point loss on the road in suburban Atlanta to highly rated McEachern. The 'Cats' 6-0 start was their best in almost a decade.

Stan Rome summarized Lowndes's rise and Valdosta's fall. "They're in hog heaven now. They're winning, they have great facilities. But a program like ours doesn't die forever. It's just taken us a little longer to find another Hyder or Bazemore."

Finally, he believed, they'd found that guy.

◆

"Good morning, South Georgia! It's Winnersville Week, baby! Put a smile on your face. I don't care what else is goin' on, if you have a big meeting to go to, bills to pay—and we all have 'em—it doesn't matter 'cause it's Winnersville Week! If you could live anywhere in the world, it wouldn't be any better than it is right here this week."

From 7:00 until 9:00 A.M. each weekday, *The Mike Davis Show* beamed out of a double-wide behind some pines at the end of an unpaved drive on the north edge of town. A red tractor sat a few yards away; a couple of horses grazed nearby. Somebody's beagle took a pat on the head from absolutely anybody.

Inside the studio, with its carpeted floor, carpeted walls, and rows of gospel CDs, the host sat and yakked from behind a lone desk like he was seated at somebody's kitchen table.

Mike Davis graduated from Lowndes, class of '93. He played ball there and was still built like a trim, sun-kissed plug. His sidekick, Monty Long, sat beside him like a next-door neighbor who'd dropped in for coffee. Monty usually left during the show's second hour to get down to his office at Cotton States Insurance.

For the two hours a day that WTHV 810 AM didn't broadcast gospel music, Davis cobbled together an unscripted, down-home, how's-your-mom sports talk show. He'd talk some about the Atlanta Braves and Georgia Bulldogs, but even more about local football, from the high schools to the middle schools to the third grade.

This week, it was all Valdosta-Lowndes, all the time.

"I have other stuff to talk about," Davis told his listeners early in the week, "but I don't want to talk about it. I know Oregon has gone ahead of Boise State in the polls—*I don't care, meatheads! Get that stuff somewhere else!*"

Caller: "What's up, fellas?"

Davis: "What's up with you?"

Caller: "Just another day in paradise . . . I'm waiting for our secondary to start showin' up."

Davis: "Get your tickets yet?"

Caller: "Got mine last night. I was out there with my tent. Anyway, I think the team that makes the least amount of mistakes . . ."

"Hopefully we'll be joined in the studio by a couple players," Davis said before he took another call. "Two players from each side. We'll see who makes it."

He paused. On the air, it sounded like he was peeking out the trailer's window. A Lowndes player was already supposed to be there.

"Looks like Braswell overslept," he said. "Well, it won't be long now, Monty. In my history with this game I don't ever remember it being sold out on Monday, but all the tickets for the home side are already gone. People waited hours. They should put some extra stands in the end zone for this game."

A few calls later, Davis plugged a couple of sponsors: Adel Outfitters ("From apparel to guns, they have it all") and D-Squared Pest Control ("It's getting cooler, and bugs try to get in when it's cooler").

Then back to the game.

Caller: "I don't think it'll be as bad as last year. I don't think Lowndes'll put up *half a hundred* again."

Davis: "The jazz has started! Keep it nice and friendly and we're good to go. Go ahead, caller."

Caller: "What's going on with Dashay March? He been kicked out of school or what? I ain't seen him in a couple games."

Davis: "No, no. He had an ankle sprain. There's no problems with Dashay. There's not even the threat of him being kicked off the team. This kid has turned himself around. Go ahead, caller."

Caller: "Just want to say I think Coach Gillespie's brought back that never, never quit attitude Nick Hyder had. Wildcats haven't had that since Hyder died."

Monty chimed in. "There's a new drug in town," he said, "and his name is Rance Gillespie!"

●

Front page, *Valdosta Daily Times,* October 7, 2010:

Lowndes student suspended for wearing Wildcat shirt

JOHNNA PINHOLSTER *THE VALDOSTA DAILY TIMES*

VALDOSTA—Winnersville has landed a Lowndes High School tenth grader in in-school suspension.

On Tuesday, Oct. 5, Mark Love Day, 15, entered his first block class at Lowndes High wearing a gray sweatshirt with the Valdosta High School colors and Wildcat paws.

Day's teacher deemed the sweatshirt a disruption and asked him to remove the sweatshirt or turn it inside out, the teenager told The Times.

The student declined to do either and the teacher sent Day out of the classroom . . .

While waiting in the hallway, he again refused the request to remove the sweatshirt when it was made by Assistant Principal Rowland Cummings, Day said.

Principal Wes Taylor also told him to remove the sweatshirt; again, Day refused, he said.

Following the encounters, Day was given in-school suspension for the rest of the week.

On Wednesday, he wore the sweatshirt again, something he said he will do the rest of the week.

The story went on to note that administrators told the sophomore he could wear the sweatshirt any other week of the year—just not this week.

Then it slipped this in: The boy's mother had attended Valdosta High and encouraged her son to keep wearing the sweatshirt after his initial suspension.

The Lowndes County school superintendent later tried to discuss the issue with the mother, the story concluded, "but had to ask her to leave when she began using profane language."

●

The team buses didn't get back from Atlanta after the MLK game until 5:00 A.M. Sunday. The coaches worked until late that night, breaking down film and doing everything else they usually did over the weekend. They were back at school early the next morning, and again worked until late Monday night.

By early Tuesday, secondary coach Taz Dixon hit the wall: fell asleep in class standing up.

"You know how when your head falls in the car when you're driving?" he said. "Just like that. Tucker [Pruitt] was right beside me, and after I did it I looked at him and said, 'Did I just *fall asleep?*'"

The coaches and players quickly caught a second wind. By now, Gillespie had programmed them to think that the only thing that should follow a hard week of work is another hard week of work. They hadn't had a weekday off from practice since the middle of July—three straight months. They'd hit each other, blocked each other, sworn at each other, laughed with each other, showered with each other, and slept overnight in the gym with each other. They'd inhaled each other's funk enough times that they'd achieved a kind of frank, macho intimacy, bound like stepbrothers in a big, brawling but defend-you-to-the-death extended family.

Nothing was off the table. When two defensive players—one of them Big Terry—got tangled in each other's pads during a 1-on-1 drill and rolled on the grass for half a minute trying to separate, Coach Rodemaker smiled from 20 yards away before he barked, "You mating over there? Those are going to be some *bad* black babies."

The players howled. Rodemaker then turned to two linebackers who ran into each other without making much of a sound.

"We're about to play Lowndes," he told them, his tone more exasperated than upset, "and I can't hear a *pop?*"

Even players called each other out now whenever somebody cut a corner—didn't extend for a pass, ran the wrong play, walked to a drill.

"Last year, it was like we had a choice: You could be average or you could be great," linebacker Justin Williams said. "This year, the only choice is to be great."

The week's last practice started like they all did, with Coach Taz standing in the middle of the 'Cats wide warm-up circle.

"This is the best Thursday ever, men," Taz told them. "We're on top and can't be knocked out."

Then: "You know what tomorrow is?"

"Game day!"

"But today is a . . ."

"Work day!"

"So we will . . ."

"Work!"

"We will . . ."

"Work!"

"We will . . ."

"*Work!*"

They then went to work. Gillespie, for once, looked pleased

"Nice job, O," he told the offense as it ran through its first set of plays.

Lowndes was on everybody's mind today.

"We don't win this one," one underclassman worried, "I think the whole team falls apart. The seniors won't know how to take it."

Others just wished Friday night would get here.

"I been waiting for this one a long time," said Tyran. "A *very* long time."

Jay couldn't walk ten feet in school without somebody asking what college he was going to play for next year. He'd narrowed his choices to Alabama, Georgia, Tennessee, and Clemson, but this week those schools seemed a million miles away.

"I don't think there'll be a game my whole life," he said, "that I'll be more excited to play in than the Lowndes-Valdosta game."

Jay was the third Rome to play in a Lowndes-Valdosta game, following his dad and his uncle Roger. He was the only Rome who hadn't won one.

Gillespie blew his whistle to end practice at 5:20, early enough that some parents didn't arrive for almost another hour to pick up their sons.

"Listen," Gillespie told his troops as they took a knee around him. "Don't get wrapped up in the distractions this week. Tomorrow will be full of them. And that egg fight"—there'd be an egg fight later that night between Valdosta and Lowndes students—"don't get involved in that. Whip their ass on the field."

Players hustled off, as if the faster they ran the quicker Friday would get here. Coaches implored them to get some sleep, to not be stupid.

"There's a lot of crap going on," Coach Pruitt told his receivers. "That's for those who don't play."

●

As the field emptied and the shadows lengthened, Gillespie turned toward midfield. There he spotted three assistants and a player circled around Edrae Gipson, a talented but temperamental junior special teams player and reserve defensive back.

Edrae had been kicked out of his foster house the night before and called an assistant coach to come get him. The coach took Edrae to a teammate's home, where he spent the night. That same evening, Gillespie got an enraged call from Edrae's foster father, who warned him, Gillespie said, that if Edrae ever showed up at the house again he'd "stomp a mud hole in his face," or words to that effect.

Now Edrae had his helmet off and big, soulful eyes lowered to the ground, like he wanted to dig a hole where he stood and crawl into it. Everybody around him was trying to figure out how Edrae could get his clothes, his books, his *life* out of the foster house he'd just been kicked out of without anybody getting hurt.

Gillespie jogged the 30 yards to where they stood and stopped in front of Edrae. He didn't say a word for a few beats, as if going through a kind of emotional play sheet in his mind for options. He needed to make the right call here.

Then Edrae looked up. Gillespie put his hands on the kid's shoulders.

"You got a tough situation," Gillespie began, his voice soft and low but startlingly firm, like a doctor delivering not-good news, as well as saying how he'd fix it. "It is what it is, okay? I want to help you through this process, Edrae. Not baby you through this process. It's bad."

Edrae's situation was messed up. Yet given the school system's swollen population of foster kids, homeless kids, and kids regularly just "put out" with nowhere to go, Edrae's story wasn't exceptional.

"Edrae," said the schools' social services coordinator, "is one of those kids who fell through the cracks."

The facts of Edrae's story can be chaotic, and Edrae sometimes confuses them himself. But corroborated by his mother and an older sister, a picture of poverty, transience, and unfocused anger emerged.

Edrae was one of four children (including a brother who died young) raised in Shreveport by a single mother. For most of his early childhood, Edrae lived in the impoverished "Bottoms" neighborhood, his mother said. He remembered the one-bedroom house with seven people living in it as "something like a shack," different enough from what other kids he knew lived in that "when I came home and looked at where I stayed, I didn't think it looked like a house." He remembered Thanksgiving as a trip to Church's Chicken.

Even that changed when he turned six. His mother, whom he called "a good lady," became a crack addict. One day he lived with her and his two older sisters, he said, and "next day I was gone."

He lived for a while with relatives, then was sent to two different foster homes in rural Louisiana. Other foster kids lived in both of them.

"People get into the adoption business because of the money the state gives you," Edrae said. "The more kids you get, the more money you get. It's all about the money."

Edrae got into fights, at home and at school, always lashing out at . . . *something*. He never heard from his mother, who by then was living in the streets. He remembered being assigned at school to write about Mother's Day or Father's Day, and how he'd leave his paper blank. When a teacher asked him once why he didn't write anything, Edrae told her, "I don't have a dad and I don't have a mom and the people I stay with don't love me." He remembered a pen dropping from the teacher's hand.

"I could feel him not thinking he's loved by his family because, of all people, his mom was not in his life," said his mother, Sonya Mitchell, who was living in Alexandria, Louisiana, where she was off drugs and cleaned houses. "I can see him thinking nobody cares."

Edrae didn't last long at either foster house. "It was like I was lost," he said.

At eleven or twelve, Edrae was shipped to Valdosta. Bruce and Roslyn Gipson, married eighteen years with no children of their own, had filled their modest four-bedroom house on West Magnolia, a tough West Side street just blocks from where Stan Rome was shot, with seven adopted children. They included Edrae and an older sister, who joined him a year later.

Bruce Gipson, still big and powerful-looking at forty-eight, said he supported himself on Social Security checks for an injury that kept him from working a steady job. Roslyn, forty, worked at a center for disabled adults. He got a check each month from the state, but Bruce noted that four of their adopted kids stayed in the house after they turned eighteen, when the state no longer gave parents money to care for them.

"We do it for love. We love a big family," Bruce said of the adoptions. "My wife had four miscarriages—had one last year."

The wood-paneled walls of the Gipsons' dim living room were decorated with family photos of brothers, sisters, nieces, nephews. A 175-gallon fish tank took up an end of the room. It used to hold what Bruce called "the cousins to the piranha" until one of them "almost bit my arm off." Now a few goldfish and sea horses have the tank to themselves.

There'd been several drug busts at houses nearby recently, and Bruce kept an eye on his kids and the block all the time. He had a sign on his door warning that earrings and baggy pants weren't allowed inside the house.

"You have to stay on them, with what goes on in these streets," he said. "I don't want them to get caught up in that."

How Edrae wound up homeless the night before the Lowndes game isn't entirely clear, but everybody involved agreed on this: Bruce came home Wednesday afternoon, found a boy under Edrae's sister's bed, and told both the boy and Edrae's sister to clear out.

When Edrae came in from practice, he confronted Bruce about his sister, and they got into an argument. Bruce said Edrae stormed out on his own. Edrae told the coach who picked him up that night that he was run out of the house, told never to come back, and threatened with violence.

Bruce called that a lie. "We is not violent people," he said. "I never hit any one of my kids. I know the kind of lick I could throw."

Bruce also said he didn't threaten anybody when he phoned Gillespie afterward. "I said to him, 'Let the coaches stay with coaching and let the parents stay with parenting.'"

What wasn't disputed: Edrae had nowhere on the planet to go. The coach who picked him up offered to bring him into his own home. Edrae asked him first to try the house of Marte Spencer, a teammate whose mother had given Edrae rides home from practice and often fed him dinner.

Edrae told Marte that all he ever ate at the Gipsons'—when he ate—was noodles. Bruce said that wasn't true, either. "I don't care what family it is, nobody cooks a meal every day. Some days you eat leftovers. If you cook enough noodles and there's leftovers and you don't eat them, then tough luck. We don't make money like that."

Marte's mother, who lived alone with her five children, didn't ask any questions when Edrae showed up. She just opened the door.

"I talked to the coach after Edrae went in and he told me all what was going on," said Denise Mathis, who managed a downtown clothing store and was separated from her husband. "He said he didn't know how long it was going to last but that Edrae needs a place to stay. I said, 'Well, he definitely has a place to stay here.'"

Now, less than twenty-four hours later, Gillespie stood with Edrae in the middle of the Wildcat practice field. The kid was a talented but problematic project for Gillespie. He had sprinter's speed and worked hard, but he also had a hair-trigger temper that had gone off a half-dozen times since spring. Players and coaches had to jump in. Among those he'd already taken on were Tampa and Jay. Afterward, Edrae was always contrite.

"He has to learn how to channel that," Tampa said. "I used to be like that. I learned to control it. But I'm not dealing with what he's dealing with."

As the sun slipped behind a lone late-afternoon cloud, Gillespie told Edrae the story of Greg Lloyd, the former All-Pro linebacker for Pittsburgh and still a legend in Peach County, where he played before Gillespie coached there.

At age two, Lloyd was taken by his mother from Florida to Fort Valley, Georgia, and almost literally dropped on somebody's steps. When he got older, he funneled the anger and bitterness he felt onto the football field and wound up with a long NFL career.

When Gillespie finished, he looked straight into Edrae's eyes.

"It's a bad situation, I know," he said, "but you have to learn how to control some of it."

Edrae exhaled slowly in the warm autumn air. His almond eyes didn't know where to focus: the grass, the coaches, that cloud . . .

Gillespie patted him twice on the shoulders, the football equivalent of cradling him in his arms. "Having said that," he then told him, "we love you, Edrae."

Fifteen minutes later, Gillespie stood in a school parking lot with the three coaches who'd drive Edrae back to the foster house and get his stuff. Edrae was in the locker room getting dressed.

"It's crazy," Taz said of the situation. "We'll just go do what we need to do."

Nobody was sure, exactly, what they'd need to do—or how they should do it, or what somebody there might do to them.

Then Edrae stepped out of the locker room with Marte and turned toward the lot. Gillespie rubbed his chin's day-old stubble and dribbled some tobacco juice on the asphalt. The night before the biggest game in any Valdosta coach's life and a third of his staff was headed off to who the hell knew what.

●

The three-vehicle caravan wound its way from the high school down to West Magnolia.

Driving behind the others, Rodemaker called a Valdosta police officer whose son was a Wildcat defensive end. Carlton Harrell Sr. gave Rodemaker the number of a cop who could accompany them, just in case.

"It's what makes the job fun," Rodemaker said after he hung up. "Keeps it interesting."

Rodemaker preceded Gillespie as head coach at Peach County. He'd had a middling 15-8 record over two seasons, and with a wife and three young kids, he decided he'd had enough of ninety-hour weeks for forty-hour pay. A bunch of his buddies had made a killing in the telecom business, and now he wanted some of that, too. So he took a job back home in North Carolina selling telephone systems to institutions like schools and hospitals. The money practically grew on trees. One year he brought home $240,000.

He liked it, for about six years. Then he missed coaching. The difference between telephone systems and football, he said, was that "the highs aren't as good as when you win a game, and the lows aren't as low as a loss. And that ain't living.

"So I checked it off and said, 'Okay, I can do something other than coach.' Then I looked for an opportunity to get back into football."

He spent a year as an assistant at a high school powerhouse in South Carolina. Then Gillespie called. Rodemaker didn't hesitate.

"I can sit in the office here and game plan until midnight and I enjoy it," he explained. "I wouldn't want to sell phone systems until midnight."

The coaches and the cop they'd hooked up with a few blocks away parked out front of the Gipson house.

Edrae knocked on his old door. His foster mother opened it and looked out at the coaches and cop standing by the yard. Edrae disappeared inside. His foster mother came out by herself a few minutes later, walked to the house next door, and returned with white garbage bags clutched in her hand. She didn't say a word to the strangers standing there, pawing the dirt in her yard.

Explained Marte, who'd come along, "She's not a people person."

Then Edrae's foster father stepped out from behind the house. The cop took a step forward. Bruce Gipson just stood there for a minute, looking everybody over. Then he boomed, "Why you need four coaches and the *po*-lice?" When nobody answered, Bruce shook his head and disappeared again behind the house.

Edrae finally pushed through the front door, a lumpy garbage bag in each hand. Without a word he dumped them both in the bed of a coach's pickup, then went back inside. A minute later, he returned with one more.

That was it. At seventeen, Edrae's life fit into three plastic garbage bags.

Ten minutes later, Edrae had a new home. Rodemaker called his wife. They talked a while, then he said "love you" and hung up.

"If it doesn't work itself out by next week, we'll take him in," he said. "How better to teach your kids grace?"

Game day. Midmorning. Swoll beamed in the doorway of Gillespie's office. His head was shaved smooth as a brass doorknob.

Gillespie nodded. Acted like he approved.

"Usually I get the Mohawk for Lowndes," Swoll told him, "but I wanted something different this year. The only thing I could think of was a baldhead. My brother gave it to me."

He hobbled off on his tender ankle.

Gillespie tore open another envelope: a hand-lettered card wishing him luck. He set it in a pile. "Guy sends a card every week. Said he started doing it with Coach Hyder."

Pruitt stepped in. "Never could get a ticket," he said.

"My wife called at ten this morning, said there was no place to park at the stadium," Gillespie told him. "Said there were three cars with tents set up last night. There's a Winnebago parked on the side of the road."

"Man, that's what it's all about," Pruitt said. "It's why you do it. I usually don't get excited for a game until after school's out, but I'm excited now."

Gillespie leaned back and opened another envelope.

"I remember the first game I coached in Thomasville," he said. "We opened with Thomas County Central. It was their version of this. The Rose City Classic. After practice I went home and was up late that night reading, so I walked over to the stadium. And I just sat there. I don't even know for how long. No joke."

Pruitt, a son of a coach, grinned.

"Your mind was already there," he said, as if it were the most normal thing in the world to sit in an empty high school stadium in the middle of a Thursday night. "Might as well just take your body."

Tracy came in.

"You have the pep rallies," she said.

There were two pep rallies today. She knew Rance would hate that. So when he groaned, she smiled.

Then she told him the Valdosta city manager would be there to unveil a commemorative coin for the game.

"What's his name?" Gillespie asked.

"Larry Hanson."

Gillespie reached for a Sharpie and scrawled on his palm: L-A-R-R-Y H-A-N-S-O-N.

●

Despite the fact that the school districts are basically separated by a mall, and that most Valdosta students have friends or relatives at Lowndes—Bee was dating one of their cheerleaders—the cultural gulf between the two high schools could be a hundred miles wide.

Exhibit A: The day before the game, each school's student body lampooned the other with a mocking dress-up theme.

At Valdosta, kids came to school in overalls and straw hats to celebrate "Plowboy Day."

At Lowndes, some kids draped themselves in bling, rolled up one pants leg, or wore baggy jeans. Their theme: "Thug Day."

As one Lowndes cheerleader posted on Facebook: "i attend LOWNDES high school, i am not a redneck and i proudly dressed like a thug today:) go Vikings!!!!!!!!!!!!!!!!!!!"

At the first pep rally, Yontell Morrison, the huge Wildcat lineman with twisted rust-colored hair, jumped onto the court with another kid and performed a kind of interpretive dance. Apparently it interpreted the night's mythic battle with Lowndes. Or something. Coach Al leaned on a railing in the stands and shook his head in befuddlement.

When Yontell finished, the cheerleaders rushed the court and got things back to normal. For the next twenty or thirty seconds, they shook it like a Polaroid picture in front of the players seated on the bottom rows.

Then L-A-R-R-Y H-A-N-S-O-N came out. To honor Valdosta's 150th anniversary, the city manager announced a special "sesquicentennial" coin would be used for the pregame toss.

Not much cools down a crowd of jacked-up teens like an adult in a suit invoking a "sesquicentennial."

"I'll make a prediction," H-A-N-S-O-N then told the students, trying to recover. "If the coin toss is heads tonight, Valdosta wins. If it's tails . . . Valdosta wins!"

Gillespie strode to the middle of the court. Coach had everybody's attention. There's something a little forbidding about the head football coach at any school, even if you're not one of his players. Like he could make you do fifty push ups just because you looked funny.

"This is a big game tonight with Lowndes and a great opportunity for the Wildcats," he began, as if clearing his throat for later in the locker room. "We need you all to be our twelfth man."

The students cheered. They'd cheer anything—short of a "sesquicentennial"—to stay out of class. So Gillespie played his hole card.

"Let me say this," he said. *"There ain't nuthin' like being a Wildcat on Friday night!"*

Pandemonium. Bee and Justin Williams grabbed a mike and shouted, "Where my 'Cats at!" Jay and Reggie did their Mutt-and-Jeff version of "Turn me up a little *HIGHer*! Just a little *HIGHer!*"

Nobody was ready for what came next. As the band blared its deafening blare and kids swayed and gyrated in the stands, out onto the floor popped Dr. Bill Cason. Buttoned up in a suit, tie, and starched white shirt, the white-haired seventy-one-year-old superintendent . . . *busted a move!* He then turned to face the girls still shimmying in the dance line and . . . *did the twist!*

He couldn't have driven the students any crazier if he'd pulled a rattlesnake out of his coat.

●

By noon, Gillespie had retreated back inside the relative quiet of his office. He busied himself the same way he busied himself every early Friday afternoon: printed out play sheets, trimmed them on a paper cutter, rolled on glue—a conscientious first grader trying to earn a star.

When he finished, Gillespie checked his texts. "Good luck this week," one read. "I love you."

"No idea who this is," he said. "This person sends me the same text every week. Got one after our first win. Thought it was my mother.

"This is a big game for this community," he added. "I want to win it for all those people. I really do."

Donna Hall, the cheerleader sponsor, walked by. A former cheerleader herself for the Hornets of Cook County, just north, she still looked the part: slim, big hair, heels that can never be high enough. The players all had crushes on her.

Donna came to Valdosta High in 1991, while Hyder ran the show. She'd seen all the highs and lows since, and her loyalty never wavered. "My philosophy," she said of the cheerleader's code, "is that when they're down they need us even more." These days she sensed that things were ticking up again.

"The excitement had been a little dry around here," she allowed, "but the feeling is back. You see the passion in the community coming back. It starts with the team, and once it goes to the student body and the community, that's what builds a dynasty."

She smiled—at herself. She knew she was getting a little ahead of herself. It's an occupational hazard for Wildcat fans. She said rivals who've tired of hearing about Valdosta's glory days have a term for Wildcat fans waiting for those days to return.

"They call us," she said, *"Those who like to dwell in the past."*

*

Players drifted in and out of the locker room. At 2:30, students poured out of classes. Until now, the day had seemed to tick by at half speed. Suddenly it accelerated.

Edrae walked by, his face serious, his eyes jumpy. Didn't say a word before he disappeared into the locker room.

"I'm sure he's struggling," Gillespie said, trimming his last play sheet, "with his . . . *existence.*"

*

Inside the crowded locker room, Justin Williams had his earbuds on, relaxing to Gucci Mane's "Go Ham on Em." Jay was splayed across the length of a bench, sound asleep.

What game?

Randy Cook stood shirtless in front of his yellow metal locker, inspecting his equipment in a careful, methodical, almost sacramental way.

He pulled out his helmet: battered, gouged . . . beautiful. He examined the black scuffmarks that pocked it, as if channeling the blow that each mark memorialized. He then kissed the top stripe before he gently replaced the helmet back atop his locker, like a priest returning a host to the tabernacle. When he finished, Randy draped a rosary around his neck.

Gillespie stepped in at 2:45, his eyes scary-alert.

"It changes right now," he told the room. *"Right now."*

Everybody shuffled out the door and off to the cafeteria, where they lined up for chicken and green beans and mashed potatoes. They ate more quietly than they did six games ago. Some players retreated into themselves. Reggie ate by himself at a table almost precisely where Hyder fell dead. A cheerleader slipped into a seat across from him. He didn't seem to notice; hard to tell who Reggie might be talking to, living or dead, inside his own head. One table over, Dashay ate alone, too.

Then the chaplain, Trea Brinson, stood up. Today's Godly message in a nutshell: Kick some Lowndes behind for Jesus!

Brinson started by reminding the players of last year's debacle. "That should make you so hungry to go after your enemy," he said. He skipped to how Nehemiah rebuilt the walls of Jerusalem and then connected the dots: the rebuilding of Valdosta, the taking on of all comers, the legacy they can leave behind—same thing.

"Do not be afraid of them," he quoted from Nehemiah, whose words now rang like one heck of a pregame speech. "Remember the Lord who is great and awesome, and fight for your brothers, your sons, your daughters, your wives, and your houses."

"What happens tonight will be remembered forever," Brinson said. "This is your last chance to wear that paw in this city for this city's championship. Just as Nehemiah said to fight for your sons, fight for your daughters—*fight for your city!*"

Every fork was down, every headset off.

"Let us pray," he finished. "Lord, allow us to be *relentless*. Allow us to be *nasty* on the field. Allow us to fight so we can remember tomorrow, remember today, and say that last year is history . . ."

The faintest smile cracked Gillespie's face as Brinson wrapped it up.

"It's us who reigns now!"

Players stood and clapped in a spontaneous rhythm.

"Amen!"

The roused Wildcats soul-shook Brinson's hand and wrapped him in man-hugs as they filed out the door.

Only Swoll lingered behind. His shaved head gleamed under the cafeteria's bright lights. He updated his Facebook page.

"Got alot to get off my mind b4 i step on that field," he tapped on his phone, "but once that first spike touch that turf ill be free from everything becuz ill be able to express myself."

He then concluded, "A poet use a pencil to express himself but ima football player so i use 9.5 pair of nikes on turf."

Swoll wasn't the only 'Cat with a fresh cut for the biggest show on the biggest night in town.

Jarquez Samuel, the bright-eyed 6'5" defensive tackle, sported cat paws carved in his modified Frohawk. Freak's dreads were rolled neat and airtight. Ryan and Zach had their blond hair barbered so razor-close their heads looked like they might start to bleed.

The week's pregame highlight film in the locker room merged past and present. Wildcats from renowned title teams, including Stan Rome, stared into a camera and spoke directly to this new breed of 'Cat—uncut, uncensored, player to player.

"You guys have an opportunity to whip the shit out of these guys," former quarterback Berke Holtzclaw, now a plate-glass salesman in Hahira, told them as he looked out from the screen. "We wrote the book on ass whippin'!"

Now time broke its leash; the two hours between the chaplain's pleas for God to bestow them with a little nasty and their final shuffle toward the buses rushed by in fast-forward. The coaches did what they could to tap the brakes.

"Slow the game down in your head," Rodemaker said during a walk-through in the gym.

Pruitt told his receivers, "I swear to you, you guys have the better team. I swear to you! So make plays."

Back in the locker room for the final twenty minutes, players slipped into their own worlds. Most listened to music: Jay to Lil Wayne's "Sky's the Limit" (*Don't worry bout mine, imma grind till I get it/ and tell all of my niggas that the sky is the limit*"), Swoll to T.I.'s "Yeah Ya Know" ("*You know we never not goin' all in/ Kickin' doors over just to let my dogs in*").

Malcolm, meanwhile, nodded his newly snipped head to Drake's "Miss Me" (*World Series attitude, champagne bottle life/ Nothing ever changes, so tonight is like tomorrow night*"). He listened while he stood face-to-face with Reggie, applying eye black to his teammate's face in a warrior gesture almost too intimate to watch in public.

Then Rodemaker burst into the locker room.

"Let's roll!"

●

The ten-minute bus ride was quiet, peaceful, removed, almost like a plane ride, a glide high above the clouds.

"We're on a business trip, y'all," one player called out as they rolled past a snow white cotton field two blocks from the school.

In a couple of weeks, the crop would be stripped clean. Bundles of the stuff would then sit in the brown field like giant soap cakes, protected by yellow and blue plastic tarps, until trucks hauled them off to a gin.

The buses rolled on: past a mobile home sales lot and an auto parts store and the Morningside Baptist Church. Past a barbershop, a piano studio, a Blimpie's. They passed the middle school and the medical center and then the semitropical lushness of Valdosta State's campus.

Then they landed, four yellow buses parked beneath the crepe myrtles on Ann Street. As soon as the doors opened, the outside rushed in.

It was a carnival. As one assistant coach stepped off the bus, some guy greeted him with a beer in each hand. Grilled-meat smell rose everywhere; even the camellias seemed to reek of it.

Williams Street was jammed with Winnebagos and TV trucks from Jacksonville and Tallahassee. College students who rented the nearby houses turned their yards into prime parking spaces, then sat in the chairs they pulled out to drink beer and keep a running commentary going on the passing human parade. Drexel Park filled with families who sat under moss-draped oaks to eat barbecue and boiled peanuts.

"Is this for *real?*" Claudette asked before heading inside the stadium.

"This is the most excited I've been since we went to New Orleans for Georgia in the Sugar Bowl," said LaVerne Rome, who waited for her son to pass on the sidewalk.

She didn't wait long. Players strolled down the block-long Cat Walk lined four deep tonight with fans. Even crimson-and-white Lowndes backers shuffled over from their own tailgates to watch. "That's the happiest you're going to be all night," one of them cracked to a passing 'Cat who smiled wide for a picture.

Everybody snapped pictures. These were the Boy Kings again.

The long line of Wildcats finally filed through the stadium's arched brick entrance. David Waller stood just inside. A few players reached out to shake his hand. Others passed without noticing he was there.

"Now we do the game part," Tucker Pruitt drawled dryly inside the closed coaches' room after the team finished its warm-up. "Which is kind of the important part."

Everyone still seemed caught up in all the prelude outside.

"It's like nothing I ever been a part of," Pruitt said. "Some of our boys were pissing in their pants."

Gillespie walked in. "It's a freakin' circus out there," he said. "How's Swoll?"

"You'd have to cut his leg off to keep him out," Loudermilk answered.

Gillespie had stood in the middle of the field during warm-ups, surrounded by the speed and muscle and cocksureness of nearly two hundred South Georgia boys. Under these lights, the display was breathtaking. Pruitt asked him how Lowndes looked. Gillespie said what coaches always say about the other team.

"They were pretty."

Now muffled shouts from players seeped through the coaches' door. Big Terry told somebody, "Hold it in, bro. We got about ten more minutes. Don't waste your energy, cuh."

Gillespie sat on a bench, planted his elbows on his knees, checked his watch, then checked it again.

"Longest twenty minutes of the day."

Then at exactly 7:45 he swung the door open into the locker room, the wide eyes of a hundred young faces not leaving him for a second.

He saw them and smiled. "Hey!" he told them. "Y'all have some fun tonight!"

Jay asked him how he felt. Gillespie didn't hesitate.

"I feel like we're gonna whip their ass, that's how I feel," he told him, and in that instant every kid in the room was reminded that Gillespie, at heart, was a warrior—that he was one of them, wanted it as badly as they did, would do whatever it took to help them get it done.

"Y'all listen up," he then started again, nothing fancy. "You've waited a long time for this. You've worked your ass off for this. Nobody's worked harder. You go out there tonight and be more physical, execute better, play hard for forty-eight minutes. Lay your heart and soul out there."

They all nodded: yessir.

"Now let's play!"

The 'Cats click-clacked their way down the tunnel as "We Ready" thumped over the loud speaker. Then that crashing rumble started. Rainwater from an earlier storm still stood on the roof, so when the players banged the tin water exploded into the air, like grease bouncing off a hot pan.

Across the way, Lowndes fans stared. *What the . . .*

Dashay led the Wildcats out as they sprinted to the other end zone. With the stands on both sides filled with fans trying to outshriek each other, and both schools' bands trying to outbleat each other, players seemed to push through an almost literal wall of sound. They then turned back to their bench, circled Gillespie, and, with kickoff just seconds away, took a knee.

Gillespie stood over his young troops, as if holding firm in the eye of a tornado. He put a hand on a player's shoulder, then waited a moment as they all followed suit.

He began, "Our Father . . ."

●

True to its plowboy heritage, the Lowndes offense ran the ball out of the Wing-T the way farmers harvest cotton: All. Day. Long.

So even after the Wildcat defense stuffed the Vikings' first two running plays following the opening kickoff, the last thing anybody in the these stands expected was what came next: a precision-guided 65-yard bomb down the middle from lanky blond quarterback Cole Parker.

They were pretty, all right.

7–0.

Gillespie stood with one hand on his hip, staring down at his play sheet and barking on his headset to coaches in the press box. He'd already moved on. The players took his cue.

"Listen to me," junior linebacker Jonathan Hester yelled in front of the bench, "we start *now!*"

They did, too, as soon as they got the ball. Swoll ripped off 10 yards on his first carry. Valdosta picked up another tough first down. Things bogged down near midfield, after a penalty left the Wildcats with a third and 12 from their own 44.

Then Ryan moved under senior center Jarquez Brown. He said hike, stepped back 7 yards—just like he'd done a million times since spring, but never once against Lowndes—and tossed a looping parabola that fullback Jarvis Roberts reached for 30 yards later and took all the way to the 1. Next play, Swoll dove off left tackle, hit a wall of white jerseys, bounced backward, and then headed right back in again—for the touchdown.

He scissor-ran down the right hash marks in his 9.5 Nikes all the way back to the bench.

7–7.

"I love this," shouted Pernell Bee Sr., star running back on the unbeaten '82 title team and father of Wesley Bee, the senior wide receiver. Pernell's older son played for Valdosta, too. His younger son played on the freshman team. "I just wish I could be out there."

Pernell had been out at a practice earlier in the week, partly to watch his son but mostly just to be around the game. He loved that green rectangle.

"Every time I step on that turf I think of Nick Hyder," he'd said one afternoon out there. "It was an honor just to be able to know him."

Then he paused, shook his head, and said what everybody here always said.

"Everything changed when Nick Hyder passed."

Pernell watched the practice fly by. Coaches and players sprinted everywhere. Even Coach Lucas, now hobbled by a torn meniscus, quick-cantered over the grass on crutches. The only time the action stopped was when Gillespie blew his whistle and shouted, "Do it again!"

"Oh, my God, he's superb," Pernell observed. "He's the first one since Hyder who resembled Hyder. He understands the game and the nowadays kid. He teaches the same things I teach at my house. Makes my job easier.

"My boys love him," Pernell went on. "He's hard but they love him. I tell my son, 'If you don't hate your coach walking off the practice field he's not doing his job.' I hated Hyder after every practice. You'd think about quitting when he's laying it on you.

"But I love what Hyder did for me," he added. "He gave me what I needed to deal with life."

Pernell played college ball at Valdosta State until he got a girlfriend pregnant, and then, he said, "one thing led to another." He now mixed chemicals at a local plant and watched the games from the field with the rest of the sideline mafia.

Tonight, the mafia was lined up two deep. As their championship rings caught the light, they'd shout out, "Cover five! Cover five!" and "The tackles are giving it away every time!"

Previous coaches had made many of these sons of Hyder and Bazemore feel like pariahs, restricting their on-field access. Gillespie made them feel like the field was still their home. As one Valdosta poster put it, THERE ARE NO EX-WILDCATS.

"Prior to this year, I didn't ever feel welcome," said Dana Brinson, a 'Cat luminary from the '80s who went on to play at Nebraska and then for San Diego in the NFL. Now forty-five, Brinson drove down for tonight's game from Atlanta.

"This coach is doing a great job, to have this team where it is at this point," he said. "People are talking about the 'Cats again."

The game turned sloppy for a while. The Lowndes quarterback threw an interception, fumbled on the Valdosta 1. The Wildcats made big gains, then stalled out with penalties and missed assignments.

"They're not that tough," offensive lineman Kendall Roberts said when he jogged off the field following one stalled drive, his short blond hair streaked dark with sweat. "We're just messin' up."

Then the 'Cats took over again when Lowndes missed a field goal. A kind of hypnotizing calm fell over the stands. Less than two minutes remained in the half.

"Gillespie's ready to open up on them now," Pernell confided to anybody who'd listen. "This ain't the same team that got beat last year."

As if on cue, Valdosta did what no other team in the state could do: got the ball to Malcolm. He caught a quick out for 12 yards, then another over the middle for 7. He jawed with a Lowndes defensive back—the ac-

cumulated teen swag on this one field could fill a three-day rap video—
and then, following a time-out, pulled in a 26-yarder with 59 seconds left.

All eyes—Valdosta's, Lowndes's—were again on Malcolm as Ryan
dropped back once more from the Viking 34. All eyes except Ryan's. He
spotted the lanky, Tinker Toy–jointed Wesley Bee over the middle and
hit him right in stride.

Touchdown.

A sideline cop had to keep Pernell from running the length of the
field to hug his son.

"That's what I'm talking about!" Pernell shouted. "I been waiting on
it. I told him he was going to have the biggest game of anyone. I told him
to be patient. 'All the talk is going to be on Malcolm and Jay. But your
time is going to come!'"

The 'Cats flew into the locker room, up 14–7.

"It's zero-zero!" a player yelled while they all poured in, flushed and
sweat-soaked and wide-eyed.

●

The Valdosta stands rattled and hummed. Folks looked like they didn't
know what to do with themselves: get up, sit down. They jammed the
bleacher aisles, unsure of where they were headed. Stuck in the middle of
one was Dr. Cason. A year earlier, he played the executioner. Tonight, he
was all rattlesnake-hunter smiles.

"We're not being outcouched this year, that's the big thing," he noted.

Bunched a dozen rows above Cason was the Mount Rushmore of
storied Valdosta coaches, along with their wives—former assistants
who dated back to Bazemore and through Rick Darlington, head man who
preceded Tomberlin. Darlington lasted three years before he sped back
to the school he'd come from, in Apopka, Florida.

That tiny section was the toughest to please in the stadium, probably
the toughest to please in the whole state.

They liked what they saw.

"These kids believe they can win. They're playing with confidence,"
said Jerry Don Baker, who played for Bazemore and coached for Hyder.
"That's a tribute to Coach Gillespie. He's out there to win a football
game. The mental edge these kids have this year over last is unbeliev-
able."

Like the sideline mafia down on the field, these guys felt respected again. They'd devoted blood, sweat, and more than a few tears to creating and then maintaining this legacy, only to be marginalized as they watched it dissolve.

Then Gillespie showed up. He invited them to come by to talk. Gave them all his cell number. Told them to call anytime.

"He's embraced us," said Bob Bolton, another coach whose roots reached down to Bazemore and Hyder.

Bolton left coaching after thirty-one years to work for the sheriff's department, in 2005, the last year of Darlington. He believed Darlington wanted to cleanse Valdosta of its traditions, to start anew, believing the place and its people had calcified.

"The others didn't embrace what this county is about," Bolton continued. "If I come into a place with tradition like this, I'm going to find out what worked before, what makes this place different than other places.

"This is not a fragile history to break," he said. "You have to respect this history. It's like the history of Notre Dame."

Bolton looked around at the packed, teeming stands, the bands high-stepping on the turf, the signs that cheerleaders on both sides hand-painted and taped up around the field: CATS OR DIE. 6-0: WHO'S NEXT? WE'RE GONNA RUN THIS TOWN!

"This is healthy for this community," he said. "It helps with discipline in school, gives people pride in what they're doing, makes people care more about each other. Even though they're competitive with each other, people look forward to going to work, they have something to discuss. They have a good time with it."

Then the former coach pointed with his chin at the scoreboard in the east end zone. He got a little ahead of himself, too.

"There's still a lot of football to play."

●

Gillespie went through his usual give-and-take with the coaches and players at halftime, anxious for their input but dispassionate in his quick dismissal of anything he thought was just plain harebrained.

"Here's what I'm going to do," he told the offense when he came out of the coaches' room. "The middle of the field is *wide freakin' open . . .*"

He addressed the entire team before they went back out. "Listen, men," he said. "There's still a bunch of stuff out there for us to do. It's a forty-eight-minute effort. We drive down and score, it's a huge turning point."

He glanced around the room. They all stared at him.

"All right," he said, "let's get going!"

Stan ambled out after everybody else left. He'd just talked to Jay by his locker.

"Jay said the defensive end's too nice," he said. "He was talking to him like, 'Good block, good block.' I told him, 'You still have to be nasty.' Jay said, 'You don't have to worry about that!'"

The third quarter played out like a physics experiment in pads, or whatever the football equivalent was of an immovable object (Lowndes) meeting an unstoppable force (Valdosta). Every hit was a thump. Near the end of the quarter, the Wildcats set up for a fourth and 1 but had to punt when a false start set them back 5 yards.

Lowndes found itself in the same spot early in the fourth quarter: fourth down and 1 on their own 42-yard line. McPherson called timeout. Sent his offense back on the field. Went for it.

Got it.

Drove the rest of the way for a score.

Tied: 14–14.

With seven minutes left, the 'Cats suddenly appeared to run out of gas. Lowndes had a bye the previous week, while Valdosta had journeyed to Atlanta on Saturday night, run their race with MLK, then returned at dawn Sunday morning. It finally caught up with them.

"We fought with all we had left," Malcolm said, "but what we had left wasn't much."

The next three minutes passed for the Wildcats like a standing blackout. By the time they came out of it, the Vikings had intercepted Ryan twice and put up a touchdown and a field goal.

24–14.

Lowndes never looked prettier.

Gillespie still paced, still stared at his call sheet, still talked through his headphones to his coaches upstairs in search of an edge. All forty-two rows of the home-side stands still roared behind him. There wasn't a boo or a hoot or a plea for Dashay.

Then lo and freakin' behold . . . on third down and 25: Ryan to Tampa, 18 yards. Fourth and 14: Ryan to Tampa, 20 yards. The Lowndes defense tightened, and Zach came on to sidewind a 29-yarder through the posts with 1:09 left. The 'Cats sat within a touchdown.

"We got a shot!" Bobby Scott shouted to his listeners, crowding closer to their radios all over town. Another 30,000 people, both locally and throughout the Wildcat diaspora, watched the game streamed on the Internet.

"Everybody in the country knows what's fixin' to happen here," Scott told them all. *"We're going onside."*

Which is exactly what the 'Cats did. Zach fell on top of his own kick at midfield.

"We got it!" Scott screamed. "The 'Cats have it! We got life! We got a prayer! We got a shot with 1:08 left and that's all you can ask!"

What Valdosta did next was no surprise: Ryan long to Malcolm. Malcolm leaped for the ball over a defender at the 15 but couldn't pull it down. He looked out of gas, too; he thought he should've had it. Tyler Hunter, the Viking whose dad had helped win so many games for the 'Cats on this same field by catching passes just like that, leaned down, yanked Malcolm up, and gave him a quick spank. He knew he'd dodged one.

Next play, Ryan dropped back to do the same thing, but this time the Vikings flushed him from the pocket. He scampered to his right, but Lowndes had little trouble taking down the field's slyest operator but slowest quarterback.

Ryan landed hard, came up holding his right thumb. The clock kept clicking. It took Gillespie almost ten seconds to get an official to give him a time-out. He couldn't believe it but this wasn't the time to give a ref the full Gillespie.

He huddled with his offense. When they broke, with 17 seconds on the clock, Dashay stood in the backfield. In the shotgun.

At quarterback.

●

Biggest play of the biggest game on the biggest night of the year . . . and it came down to Dashay—the "next Michael Vick," the "pure thug," take your pick. Make this one play, even he had to realize inside a stadium that was now as frenzied and ecstatic as a tent revival, and all would be forgiven, all would be forgotten. All the bad behavior, bad choices, badass-ness—it would all be made right.

He dropped back. Planted his right foot. His girlfriend stood in the Lowndes bleachers with her friends from school while the father of her daughter tried to pull out a final-second miracle for Valdosta, and maybe for himself.

Who to cheer for? Being a teenaged mother in this town was a lot more confusing than anybody knew.

LOL.

Dashay's dark face glistened inside his helmet. He planted that back foot and then—nothing. So he bounced on the balls of his feet for a while and searched for something, anything, downfield. Minutes seemed to slide by. Dashay waited.

A Lowndes defender finally broke through. Reached for him, pawed at him, like he'd eat him if he caught him. Dashay spotted the dude without ever really looking his way and scrambled to his left, like he was out on Claudia Circle dodging a car—or bullet from a .22—his black face mask pointed the whole time toward the end zone.

Then finally he let it fly and with his rec-league, rear-back-and-wing-it motion, Dashay unloosed a spiral, high and long. Maybe 45 yards in the air. Nose up, then down. A mortar shell. Aimed imprecisely, at some general target.

Good enough: Tampa was there.

He sighted it. He backed up like an outfielder on the warning track, surrounded by five scuffling defenders, all absorbed in the same spiraling object. He took aim. The voice in his head that took over at times like these—the voice that had told him to straighten his life up, to go back to football, to trust Gillespie—now told him this: *Go get it!*

He rose. Climbed. Scaled.

Ascended.

Until the wall of white jerseys collapsed beside him. An unseen teammate, the newly emboldened Tyran, got buried beneath it, too. The ball hit the turf, bouncing that stupid way that footballs can bounce. Players on both sides kept grabbing for it, circling it, pushing at each other. Like they didn't want what they'd been doing all night to end. Like they knew it would never get better than this—twenty, thirty years from now, this was what they'd all still be talking about.

Even the officials stood there and stared at each other for a brief second, like even they weren't sure whether they should stop this yet. Then one of them threw a flag: interference. Valdosta would get another shot from just past midfield. Six seconds left.

Ryan jogged back out, Dashay's chance past. Launched his own high, looping mortar. Another big crowd gathered under it. A thousand hands, it seemed, reached out.

A Viking came down with it.

Interception.

Over.

24–17.

The scoreboard lights went dark an instant later. Stunned 'Cats shook their rivals' hands, then drifted toward the end zone, surrounded their coach, and took a knee. Gillespie looked spent but still composed in his Valdosta polo and light khakis; he could step into an Alabama grandmother's house right now and still recruit her grandson. The Lowndes band drowned him out for a minute, bleating away in the visitors' stands like they'd just won World War III—which, well, hell, they had. Give 'em that.

"You cannot let this night define your season," he told his upset kids, who leaned in to hear him. They looked less interested in what he had to say than in knowing he was still there to say it.

"You have a region game next week. Win enough of those and you get another shot"—his eyebrows narrowed like two poison-tipped arrows toward the white jerseys still mobbing each other downfield—"at them."

When he finished, Monty Long put a mike in front of him. Gillespie's eyes darted, looking for Claudette and Kennedy. He couldn't find them. Security wouldn't let anybody on the field. Too crazy.

Gillespie's mouth moved. Words fell out.

"We battled the entire game . . . had a tough time offensively in the second half . . . we got to be able to rebound . . . got a tough Coffee team next week . . ."

He finally found his own way off the field and up the concrete walkway outside the stadium locker room. A trainer peered into Reggie's bloody mouth: A front tooth had been knocked loose and now hung there by its root.

Reggie was too disappointed to care about a tooth.

"Even if we win the championship," he said, wiping blood from his goatee with a towel, "we still can't say to our children we beat Lowndes our senior year."

Stan stood over Jay inside the empty locker room. Jay sat there on a bench, still in his pads, his head down and round eyes filled with tears.

"Listen," Stan told him, bending down on his cane to get closer, "this team has the opportunity to be great. Take this and make it better."

Jay shook his head. Stood. Towered over the greatest athlete in the history of South Georgia, then turned and pushed through the door. Didn't look back.

"Jay, *c'mon* . . ."

Then Kennedy rushed out of nowhere to bury her face in her daddy's chest and have a big, shoulder-shuddering cry. A red-eyed Claudette, right behind her with a pom-pom, stood in front of Rance. They'd been here before, but it was never easy. What can you do? First thing they did: fist bumped, like middle school kids who really, really like each other. Claudette then reached over the big white bow in Kennedy's hair and gave her husband a long, long hug. She tilted her head up. They kissed.

"It's all right," Rance said softly, to both of his crying girls.

Another one of his girls stood a few feet away: his mother, who came down from Clayton. She looked about all cried out herself.

"I can't hardly stand it anymore," she said, "but there's something special here for him. He has the desire to bring these people back together."

Claudette moved aside while a string of others—parents, students, former players, boosters—queued up like a funeral-home receiving line to tell their coach that they were proud of him, that they were grateful for him, that this was the first time they'd felt like a real Wildcat since . . . well, they couldn't hardly remember anymore, but it sure felt good.

Claudette looked on, her arm tight around Kennedy.

"I'm sad for our sweet little school system," she said. "For this community, this is the state championship. So this is a test of our endurance. Of our faith."

Then the sweet community consoler morphed back into the coach's wife—the first lady of Valdosta football.

"They have bragging rights for a year," Claudette said, "but they can't say they whipped us!"

This year, nobody will ask a Wildcat to pass the Heinz 57-to-15 sauce.

Suddenly Rance had enough. He broke away from the line and reached for Kennedy. "Come here," he told his daughter. He hugged her, kissed her on top of her head. "I love you."

Kennedy beamed: Right away she felt a hundred times better. She then took her daddy by the hand and pulled him into the deserted locker room. Away from everyone, she led him to a whiteboard still smeared with the X's and O's of plays diagrammed at halftime.

It was just the two of them in there. She grabbed a marker and drew something up: squiggles going this way and that way and up and down. When she finally finished, she stood back and looked over what she'd done. The meaning in that mess, her satisfied look suggested, was obvious.

"If you would've done *that*," she then told her daddy matter-of-factly, "you would've won."

●

Rance didn't let Kennedy go after that. She rode back to the high school with him and a couple of other coaches in one of the coaches' trucks. The mood on the drive inside the dark cabin was quiet, still a little charged, but not at all angry or upset. It was what grown men sound like when they've left it all on the field.

Kennedy was the first to speak up. "It was sweet of the Wildcats to let the Vikings win," she said.

The words roused Gillespie from a reverie. He took a minute to work them in his head until they made sense. His reply was soft and twangy, with clear mountain air blowing through it.

"I assure you they didn't try to let them win," he said, "but I appreciate your trying to be positive."

Having talked, Gillespie kept on talking, as much to himself as to the other men in the truck. "If we could've just come out at halftime and gotten one more . . . You know, I really thought 21 points was going to win this game. And it should've . . ."

Ten minutes later, the truck rolled up behind the school. The buses were empty, though people still milled around. Tasha Williams, the junior who helped film the games, looked lost as she roamed around in the dark, like she wasn't sure where to go or even where she was. She cried big, anguished sobs, with her hands held up to her face, a South Georgia rendition of *The Scream*. It had been the worst night ever for her: 'Cats lost to Lowndes, and she and Tampa broke up.

"I just can't *handle* it," she cried.

Inside the locker room, stinking now with an elevated level of funk— what a locker room smells like when a hundred teenagers have left it all on the field—players and coaches went through the motions of showering and dressing and shelving equipment and shuffling things around in their lockers and offices.

Players didn't hang around long. "It was fun until a little while ago," Ryan said before he bolted for the door, his hair wet, his face flushed. "But it ain't the end of the world. It just feels like it now."

Tucker Pruitt stood in the narrow walkway in front of Gillespie's office, watching and listening to it all. It wasn't tonight he was worried about.

"Now we have a long weekend," he drawled, "of just *thinkin'* about this shit."

Rodemaker glistened with sweat and was even hoarser than usual. He told the other coaches that Jack Rudolph, the defensive coordinator against whom all Valdosta defensive coaches are judged, walked up afterward and assured him, "It's only a game."

That prompted Al Akins, who coached with Rudolph, to reach deep into his institutional memory. He recounted another tough loss, back in 1989, against Colquitt, 7–0.

"Woke us up," he said. "We came back and won state."

"What we got to do is go to work on Monday," Pruitt put in. "They're not going to forfeit next week."

Akins said, "That would be the only loss of the night: if we don't learn from this how to be better."

Gillespie sat in his office, neatened piles on his desk, glanced at a replay of the game flickering soundlessly in front of him. It was being copied for next week's opponent.

"Is that tonight's game?" Kennedy asked. "I don't want to watch it. It's too sad."

Gillespie nodded. Kept watching.

"I love you, Daddy," Kennedy said.

"I love you, too," he answered.

"Where you going to be tomorrow?" she asked him.

"I'll be with you," he said.

Kennedy smiled. "You're going to take the day off?"

Gillespie's eyes never left the screen. He nodded again.

Yes.

In the small hours of the next morning, on the *Valdosta Daily Times* Web site, a man who identified himself as Mark Wood posted a comment.

"I am a Lowndes Viking fan and sat on the home side tonight," he began. "On my way out of the stadium, I walked past the area where the Cat players were meeting their family members and friends. I walked within a few inches of a young Cat player. I could not see his number because his shoulder pads were off, and could not see his face, because it was buried in his Mother's chest, with her arms holding him tight. You could hear the uncontrollable sobs of crying coming from this young man, and his Mother telling him it was Alright and it would be OK. I could literally feel the pain of emotion coming from this young man.

"I am a 2 tour Iraq combat vet," Mark Wood concluded, "hit by 2 IEDs, been to dozens of military funerals, and have a heart about as hard and cold as a steel rod. And it was all I could do to not break into tears myself over this young man's pain. If not for fear of being thought to be rubbing salt in a wound, I would have grabbed this young man and hugged him myself."

The player Wood saw was Randy Cook.

The kid who always wanted to be a Wildcat. Who ran all those gassers by himself after practice back in August, with the coaches long gone. Who understood every time he stepped onto the field that another Wildcat had stepped on it before him, and probably won—probably won big. Who thought the least that he could give back to the town that let him play the game he loved so much was a W—a win.

It was Cook who hurt enough tonight to break the heart of a two-tour, twice-wounded Iraqi War veteran because he thought that he'd failed to give Valdosta what he knew it wanted most.

That damn W.

19

Boosters, 'Cruiters, Funerals

or Grinding

The Monday after he lost the game that the last coach was fired for losing, Gillespie went one-on-one with the Touchdown Club.

He stood in front of a stage inside the high school's performing arts center for his weekly game review—its own kind of performance art—which tonight featured clips of the Vikings outscoring the 'Cats 17–3 in the fourth quarter. If there was a list of high crimes in Valdosta's founding charter for which one could be bum-rushed out of town, blowing a fourth-quarter lead to Lowndes would rank near the top.

Gillespie didn't know what to say. So he just said what he felt.

"I'm sorry."

A low rumble rose from the seats filled with the season's biggest crowd of notoriously hard-to-please boosters.

Gillespie continued, "I'm sorry because of the seniors. They deserved to win. I'm sorry for y'all. I know how much you wanted to win that game. I wanted it, too."

It was a litmus test of sorts. These weekly meetings had become infamous in recent years for their Looney Tunes–esque confrontations. Five years ago, at a session inside the Wildcat museum, a then soon-to-be-former coach became so incensed over what he considered a booster's disrespect that he tossed a folding chair clear across the linoleum floor. "The moment I saw that," David Waller recalled of the incident, now as much a museum relic as the Peanut Bowl trophy behind glass, "I knew he wouldn't be back."

He wasn't.

During the troubled Tomberlin reign that followed, sessions sometimes got so heated that Touchdown Club officers started to check membership cards at the door to make sure only members got in, and not irate fans just dropping by to heckle.

Things hadn't always been that hostile. Like most everything else surrounding Valdosta football, these weekly gatherings had fallen a long way since the Hyder era. Back then, the charismatic coach sometimes held them at the First Baptist Church and turned the nights into something more like advanced lectures on the theory and theology of high school football. He'd unreel the *entire* game, providing commentary after virtually every play. The sessions often dragged on so long that some boosters took to sitting in a back row so that Hyder wouldn't spot them if they sneaked out early.

To stay a step ahead of his critics, Hyder also came armed with intelligence on what boosters griped about among themselves. When he learned that a Wildcat's father had complained about a play call, the coach stopped the film during one meeting to point out a block that the dad's kid missed, botching a run that otherwise would've gone for big yardage. Boosters were more careful who they whined to about Coach after that.

Gillespie's mea culpa, while a bit of a risk, also kept him ahead of what some boosters had already talked about privately. He admitted that he probably got too conservative in the second half, that he should've thrown more on first down.

Gillespie finished. Yet rather than turn on him, the grizzled 'Cat followers who'd crowded inside the 900-seat auditorium looked almost on the verge of tears. They'd clearly come to praise their new coach, not to bury him.

"It feels like you've been here forever," one man stood up to say. "We're in love with you and your family. You showed the guys on the other side of town there's no more laying down."

"Keep your vision," a middle-aged black man then rose to tell Gillespie. "You got one. Don't lose it. The Bible says, 'Where there is no vision, people perish.'" The man turned his head slowly around the room for dramatic effect before he added, "The last three years, we've perished!"

The room erupted in laughter, then applause.

It was clear that seven games into the season, Gillespie had managed to pull off a rare bit of coaching stagecraft: raised expectations for this year's team (he told this same group earlier he had enough talent "to win state") while he kept his emphasis on the future. A single good season wasn't why he'd come here. Consumed as he was with getting this team ready to win each week, Gillespie's goal was to rebuild a program that could sustain itself through the inevitable cycles of lesser talent, major injuries, and bum luck—as Valdosta had done for nearly seventy years.

While not intending to, Gillespie also seemed to have revived Valdosta's long-dormant cult-of-the-coach yearnings. With his smarts, marathon work habits, and form-fitting religiosity (as well as his immensely popular wife), comparisons around town to Hyder were rampant. So it didn't sound all that weird when longtime fans characterized his half-season turnaround in terms of a Second Coming—not a literal one, of course, but, well, close enough.

"Remember the first time people seen Jesus, what they were saying?" the same middle-aged black man said later in the lobby. "What they were saying was, 'Praise the Lord!'

"That's what we're saying about this man," he said of Gillespie. "Praise the Lord!"

A similar scene unfolded Wednesday night at Gillespie's radio show inside the Smokin' Pig. More fans filled the back room than had shown up all year. They doubled up at the tables, their chairs knocking against the pine walls and stacked cases of barbecue sauce.

It looked more like the ad hoc setup of an open mike night than a radio show, and Gillespie, Bobby Scott, and Monty Long ran through the hour as harried waitresses scrambled to fill orders. Some folks drifted in late from church—or left church early.

Reggie, Justin, and Jay slipped out after the show, feeling good about themselves again as they piled into Jay's roomy Lincoln Town. Before Jay turned the ignition, his cell went off: John Lilly, one of Jay's regular once-a-week suiters.

"Yes, sir. We lost that one," Jay said to Lilly, Georgia's tight ends coach and point man, along with offensive coordinator Mike Bobo, in the Bulldogs' round-robin prize fight with every other college that mattered for Jay and Malcolm. "But all our goals are still there."

Reggie and Justin already knew who was on the other end. They'd heard Jay take enough calls to identify both the college and the coach just by his inflections.

Then Justin's phone went off: an assistant from Georgia Southern.

Seated in the back, Reggie glanced down at his own phone: nothing.

"Tell him about me," Reggie called out to Jay and Justin. He looked down again. "How come my phone line ain't lightin' up?"

Justin stretched his legs in the passenger seat and finished his call. LSU was interested early, but they'd since vanished, spooked by his undersized linebacker frame.

"Everybody knows about LSU," Justin said. "So even though Georgia Southern is a Division I-AA school, I'm happy they took the time out to call me."

Jay finished his call, too. Instead of hanging up, he handed his phone to Justin, who again leaned back in his seat and looked as relaxed talking with the Georgia assistant as Jay had just moments earlier. With recruiting now so ubiquitous—daily updates on dozens of Web sites, signing day on national TV—everybody knew its rituals and how the game was played.

"Nothing, Coach Lilly," Justin began. "Just chillin'."

Their faces glowed orange in the car, lit from above the parking lot by the Pig's neon flames. Customers smiled as they walked by, proud of their boys and happy to peek in on the process. One imagined that variations of this scene played out tonight in towns like this across the country.

Reggie's mock outrage continued from the backseat.

"Man, UGA, Georgia Southern—it don't matter," he shouted out again. Justin tried not to laugh while he was still on the line with Lilly. Jay had to cover his face.

"Just pass the phone to me! I'll take it! I'll take it!" Reggie went on. "I'm taking all offers!"

The Tennessee coach showed up on Friday as Gillespie trimmed play sheets by his desk for the 'Cats' region game against Coffee County, their first since the Lowndes loss.

"I should have somebody else doing this," Gillespie told him without looking up, intent on not lopping off a thumb with the paper cutter, "but fact is, I really enjoy it."

The assistant from Tennessee smiled. Eric Russell, Vols tight ends and special teams coach, came to Valdosta to restock his team's depleted stable. New head coach Derek Dooley took over a program abandoned overnight by Lane Kiffin, and so far he'd had a rough go of it. Tennessee had a losing record halfway through the season, and it wouldn't get easier. The Vols' next two opponents: Alabama and South Carolina.

"That'll motivate you to get on the road," Gillespie half-joked.

Recruiters were part of the continuous stream of people and problems that walked through one of Gillespie's two office doors all day, every day. Seated behind his desk, he was equal parts air traffic controller, counselor, disciplinarian, babysitter, shrink, administrator, good cop, bad cop, and, when time allowed, head coach atop one of the hottest seats in high school football.

Players drifted in during the afternoon to watch film with him on his wall's pull-down screen. Others just drifted in, took seats nearby, and hung out while Gillespie tweaked game plans on his computer; they just liked being around him, whether he said anything to them or not. Others would walk in with a hat on, or open a closed door without first knocking, and be told to go back out and do it again, this time the right way— hat off, knocking first.

"Coach G, man, somebody stole my—" Dashay barged in one afternoon without knocking.

"Dashay, first of all, I'm not your drinking buddy," Gillespie shot back before he finished. "So don't come in here and 'Coach G, man' me. Go back out and do it over."

Gillespie explained the hot-and-cold climate of his office. "I don't want it to be so shut down they don't come in. But if they come in for the wrong reason, it should be uncomfortable."

Recruiters were always welcome; Gillespie jokingly referred to them as "squatters," but he'd been in their shoes. Few of them ever sat in there long without remarking on the framed photo of Kennedy hugging her dad with her feet off the ground on the Georgia Dome field back when Rance coached at Peach. Talk would turn to wives and kids and life on the road.

The real stampede wouldn't come until after the season. That's when Nick Saban and Mark Richt and the rest of the elite schools' head honchos would take advantage of the NCAA's "contact period." They'd fly in to replace their assistants, plant themselves in Gillespie's office (or move Tracy out of hers), and try to close deals. Word of their arrivals would run through the school and then through town the moment they arrived.

When the head coaches flew out, their assistants swooped back in and circled Gillespie's office and the players' homes like planes over Atlanta's Hartsfield-Jackson. One morning in December, Gillespie's office would be filled with assistants from Georgia, Florida, and Clemson—all at once. They yakked with each other for half an hour about the plusses and minuses of various dipping tobaccos as they tapped their feet and waited for Jay or Malcolm to show.

One freezing night, Lilly sat in his car with the heat on until past nine, parked at a gas station beside the Smokin' Pig as he waited for a call from Stan to tell him the Tennessee coach had left and it was clear to come by the house. Lilly left Jay's home around eleven and headed straight for I-75 to make the five-hour drive back to Athens that night and be with his own family.

It could be a grinding, swallow-your-pride existence. One Florida assistant waited in Gillespie's office almost half an hour one morning for Malcolm, until he finally figured out he'd been stood up.

"Thanks for letting me sit in here, Coach," he said to Gillespie before heading out the door empty-handed. "Beat waiting in my car in the parking lot."

Moments after he left, Malcolm appeared. He'd hidden in another room, then sat down with Georgia's Mike Bobo.

Malcolm had decided against Florida but hated telling their coach face-to-face; he'd talked to him for almost a year. For a lot of players, it was like breaking up. You half expected to hear one of them say, "It's not you, it's me." For Malcolm, again, the decision had come down to trust.

"I looked them in the eyes and they didn't seem real," he said of his previous talks with Florida. "Like there was something up they weren't telling me. I just sat and stared at them and it was like something about them just didn't seem right. So I left it alone."

Malcolm's intuition proved dead on. Another morning, the Florida assistant sat across from Gillespie, waiting for Malcolm, when his cell vibrated with a text.

The assistant whistled after reading it. "Well, what do you know . . ."

Gillespie knew: His cell had already blown up with texts telling him that Urban Meyer just resigned as Florida's head coach. Gillespie never said a word; wasn't his place to tell the assistant his future had just been upended. When the coach read the text aloud, Gillespie gave him his condolences.

"Been there," he said.

For Malcolm, Meyer's out-of-the-blue resignation sealed the deal. Florida was out.

Soon, Alabama was out, too. Again, for Malcolm it came down to a feeling. Having barely watched an entire college football game in his life, he only vaguely knew who Nick Saban was until he had to meet him. He wasn't star-struck. Instead, he simply watched and listened.

"A lot of the stuff they said was true, but sometimes I looked at them and it didn't seem real," he explained of his visits with Alabama's staff. "At a certain point I got a bad vibe. The coaches did a good job recruiting me, but I think they stated the truth a little too much. They overdid it. When they tell you you're a good player, that might be true. But then they tell you you're the best player ever . . . stuff like that, something felt wrong."

Not everyone who would step through Gillespie's doors was named Saban or Richt—or Kirby Smart or Mike Bobo or Jim Chaney. There was a whole other level of recruiter who walked in as well.

They came, as an assistant from a Mississippi junior college said, to "recruit 84," the talent-rich high schools along Highway 84 that ran east-west across South Georgia from Bainbridge to Brunswick. That same assistant finished his pitch to one Wildcat while Gillespie was out of the office, then fished through his pockets to give the recruit one of his cards. When he couldn't find one, he sneaked one of Gillespie's cards from the desk and put his own name and number on the back.

Later he'd ask the recruit, "Mind not telling anybody about that?"

October was what the NCAA labeled its "quiet period." From August to the end of November, college coaches could call a recruit only once a week. They could also make one visit to the recruit's school to evaluate him but not to meet with him. Recruits, meanwhile, could make official visits to meet with a coach on a college campus.

Malcolm and Jay checked out a lot of schools together over the summer: Auburn, Alabama, Florida, Georgia. Once camp started, they made a joint decision to forgo their official visits until after the season. They didn't want recruiting to distract them from the team.

That's why the Tennessee assistant was here. The Vols had an off-week, and Russell, whose Vols were desperate for "difference makers," as he put it, wanted Malcolm and Jay to know he was interested enough in them to be there. So far, he'd had trouble getting their attention.

It wasn't always easy for a recruiter to separate himself from the pack, especially when the pack was the SEC. Waist-high stacks of unopened college letters sat in a corner of Jay's bedroom, and they grew higher daily. Unless an envelope had something that caught his eye, or looked personal instead straight off the recruiting assembly line, Malcolm tossed out almost every letter he got.

"What do you think is going on with Jay?" Russell asked Gillespie.

"I thought he was slotted to Georgia, but I don't know anymore," Gillespie told him.

Then Jay walked in with two girls who filmed the 'Cats' games, one of them Malcolm's ex.

"You been hiding from my calls?" Russell asked him, doing his best to smile. Jay hadn't answered one of his calls in a while.

"Oh, no," Jay told him. "My phone broke."

"Well," Russell said, "I'm down here on my off-day."

Malcolm walked in.

"The invisible man," Russell announced, again forcing a smile.

Malcolm barely shrugged, sat down, picked up something off Gillespie's desk, read it.

"The ghost," Malcolm corrected him, absently.

Russell asked Jay if he was ready for the game tonight against Coffee, a big, rugged, historically underperforming team from Douglas, sixty miles north. Gillespie once coached there for a year.

"I'm just ready to get back on the field after last week," Jay said, "and make somebody pay for it."

Russell asked both of them if they'd seen Tennessee's recent game against LSU. The Vols nearly upset the Tigers in Baton Rouge, losing on the game's last frantic play.

They both kind of nodded.

"Who were you rootin' for?" he asked Malcolm.

"Nobody," Malcolm told him honestly.

"You can lie, you know," Russell said, doing his damnedest to stretch yet another smile across his face. "I'm sitting right here."

"Okay." Malcolm shrugged. "You. I was rootin' for you."

Russell smiled.

"I can't visit with you all today," he then told them. "I just wanted to let you know I'm here."

Malcolm and Jay kind of nodded again: Message received. They disappeared into the locker room.

Russell leaned back in his seat. "They seem like good kids."

"They're *awesome* kids," Gillespie said.

"Malcolm's been a tough one." Russell sighed. "I don't get much out of him."

Russell walked with Gillespie to the team's pregame feed and devotional. Dinner tonight for the SEC assistant was cafeteria chicken, mashed potatoes, green beans, and all the weak sweet tea he could drink.

Afterward, Russell watched film with Gillespie in his office behind closed doors. Loudermilk knocked forty-five minutes later, same as he did every week, at 4:15.

Squatting time was over.

●

That night at the stadium, Russell stood on an end zone sideline as the Wildcats left their locker room to bang the tin and rock the roof. The energy level was lower and the crowd a little sparser than it was for the Lowndes game, but it was still Friday night in South Georgia. Russell stepped back as the first dark jerseys seeped from the tunnel. Soon more jerseys crowded behind them. When Gillespie finally released his team to sprint the length of the field, students hopped on top of their seats while the band pounded out the fight song.

Russell continued to stand and stare and soak it in. The Spanish moss behind him barely fluttered; pairs of graying heads belonging to the sideline mafia talked with each other in the easy shorthand of boyhood friends grown up together into middle age.

Next week, Russell would be back in Knoxville, standing inside 102,455-seat Neyland Stadium, its sky-high stands stuffed with orange-clad fans who'd dance to "Rocky Top" for the Vols' game against the Crimson Tide. Intimacy would be replaced by spectacle; timelessness by transience and bloat and restless ambition.

Russell stood alone on the Bazemore-Hyder turf. He continued to stare ahead, watching the 'Cats reach the other end of the stadium, circle back to their coach, take a knee, shout "Amen!" and trot back out onto the field—their field, their daddy's field, their uncle's field, their brother's field.

In his heart, Russell had to know that Malcolm and Jay, the two kids Tennessee needed most, were long shots at best. He also had to know that on this warm autumn night nobody on that field in a black jersey and yellow hat needed any kind of validation from Tennessee—or Alabama or Florida or Georgia or anybody else. On nights like this, the players out there in the black and gold had everything they needed. It was all here.

In Valdosta.

"These kids," Russell acknowledged, four hundred miles south of where he'd be next week yet not looking like he was in any hurry to get back, "don't know how lucky they have it right now."

The 'Cats beat Coffee 42–24, then won their last two games on the road to finish 9-1, the school's best regular season record in nearly a decade.

During the season's last three weeks, the team's biggest bumps came off the field. Bee was mugged the night before one game in the Walmart parking lot. Another week, a distraught Odell showed up in Gillespie's office just before the players boarded the team buses for their hour-long ride to Tifton. The son of a man who was close to Odell—Odell referred to the son as his brother—had been shot and killed in Homerville five days earlier over an argument about a car door. Odell's mother wanted him to stay home that night for the wake. Odell, who'd yet to see any action this season, wanted to dress for the game.

Gillespie shut his door to talk with him while the buses idled in the parking lot. His experience with Odell had been up and down—mostly down. When Odell was unable to make it through spring practice, Gillespie wrote him off. Then the kid showed up again in the summer wanting to play, and Gillespie decided to give him another shot. By camp, Gillespie was convinced Odell was "fixin' to turn a corner" in his life. Then he violated probation and was thrown in jail.

"I was at a crossroads of how to handle that," Gillespie said. "Here was a kid getting punished for something he'd done in the past, but since I'd had him he'd been good and come a long way from what he was to what he is now. So I made a decision to let him come back when he got out.

"Whether he played another down or not wasn't the point. I wanted to let him be a part of something, give him something to be involved in every afternoon.

"The easier thing to do," Gillespie said, "would have been to tell him to just concentrate on school and not play football. But is he really going to finish school if I do that? So I let him come back."

So far, Odell had not played a down. Yet the kid who'd bought a radio at the jail store to listen to the Wildcats season opener wanted to be on the sideline for tonight's game in Tifton.

Gillespie walked out of his office and across the parking lot almost a half hour later. Odell boarded a bus. Beneath his jersey, another tattoo was inked in looping script across the top of his chest: BLESSED.

"It's therapeutic for him to be here," Gillespie said.

◆

Life just kept breaking out. One starter's girlfriend was pregnant. When another starter learned that his girlfriend wasn't, Coach Al warned him bluntly after a practice to quit while he was ahead.

"In four years, you can either be a gazillionaire or drive a forklift at Langdale. Which you want to do?"

Malcolm started to see Brittany Yoder, a very personable, very white senior cheerleader. He came over to her house with a bunch of other players on Thursday nights all season. Brittany's mother, Sheri, cooked for them while they watched *Wildcat Tradition*, Gillespie's weekly TV show.

Rumors that the two of them were seeing each other circulated for weeks. Then Malcolm and Brittany showed up together all over town—the Waffle House, the mall, the movies, a haunted house on Halloween ("You'd think he'd be all macho," Brittany laughed, "but he left me and another girl when a guy with a chain saw started chasing us").

Few students or parents blinked, even though the black-white dating thing was still mostly taboo at the school. To Malcolm, it was no big deal, "just a football player–cheerleader thing." Like any girl dating a star player, Brittany put up with the steady parade of girls in the halls or at the mall who wanted to talk with Tampa *all the time*. At least outwardly, race wasn't an issue. Most chalked that up to the power of football.

"Because it was him," Marquise Mitchell said of his popular younger brother, "people overlooked it."

"Some people who are Deep Southern didn't like it all," allowed Brittany, whose parents were originally from Pennsylvania, "but all my friends I'm close with didn't have a problem. As long as I was happy they were fine.

"In fact," she added, "this year you see that [black-and-white high school couples] more than ever before. I don't know if it's in the water or what."

During those same three weeks, Gillespie gave two eulogies.

One was for a freshman coach who died suddenly at age fifty. At the funeral service, Gillespie quoted from Ralph Waldo Emerson.

"It is not the length of life," he said inside the nearly full performing arts center, where rows of players wore their home jerseys, "but the depth of life."

The second one was for the father of his closest boyhood friend, a tough-as-nails Renaissance man who'd coached youth league football and taught Rance what grit on the field really meant. He died, at sixty-three, while walking to the parking lot after the Georgia-Florida game.

Gillespie gave that eulogy inside the redbrick church in which he grew up. He drove the length of the state with Claudette and Kennedy right after a Wednesday practice. It was after midnight when they pulled past the fishing boat parked in Claudette's parents' driveway.

Next morning, a familiar mist shrouded the landscape. Rance rode by the cabbage fields he steered a tractor through when he was seven. He rolled down a window to inhale the dead-leaf scent carrying in from the woods ("There isn't another smell in the world like it"). Not far away, when he turned thirteen, a preacher baptized him in the clear, cold waters of Betty's Creek. Born again, Gillespie had wrestled with the consequences of that day ever since.

"Has my life been a spiritual roller coaster? Absolutely," he said. "There are times I've been closer to God than others. Fundamentalists call that backsliding. It's a daily process."

Later, dressed in their Sunday best, he and Claudette fell right back into this mountain community's easy, pausing rhythms over covered dishes in the church basement. After the service, it wasn't two minutes before talk among the men on the church's front steps turned to football. The man who gave Rance his first job down in Thomasville was there. George Bobo, father of Georgia's offensive coordinator, remembered being one of those South Georgia kids who once watched Valdosta play from the branch of a magnolia tree outside old Cleveland Field.

Rance, Claudette, and Kennedy then drove the nearly six hours back to Valdosta that night. He missed Thursday's practice—first practice he'd ever missed as a coach.

●

Football season for Claudette was an endless series of notes to self to make sure bills were paid, checkbooks balanced, groceries bought, Kennedy's drop-offs and pick-ups at school accounted for, and, if there was time, her homework checked.

Then there was her day job. Some teachers were grateful for her help. Others felt too harried to view Claudette as anything but one more parachuting outsider telling them how to do jobs they already knew how to do.

She put out one fire after another. It wasn't uncommon for the first words to greet Claudette whenever she arrived at a school to be, "Wish you'd been here half an hour ago. He was *horrible*."

"That's my day," Claudette said. "Everything's the end of the world."

It was exhausting—fulfilling but exhausting.

"It's called being a mom and working full time and doing the best I can," she explained. "It has just about worn me down. I'm playing the lottery. If I win, I told Rance I'd have dinner on the table every night."

Rance's reaction: "He tells me I'm not coachable."

The next evening Rance was on the sidelines inside Colquitt County's sold-out Hog Pen, in the agricultural crossroad of Moultrie, where his father lived. The 'Cats scored 29 of the game's first 36 points, then held on to win.

The victory assured Valdosta of a home game next week in the play-offs' first round. It also humbled, if only temporarily, the Packers' high-profile coach, Rush Propst, whose celebration after Colquitt won in Valdosta last season still stuck in many Wildcat fans' craw. Propst had fled to South Georgia two years earlier following his five-title reign in Alabama.

Propst was widely recognized as one of high school football's top offensive wizards. All you had to do was ask him. Nevertheless, on this cool, crystal night before a raucous crowd out to watch the region's oldest rivalry, Gillespie outwitted the wizard. When the game's last seconds had ticked off, Propst met Gillespie on the giant hog painted across the middle of the field and warmly shook his hand.

"Nice job," he told Valdosta's newest coach.

Later, he'd give Gillespie his highest compliment. "He reminds me," the silvering fifty-one-year-old said, "of me—ten years ago."

Gillespie was just glad to get these last three weeks over with. The funerals hit him hard, and his office had become a nonstop stream of player problems, hassles, and setbacks. During the team's lone off-week, he'd planned to get a slow leak fixed in one his tires so he wouldn't have to stop at a gas station every few days for air, like he had almost all season. He never did get around to it. Rebuilding a program never got easier.

"Sometimes I wonder," he said in a rare moment of frustration, "how can I do this another fifteen years?"

Yet all of that lifted with the victory in Moultrie. He'd blown his stack over two calls, to the endless delight of Valdosta's fans ("That was the second worst call I've ever seen in my life," he said afterward of one, deadpan. "The worst one I ever saw was the one before it"). Then he argued with a cop after the game who wouldn't let Claudette and Kennedy onto the field.

His juices flowed again. Suddenly, he was anxious for the second season.

The playoffs.

20

Pretty Boys and Mohawks

or Back in the ATL

The opening playoff round was a stone-cold gimme. Valdosta hosted Windsor Forest, a Savannah school of about 1,100 kids. That number qualified the Knights for a classification two rungs lower, but they "played up" to cluster with other city schools on the Georgia coast. Their reward: They'd never won a playoff game.

That wasn't about to change this cool Friday night the second week of November, the air cripsed by smoke from a swamp fire in an adjoining county. Windsor Forest sprinted gamely onto the Bazemore-Hyder turf with about sixty players, barely the Valdosta Marchin' Cats' woodwind section.

The Wildcats, meanwhile, dressed out freshmen for the postseason and swelled their number of tin bangers to about 135. Buck Belue, Hyder's first quarterback, remembered how back in the day Valdosta dressed so many kids that the fight song had to be played twice while the team ran onto the field. Now the band played overtime again as the parade of black jerseys that poured out of the tunnel stretched from end zone to end zone.

It was the seniors who banged the tin hardest this night. The 'Cats' second-place finish in the region guaranteed them just this one home game, even if they continued to win. They'd only play here again if a higher seed in their bracket lost. So seniors stepped between the white lines in Death Valley for what they assumed was the last time.

Jay came out before warm-ups. In the dimming autumn light he headed straight to midfield, dropped to his knees, shut his eyes, and then ritually kissed the gold paw on the 50—the same carpeted-over ground where Stan and Roger begat the royal Rome lineage four decades earlier. When he stood up and turned back toward the locker room, tears streaked his face.

"This is the first year playing for the Valdosta Wildcats that I felt like I did when I was a kid, looking up to all those players," he explained. "It reminds me of old-school football again, the kind you see in movies. It feels like Valdosta football. I haven't felt that until this year."

Reggie waited until right before the game, after he'd stepped out of the tunnel. Then he got down on all fours, flipped back his dreads, and pressed his lips to the turf while the rest of the team pooled and bopped to "We Ready" behind him.

Yet for all its back-story emotion and drama, the game was as close to a sure thing as Valdosta had all year. Short of a nuclear-style meltdown, there was no way the Wildcats could lose.

That's what made Gillespie nervous.

"Thing that bothers me about this game," he told his assistants after warm-ups, "is even the ref said, 'Coach, if you're up by 30 in the first half, we're going to go with a running clock.' I never had a ref say that to me *before* a game."

The official's words proved prophetic. Valdosta had jumped ahead 34–0 at the half. *Everybody* made plays. Even Chance McMillan, a big, rarely used white lineman nicknamed "Cheese," had the starters whooping on the sideline in the fourth quarter when he was sent in to block on a Windsor Forest kickoff.

Startled by a short, looping kick, Cheese caught the ball on the fly and lumbered upfield like he was hauling a melon out of Mr. McGregor's garden. Twenty yards later, he plowed into a group of bewildered tacklers rather than wait for them to tackle him. The senior couldn't remember the last time he'd touched a football.

"I was confused," he explained later as his teammates howled. "The kicker hit it right to me. I thought, 'Guess I should run *forward.*' Then I saw a pile. So I put my shoulder down and ran into it.

"All's well that ends well," Cheese smiled, talking about the 'Cats merry 34–13 victory. "It was random, to say the least."

The night's most exhilarated Wildcat, in his wary-alert, super-serious way, was Edrae. Five weeks after he'd toted everything he owned out of his foster house in garbage bags, he made his first start in the secondary, replacing the injured Devontae Foster, the team's leading interceptor.

Edrae played well enough; the game wasn't exactly a tester. How well he played was almost beside the point, though.

The point: He played.

He . . . *belonged.*

"The feeling, standing out there for Valdosta High School, it felt off the chain," Edrae enthused afterward, still breathing hard. "I told Coach, 'I'm not done.'"

●

Next game was a whole other story. The Wildcats had to travel up I-75 again, this time to Powder Springs, a leafy suburb northwest of Atlanta, to meet the slick, sleek McEachern Indians—third-ranked team in the state and early-season vanquishers of Lowndes.

McEachern had won ten straight games following an opening loss and scored more than 50 points in four of them, including 64 against a top-rated rival. Among their Division I prospects: an all-state kicker and a tight end rated second in Georgia behind only Jay.

Reggie was underwhelmed.

"They a bunch of pretty boys and Mohawks," he summed up the 'Cats Cobb County opponent. "We grimy. Down here, we get in the *dirt.*"

Only the way Reggie said it, it came out *git in da duhrt.*

Players had the weekend off, but coaches barely got a night's sleep. Gillespie drove two hours north to Perry the next morning to trade film, then turned right around and started to break it down as soon as he returned.

The rest of the staff came in early Sunday. Teams typically request three game films from an opponent, but this was playoff time in South Georgia, and Gillespie wasn't messing around. He asked McEachern for film of all eleven of its games, each to be meticulously deconstructed by pairs of coaches to chart every offensive and defensive tendency imaginable—down to, it almost seemed, whether or not McEachern wanted fries with that.

"Hol-ee *shit*," Tucker Pruitt whistled when he arrived at the high school that Sunday and learned of Gillespie's haul. "I forgot my sleeping bag.

"You have to be out of your mind to trade eleven films with this guy," he added. "Him being able to break down the percentages for eleven games? You're just asking to lose."

They got right to work, like college kids cramming for finals. Gillespie was in full, glorious nerd mode. Jeans, T-shirt, unshaven face, he programmed Pandora on his computer for '80s rock and ground away. He rarely lifted his head the rest of that Sunday. His desk, otherwise in order, was littered with samples from a football coach's three primary food groups: bottle of Diet Coke, bag of sunflower seeds (dill pickle flavor), and can of Grizzly Wintergreen Long Cut.

"Breakfast of champions," he said.

Power chords cranked all day long out of his computer: Guns N' Roses, AC/DC, Slaughter, Bad English . . .

No T.I. in here. No Rick Ross. No Gucci Mane.

"Boss man is rockin' out to some hard rock in there," Coach Lucas, in the defensive coaches' room next door, said with a smile.

An hour later, Boston's "More than a Feeling," circa 1976, blasted through their door. "Best of all time," Coach Taz proclaimed. Heads bobbed, legs pumped under tables. Taz added, "The whole band is vegan."

"How you going to listen to a band that don't eat meat?" a flabbergasted Lucas asked. "This is America!"

Yet for all the air guitar and head banging they mimed as they watched film, the coaches rewound plays half a dozen times or more to hunt down clues to something they could exploit Friday night.

"That's the first time I've seen that empty set with two tight ends," Taz noted hours into the process. "That's pretty sporty, there."

By the time he'd stared at a half-dozen games, Rodemaker had a pretty good feel for McEachern.

"They look a lot like us," he said. "They find a way to win every game."

Gillespie stepped into the cramped office that the four defensive coaches shared, like a camp cabin, their desks practically on top of each other.

"How good are they?" he asked, tilting his head toward the kids on the screen in royal blue and gold—the tall, speedy ones.

"They got better wide receivers than Colquitt," Rodemaker told him, "but they don't really like to run into people. If it turns into a smash-mouth game, I think we'd win it. But I don't know. They're not the most physical team in the world, but then they don't have to be."

McEachern's field goal unit set up.

"Holy smoke!" Taz exclaimed, rewinding what he just saw. Once again, he watched the McEachern kicker knock home a 54-yard field goal, with room to spare. "They get to the 36-yard line, they got points on the board."

Gillespie nodded, disappeared.

Blowing out of his office now: "Don't Go Away Mad (Just Go Away)."

Taz fingered an air guitar.

"I *knew* it wasn't going to be long before they put some Mötley Crüe on us!"

A grizzled Coach Akins belched, popped a Zantac, and rubbed his rumbling belly. Then he cocked an eye at Taz.

"You smoke much dope when you were in college?"

●

Day slipped into night. Night into late night. Three of the staff's youngest coaches, each unmarried, charted film in the windowless, funk-filled locker room. They'd been in there since early afternoon—long enough to question their lives.

"I need to start coming up with a get-rich-quick scheme." That was Pruitt.

Coach Hen was way ahead of him. He'd thought up a computer program to sell to Microsoft that automatically logged in the down and yardage for coaches doing what they'd been doing all day. Pruitt said he thought a program like that already existed.

"Shit," Henderson said. "With these hours, I got to come up with *something.*"

They kept watching, kept taking notes, kept rewinding a good play over and over because, for all their carping, there was nothing else in the world they liked better then watching a fine, well-executed football play.

"There's a bunch of ways to do this," Pruitt said as the hours dripped by, "but this guy has us at 10-1, so I'm gonna do it this way with a smile on my face."

He smiled. "Next week, *twelve* films."

●

Late Sunday night dissolved into early Monday morning. Gillespie still sat hunched over his computer, the overhead lights bathing him in a washed-out interrogation-room glow. Everybody plugged away.

"I feel like I'm sitting at the lunch counter and everybody's walking by going, *'Nerd!'*" Rodemaker said at one point. "And that nerd up there at McEachern"—straitlaced Indian head coach Kyle Hockman—"he's up there doing the same thing. I'm just trying to outnerd him."

The Wildcat coaches finally finished their charting and started to go over match-ups. The defensive coaches didn't like what they saw. McEachern had a stable of long, fleet wide receivers; Valdosta had a flock of not-so-long, not-so-fleet defensive backs. They started to feel outgunned.

"Can I ask a dumb question?" Lucas finally asked at 12:16 A.M., now Monday, late enough to ask a dumb question. "Can number 1 play corner?"

He meant the kid with 1 on his uniform: Dashay. Lucas proposed that Dashay, because of his speed and quickness and instincts, be inserted at cornerback.

"I'm just saying," Lucas continued as the other coaches blinked back at his audacity, "if our goal is to play the best asses we have on the field . . . I mean, Dashay, like him or not, if our goal is to play fifteen games . . ."

Taz, who'd been desperate for secondary help all season, lifted his head and piped right up. "The answer is: 'Yes he could!'"

If the 10-1 season had a dark side, aside from the distant thunderclaps of school consolidation, it was the Wildcats' pass defense. Those 62 points given up to Brunswick, those 17 second-half points put up by Lowndes, and a general sense that too many yards were gained through the air—it had worn on both players and coaches.

Valdosta's defense did shut out three teams and held another to a lone touchdown while playing one of the stoutest schedules in the state (nine of eleven opponents made the playoffs, and Lincoln would go on to win a title in Florida). Scoring was up everywhere, too; more high schools had adopted the spread offense, part of the trickle-down effect from the pass-happy pro and college games.

Yet a lot of Valdosta fans still ranted about the defense when they called up radio shows, sat inside barbershops, walked in and out of church. The second-guessing drumbeat, along with the killer hours and up-and-down emotions that came with even a successful season, had already strained at least two coaches' marriages.

"It's a proud, proud culture here," said Taz, an undersized All-American defensive back on three national championship teams at Georgia Southern. "Folks here have a hard time accepting that times do and have changed. You're not comparing apples to apples anymore, but they don't want to hear that. They just say, 'Yeah, Coach, I hear ya. Now win a championship.'

"I heard multiple times before I took this job, 'You gotta be nuts to coach at Valdosta.' If you don't win a championship, you better bump your retirement up to the highest three years you can, because they'll fire you in three years."

He shrugged. "But, hey, if it wasn't broken we wouldn't be here."

So after Lucas's suggestion, Taz shot out of his chair and headed straight into Gillespie's office. He then announced to the stubble-faced boss man what they'd just come up with: Dashay at corner.

Gillespie stared back at Taz like his head was on fire.

"*Sheee-it*," he finally drawled, "I think y'all are *crazy*."

Taz blew out all the air he had and returned to where he came from. The three coaches looked up as he walked in.

Taz shook his head no. "He said, 'We'd be pissing down our leg with 1 back there.'"

More minutes ticked by. Lucas had another idea.

"What about 11 at defensive end?"

He meant Jay Rome.

Now it was Taz's turn to stare at somebody like his head was in flames.

"*You* go in there with that," he said, moving his eyes toward Gillespie's office. "I'm not touching it."

Lucas swung back around in his chair and let it go.

Gillespie stuck his head in the doorway fifteen minutes later. "You got 'em all shut out yet?" he asked, grinning. "You all get 'em stopped or don't go home."

Then he left: 12:35 A.M.

Rodemaker locked his own door almost an hour later.

❦

Players shambled toward the practice field that Monday afternoon while the rest of the school emptied out. With the biggest game of their lives five days away, the Wildcats remained a relaxed, unflappable, if still slightly scattered bunch.

James Eunice, an air force baby home-schooled until ninth grade and owner of the team's highest GPA, walked out with Dashay, whose own grades were slipping and already threatening his graduation. This deep into the season, even conversations between polar opposites like these—blond God-squad yell leader and tatted street-cool icon—were loose and easy and anything-goes.

"I had a dream about you the other night," Eunice told Dashay as their cleats clacked down the sidewalk.

Dashay shot him a crooked look.

"I had a big bag of weed on me and I was scared to death," Eunice went on in his endearingly earnest way. "So I called you. And I sold it to you . . . That's all I remember."

Dashay didn't say a word. Just lowered his head and let out a deep, booming belly laugh.

"Honest!" Eunice insisted as Dashay jogged off ahead.

When they arrived at the field, a handful of players were circled around a stray frog looking for cover on the sideline's autumn-brown grass. Most of them looked at it quizzically, like they were afraid to touch it, until Tyler Yelito, the lanky yellow-haired punter, picked it up, examined it for a minute, then carefully tossed it out of harm's way.

Now Dashay stared at him.

"Yelito, you . . . you . . . *white.*"

Bee then assumed a hand-on-hip pose and stared at Dashay.

"Dashay, you darker than a shadow," he said loud enough to be heard halfway down the field, sounding like Brer Rabbit dressing down Brer Wolf. "Look at Dashay, he look like a burnt pickle! Look at him through his helmet—his face look just like his face mask. You can't see nothin'!"

On they went, back and forth, riffing on players' skin tones as if they were conjugating verbs.

Fullback Jarvis Roberts, a junior whose uncle was a Hyder 'Cat, tapped his two taped hands together. He'd played with one broken thumb for weeks. Now he'd broken the other one.

"I thought a woman was the bravest person in the world. They have to push out a baby," he said. Then he raised his two blunt mitts and rapped them together one more time. "But playing football with two broken thumbs—that makes me the bravest person."

Ryan and Alex, meanwhile, stood talking together in the end zone, waiting to start their drills. A couple of girls from school were jogging in shorts around the track. Both players' heads swiveled to follow their progress.

"My dad told me the best way to get girls," Alex said when the joggers finally made their way to the far end of the field, "is either be the quarterback or score a lot of touchdowns."

Ryan let that marinate a minute. Then he gave one of his quick shrugs before he unloosed a Ryan-ism.

"My dad said the best way to get girls," he let out slowly, "is look good."

Nobody could boil it down, whatever *it* was, like Ryan. Alex was learning that. Four months earlier he wouldn't have even been standing here with Ryan. In his fantastical quest to become the starting quarterback for the Valdosta High Wildcats, and then master of everything that lay beyond, he saw Ryan only narrowly, as simply competition, as somebody who stood in his way to getting what he wanted and who needed to be shoved aside. Ryan was the enemy.

"I was not going to be friends with him and let him take it from me," Alex recalled now. "It was that way the whole time we were competing. There was never a friendship."

Ryan, for his part, couldn't have cared less. He'd ask Alex to hang out and Alex would blow him off in his jittery, gotta-work way. Ryan would just shrug, of course, and go about his own business. That 'tude didn't endear Alex to the rest of the team, who'd embraced Ryan as their one-of-them leader.

Alex saw the foolishness of that now.

"It was just part of me being fifteen years old," he said. "I messed up. I play it back all the time. My drive was my family. I did not want to disappoint my dad and mom. I wanted to make sure my family didn't move over here, spend this money, go through all this exhaustion, for nothing. I got too serious about it and quit having fun."

Eventually, Alex came to see what others saw in Ryan—"a cool cat, man." Like many in town who'd been reluctant to accept the inexperienced, slow-footed senior as point man for this storied program's revival, Alex was won over by Ryan's perseverance, his fearlessness, his dogged screw-you-ness in the face of all those fans who'd hooted for his head.

Alex recalled how Gillespie told him to warm up with three minutes left in the first half of the season's second game, after Ryan threw yet another interception. Alex remained on the sideline only because the hapless Hardaway Hawks managed to run out the clock before he got a chance to go in. At halftime, Gillespie was ready to hand Alex the ball as they left the locker room, then decided at the last minute to give Ryan one more shot.

"Sure enough," Alex said, "Ryan went in and did right."

The turning point for Alex—the moment when he finally understood what Gillespie meant when he said Ryan "does a lot of things you can't put your finger on"—came during the Wildcats' comeback against that hostile, talented crew at MLK. At one point, Ryan was knocked nearly cold after tossing a touchdown pass. His linemen ran back to help him, lifted him up, and steered him in the right direction when Gillespie ordered the offense to go for 2. Then he got the 2.

"To come back and win that game, that takes balls, man," Alex said admiringly. "To go back out there every single down, not give up on the guys, keep saying we're going to win this game—not just anybody can do that. He's always calm no matter the situation. He could throw six interceptions and it wouldn't faze him.

"I was different, and that's probably what separated us," Alex added.

His practiced, camera-ready wall of self-confidence had finally lowered enough for him to see his own deficits. "A lot of it was about me being so serious about it, not being able to flush the previous play down, to dwell on it and think too much instead of just reacting."

Alex ran a hand through his scalp. "Think I got a couple gray hairs in there."

Then his dark features brightened before he padded off to throw some passes. He chuckled as he repeated Ryan's latest words of wisdom.

"Best way to get girls is look good . . ."

The week now had its own momentum. There was a different charge in the air.

E-mails from coaches at colleges around the Southeast—Auburn, Florida, Tennessee, Georgia—popped up on Gillespie's computer screen to congratulate Rance and his staff on their playoff run. Each one sounded like the other, as if copied from the same "Congratulations, Coach!" template (one, from Nebraska, did include a convincingly personal touch). Gillespie knew what all the warm wishes were really about: The recruiting of Jay and Malcolm never stopped.

"I imagine there'll be a lot of people through here this week," Gillespie said of the recruiters who were after his two stars, as well as the coaches from schools a rung or two lower interested in Freak, Jarquez, Justin, Reggie, and, lately, even Ryan. "If we get to the next week, there'll be a *ton* of people through here."

Gillespie was a little baffled that there wasn't more interest in Swoll, who he said might be his favorite player he ever coached. Swoll's tender ankle had slowed him for a portion of the season, and his size and speed didn't meet a lot of recruiter's preset specs. Yet he'd had a monster year anyway, was strong as an ox, and got every tough yard on every tough play he was asked to make.

He'd become the beating heart of the Wildcats.

Gillespie knew the cruel rule of thumb followed by recruiters who'd been burned by too many indomitable but undersized prospects.

Their maxim: Never recruit heart.

Still, Gillespie believed that Swoll could find a home at the next level and that the playoffs would help showcase him. Friday night was sure to showcase everybody. A reborn Valdosta traveling north of the Gnat Line to play a suburban Atlanta powerhouse that looked locked and loaded to win its first title—it was the most talked-about game in the state.

Stan sought out Dashay during a practice.

"This is going to be the greatest stage of your career," Stan told him. "You have the ability to turn some heads. There'll be more recruiters at this game than there's been around here all year.

"Now don't get into trouble or anything," Stan added as Dashay looked off into some middle distance out by the pines. "Don't do anything that'll interfere with this opportunity."

Dashay seemed to have dropped off the recruiting grid. His suspension last year, the shootout at his house, his own ankle problems—none of it helped. Deep down, he'd admit later, he wanted to quit. He'd wanted to quit all year. He was tired of everybody talking at him, tired of coaches yelling at him, tired of being the next Michael Vick. He just wanted to be left alone.

Letters piled up daily in his mail slot outside Tracy's office, but when a teammate grabbed a fistful after one practice and tried to hand him the letters—the top envelope was stamped URGENT: *Auburn University*—Dashay waved him off and walked away.

"Most letters I just throw in the trash," Dashay explained. "They're just a letter. Usually they're telling you they're watching you. If you want me, you can come see me."

On a bright, crisp Saturday morning just weeks earlier, a twenty-five-year-old black man who said he was a University of Texas alum had stopped Gillespie in the Boys and Girls Club parking lot as he, Claudette, and Kennedy were leaving one youth football game and heading off to watch another. The guy from Texas, who'd moved recently to Valdosta, where his brother was stationed at Moody, stuck out his hand and introduced himself. He then told Gillespie that Longhorns head coach Mack Brown wanted to talk with two of his players, Jay Rome and Dashay March.

The brief, unfancy scene in that everyday setting seemed to affirm Valdosta's continued hold on the football world's imagination: a courier for one of America's most celebrated football factories, a thousand miles west, standing with the Wildcats coach in a paved parking lot crowded with pickups for a game between eight- and nine-year-olds.

This was still one of those places that determined who the rest of the country watched on Saturdays and Sundays. Valdosta remained a spot where men still came to seek a particular kind of athlete—one developed in this dirt, in this heat, in this relative isolation, and who'd been coached or raised or simply encouraged enough to play a kind of football, as *Sports Illustrated* put it decades earlier, "like nowhere else in Georgia—or maybe the rest of the known world."

Yet Gillespie's response to the encounter was just as telling. It affirmed the double-edged nature of a hothouse like this: Football could take a kid only so far. It was easy for an eighteen-year-old to forget that, with all the hands reaching out for him during the Cat Walk and the boosters grilling him up sausages after practices and the girls Googling his name.

It was easy to luxuriate in all that at the expense of the hard, off-the-field stuff that needed to get done if a kid was to play beyond Valdosta High. For too many, Wildcat football was not just an end in itself but *the end*. "See that one," Carlton Harrell, a Valdosta cop and father of a Wildcat, said one weekday afternoon, pointing out of his squad car window at a young black man stepping across a street on the town's East Side with a bottle wrapped in a paper bag. "Used to be a Wildcat. Good one, too."

In Dashay's case, if his grades didn't improve, he wouldn't get through the door of anything but a junior college—and he'd only get in there if he stuck around long enough to graduate.

"Dashay get that from me," his mother La La conceded. "I wanted to do what I wanted to do and that was the end of it."

So now, standing in the Boys and Girls Club parking lot, Gillespie said the hard thing to the guy from Texas the same way he always said the hard thing: straight up, no chaser.

"That'd be fine," he said over the sound of pickups backing out and pulling in, "but Dashay's not going to qualify."

Later, back in his office, he'd add, "With Dashay, you hold your breath and say, 'If I can get that kid through high school, what an accomplishment.' And then you say, 'If I can get him into a junior college, that would be a major accomplishment.'"

That Saturday in the parking lot, while kids strapped in oversized helmets ran like cool breezes across the grass nearby, with their mamas and daddies shouting at them to keep going, keep moving, keep trying, keep hitting ("Michael, use your hands! Take him down like you do your sister!"), Gillespie's words to the guy from Texas dropped out of the morning air like cold, sharp stones.

The guy from Texas nodded. Walked off, got in his car.

Gillespie got into his. Headed off to another kids' game.

◆

Everything about McEachern High was strikingly, unnervingly impressive.

Flush with an endowment reportedly in the tens of millions of dollars from old Georgia insurance money, the public school's rolling campus looked like a place just itching to spend its dough. Right now the school was dropping $12 million on a 115,000-foot, glass-encased fitness center for faculty and students. Expected to be ready by the next season, it already rose outside the corner of one end zone like an unfinished Taj Mahal of Wellness.

The boys' weight room alone covered 8,000 square feet—almost more than Valdosta's own weight room, locker room, and coaches' offices combined. The women's faculty lockers were built from rich dark mahogany.

The fitness center was just part of a wider $25 million improvement package. A press box that included a pair of VIP suites reached all the way up to Mount Olympus, or at least that's how the thing looked from the 12,500-seat stadium floor. From up there, Atlanta's skyline winked twenty miles away.

The campus looked and felt like a small Southern college. It held thirteen separate academic buildings, as well as men's and women's field houses, an in-house TV station, and a nature trail with a cottage and restored pond. It served 3,500 students until four years ago, when a new high school was built up the road to accommodate Cobb County's boom. The student population then dropped to about 2,500, though the demographics flipped, from majority white to majority minority. But little else changed. The school still spent money with both hands, graduated more than 80 percent of its kids, and won a whole lot of football games.

The place, in short, was gorgeous. So, too, were its players, who now high-stepped out into the North Georgia chill and onto their turf. A bare-chested, two-story-tall Indian with six-pack abs hailed them with a perpetually raised hand from just outside one end zone.

"First time I've looked at another team and been intimidated," confessed senior cheerleader Kathryn Cody as the McEachern players lined up to stretch. She and the other Wildcat girls were bundled against the cold in black sweatpants and hoodies. The Indians sported burnished gold helmets, glossy gold pants, and deep blue jerseys.

Kathryn added, "They look all big and pretty and shiny."

Yet pretty as they were, nearly every one of those gold-helmeted heads turned when the 'Cats took the field. They stared at the 135-player army as it formed a circle that looped from sideline to sideline and from the back of one end zone to out beyond the 40. The head-bobbing 'Cats then began to pound their thigh pads and clap their hands in a singular chant that announced *Boys, we're here.*

"Aren't you glad to be a Wildcat!" Coach Taz called out from the middle of the ring.

"Hell, *yeah!*" Malcolm called back, and moments later the stadium echoed with the players' deep, loud thumps, like they were waking the ghosts of those Wildcats past who'd formed the same circle back in the '90s and wasted McEachern four straight games—the last time for state, in 1998.

Boomph! Boomph! Boomph boomph boomph boomph!

Again, these crazy 'Cats were loose. When someone informed Ryan that the game was being televised, he responded with a straight face that it might help his recruiting chances. "About time for me to go from a one-star to a two-star," he said of his rating.

"That's the personality of this team," observed Coach Al, wearing his own championship bling from that last title game against McEachern. "When the lights come on, they seem to rise to the occasion."

Back inside the locker room following their pregame ritual, players put the finishing touches on their equipment, their eye black, their focus. Jarvis Roberts inspected the tape wrapped mummylike around his two busted hands.

"Big-time players make big plays in big games!" Reggie shouted out.

Meanwhile, back in the makeshift coaches' room, Gillespie paced.

This was the only time he got nervous, after warm-ups and before he addressed the team. Once he hit the sideline he'd be sky high, lost in his own world of managing chaos and thrilling to the competition. Right now there was nothing to do but wait. It ate him up.

"It never changes," he said to the other coaches, deep in their own thoughts but always alert to his. "How many times can you do this to your body? 'Cause it *can't* be good for you. Each Friday night probably takes six months off my life."

He checked his texts: Claudette and Kennedy got caught in a traffic pileup outside Atlanta and still hadn't arrived. He'd miss Kennedy's pregame kiss. So he headed into the locker room.

Gillespie told his players straight off that tonight they had to play physical, on both offense and defense. That's what he saw after a week of unreeling those eleven game films. He had kids who could out-tough the other team's kids, no matter how talented those other kids might be or how many shiny resources they might have. He had kids willing to *git in da duhrt.*

"Men, I can't promise you what's going to happen tonight," he then said to the sweaty sea of game faces that knelt in front him. "But I can promise you this: *Somebody's gonna get their ass hit!*"

The 'Cats roared and rose and massed around the door.

"Turn the lights on!" Jay shouted, and the whole bunch of them streamed out. After they hit the field, Jay's eight-year-old brother, Justin, a Wildcat ball boy, hugged his big brother and wished him luck. Jay leaned down to kiss the Rome dynasty's next prince-in-waiting on top of his head.

The sky looked brittle-black, the lights bright as day. The Valdosta side was full. It looked like the whole town was there, swaddled in big coats and gloves and scarves. The night's forecast: 37 degrees.

Nub sat squished among them near the 50, about halfway up, warm and cozy in his insulated pants and camo jacket and cap with ear flaps—a rogue duck hunter sitting in the middle of Atlanta's 'burbs.

●

Then . . .

The 'Cats did what they do, fell behind 14–0 before the first quarter ended, before Claudette and Kennedy even made it inside the stadium.

"We couldn't find a parking place anywhere, so I parked the car right under that Indian man," Claudette said, rushing in, nodding at the statue, her nose pinked from the cold. "Some man told me I couldn't park there. I told him I wasn't walking all the way from Timbuktu to get here."

Valdosta got a little more creative this time in the way it dug its own hole. The Wildcats actually thought they'd scored first, on their opening possession. Swoll started the game with a brilliant 40-yard sprint, then took the ball again on a fourth and goal at the 1 and disappeared into a massive pile. When officials finally excavated him, they spotted the ball just inches short of the goal line.

The Wildcat sideline went berserk.

"That call was so bad," Jay said as he came off the field. "I pushed him into the end zone *myself*."

Rotating two quarterbacks, the richly endowed Indians then drove the entire length of the field, cleaning it up with a 10-yard touchdown pass. They scored again with less than a minute left in the quarter. The other quarterback dropped a 25-yarder into the hands of yet another of McEachern's stable of beautiful tall drinks of water.

Yet if the Wildcats appeared unflappable after getting themselves in this same kind of mess against Lincoln and Brunswick and MLK, this time they looked . . . *unconscious*.

Helmet off, Swoll leaned back on a bench against the visitors' stands and chatted with some wide-eyed Valdosta kids. When a coach barked for the offense to get back on the field following McEachern's second score, Swoll first told the kids that he enjoyed talking with them but that he had to go. He then slipped on his helmet and ambled off, as if a maître d' had just signaled him that his table for one was now ready.

Ryan went to work. Looking every bit like a two-star instead of a one-star, he dropped back and waited until he found his five-star receiver slanting across the middle. Malcolm slowed for a second so he wouldn't outrun the pass—always a hazard for him—then turned it back on and raced untouched for 47 yards, until he ran out of room at the 7. Ryan hit him again from there for the touchdown.

Gillespie's biggest pregame call, sticking Malcolm back on defense, looked like genius on McEachern's very next possession.

A yellow helmet popped the football loose from an unwary Indian running back, who then juggled it almost comically while he continued to dance up the middle. Malcolm had rushed up from the secondary the moment he saw the run, pushed by the voice in the back of his head that he said this season spoke to him louder and more directly than ever.

Others might call the voice he heard instinct. Malcolm called it "a gift."

"I want to say it's God telling me that something's going to happen," he once tried to explain, "but it's *something* telling me. I don't know *what's* going to happen. I just know something's telling me it's *fixing* to happen."

Then it happened. The ball flew up, and the game's action suddenly did for Malcolm what it always did for him in these split-second situations: It came virtually to a halt. The football just hung there, in midair, almost still, like a ripe, low-hanging peach. The narrator in Malcolm's head then said, "Grab it." So he grabbed it. Then the voice shouted, "Go! Go!" So he freaking went.

All this happened in real time, of course, so before Malcolm knew it, one of those speedy McEachern receivers had reversed field and run him down and was trying to take him to the turf. Poor kid didn't know what he was dealing with. "Stick your arm out!" the voice in Malcolm's head ordered now, so Malcolm stiff-armed the kid in the face with his left hand and kept on moving.

By this time, Reggie was running right beside him, his dreads flying, trying to block, trying not to get a penalty, trying like hell to keep up. Reggie had his own chorus of voices going in his head: dead cousin, dead aunt . . .

Lord, with all the voices out there, ref could've flagged the 'Cats for too many men on the field.

Malcolm, meanwhile, just kept lifting his feet, obeying his first law of carrying the football: "Just because someone grabs you don't mean you have to fall."

He never did go down. Malcolm carried that frustrated, outmanned McEachern receiver for more than 30 yards, pirouetting with him somewhere around the 20, yet staying upright until finally he was wrestled out of bounds at the 3. Swoll poked it in from there.

With less than four minutes gone in the second quarter, the game now was tied, 14–14.

"We never quit!" Jay yelled as he jogged to the sideline after Zach's extra point, channeling yet another Valdosta voice from the beyond. He yanked off his helmet; steam spiraled from his head. *"Never, never, never, never, never, never quit!"*

They didn't quit. The defense forced a punt, and the 'Cats charged back down the field. On second and short from the Indian 21, Ryan faked a handoff to Dashay, stepped back, and unloaded a high spiral down the middle. Tyran Watkins stood on the goal line, back to the end zone, defender draped around him, and reached both hands as high as he could.

Tyran had a different voice rattling around in his head: Mr. Stan's.

"You gotta pull that shit down!" he remembered Stan counseling him in the locker room during the Brunswick game. "You can't hold it up there! Picture yourself making great plays!"

Tyran grabbed the ball with his fingertips—and pulled it down. He tumbled into the end zone, a royal blue jersey still on top of him, both of them wrestling on the turf. An official stared for a second as they rolled over, waiting to see who'd come out with the ball.

Tyran did.

21–14.

Ryan trotted to the sideline, plopped down on the bench, and toweled his head.

Still deadpan, he asked, "How we look out there?"

●

Valdosta fans huddled under the stands at the half, stamping their feet and clapping their gloved hands to keep warm.

Nub stood just beyond them, on the other side of the gate, burning one.

"It oughtta be 28–7," he muttered between drags on his smoke. "But things are going great around the state."

Looking ahead was a habit Valdosta fans couldn't break. In the county just east of here, playing in Valdosta's bracket, unbeaten and second-ranked North Gwinnett was losing 10–0 in the first half to Grayson, a 3-loss team also from Gwinnett County. If North Gwinnett rallied and the Wildcats won, Valdosta would have to bus all the way back up to play there next week. If Grayson held on and the 'Cats kept their own lead, next week's quarterfinals, the day after Thanksgiving, would be at Bazemore-Hyder. The road to the Georgia Dome was starting to look straighter.

More good news: Lowndes was winning. Valdosta fans were actually pulling for the hated "Low Ends." The way the brackets were set, if the Wildcats and Vikings both won the rest of the way, the two teams would meet one more time: in the finals, in Atlanta, for the state championship of South Georgia.

Inside the Wildcats' locker room, however, nobody was thinking beyond the second half.

"We gotta find more points," Gillespie told his players. "You did a good job not hanging your heads. Like I've told you before, you're the best team in the state. So let's put up some more points."

Some of the offensive players talked among themselves about McEachern's defensive line being "soft." On the other hand, they'd also seen how explosive the Indians were on the other side of the ball. Dudes could *move*. The 'Cats just needed to focus on what Gillespie said before the game.

"Ain't *nobody* going to out-tough us," guard Yontell Morrison declared as a trainer taped together two of his bent fingers. "They ain't witnessed hell like we have at camp."

Then Jay's voice boomed across the room.

"Twenty-four more minutes of hell, baby," he called out. "Twenty-four more minutes of hell!"

He threw on his helmet, headed out the door.

"Let's *snatch* us some!"

Valdosta got the ball first and went right at that sissy defensive line. Swoll scooted for 20 yards. Dashay picked up a quick 5.

Then Ryan backslid and heaved an interception. It didn't take McEachern long to make the 'Cats pay. The Indians' quarterback searched for Malcolm, spotted him, then went the other way, tossing a high strike on a fade route to his tallest receiver. Reggie leaped as high as he could and still came up a foot short.

Game tied: 21–21.

Then Swoll took control. He darted behind Jay and the rest of the offensive line, who were just wiping defenders out. Valdosta killed off nearly all eight minutes left in the third quarter with a fourteen-play, 80-yard march. Running backs humped the ball eleven times, including the drive's last play: Swoll dove up the Indian line's gut from the 3 and came out the other side untouched, airborne like a missile, landing almost 5 yards deep in the end zone.

The Marching 'Cats paid their homage to Pastor Troy. Players swayed on the sideline. Jarvis Roberts, the hard-as-nails, tough-as-a-boot fullback who'd taken out a defensive end on Swoll's touchdown, found a seat on the bench. Sweating, gulping air, steam curling from his head like it was being boiled, he rested his two broken hands on his knees.

McEachern had too many weapons to let it end like that. So, first play of the fourth quarter, they struck: An Indian receiver pulled in a short screen and jitterbugged 33 yards for McEachern's fourth touchdown. Behind the Indian bench, their fans squealed and sang and danced, creating a steep wall of sound that ran all the way up to those sky-scraping VIP suites.

Tied again, 28–28.

As Ryan loped back out onto the field, his family sat bunched together in the middle of the stands, near Nub. They shivered from the cold and the tension. His older brother's leg jiggled up and down. "Hasn't stopped moving since we been here," he explained, staring at it, like it wasn't exactly his. "These games drive you crazy."

Stan had already bolted the stadium to sit out the rest of the game in his car. He couldn't take it anymore.

Now, having just thrown the biggest interception of his life, cool cat Ryan stuck his hands back under center—both sides of the stadium in full roar, his barked signals floating out of his mouth and above his linemen's rumps like smoke rings—and promptly led Valdosta on a spotless twelve-play, 71-yard drive.

Ryan's parents stood up through most of it. His dad tugged at his ball cap; his mother waved a pom-pom. The drive stalled inside the 10. "He had Jay open in the back of the end zone!" somebody yelled behind them when Ryan misfired. His parents shot each other knowing looks, then turned their attention back to the field. They'd heard worse.

The situation now: fourth and goal at the 11.

Out trotted Zach. Gillespie knew all about those three missed field goals in the 'Cats' big loss last season. He also knew Zach had kicked with a bad back. This year he'd been almost perfect. In a pressure situation like this, the kid's dudeness was an asset; he had *no* voices in his head, unless maybe you counted some random riff from Widespread Panic.

Zach didn't sweat it. Knocked the ball plumb straight from 28 yards out and put Valdosta back up by 3. Clock showed 6:44 left.

LaVerne phoned Stan in his car and told him Valdosta just went ahead, that it was safe to come back in. Stan told her 3 points wasn't enough. He wasn't budging.

It looked like Stan was right. The Indians got the ball again and rolled up near midfield. They needed less than 20 yards to get in range for their diva kicker. Nick St. Germain had already transferred from two other high schools before arriving at McEachern. He'd trashed his last team in the local paper, saying their players were jealous of him and calling their field a "pigpen."

McEachern's state-of-the-art facilities better suited his taste. In a game against one rival he kicked two field goals over 50 yards. He boomed touchbacks so regularly that his coach admitted he hardly ever watched kickoffs anymore. St. Germain's personal Web site detailed his every accomplishment.

The Valdosta coaches' jaws had dropped when they watched him kick before the game.

"Kid's going to be making a couple million dollars in a few years," Taz said as he whistled after one boot from beyond the 50.

Yet on a fourth and 7 from their own 45, with less than four minutes left and three time-outs, McEachern chose to punt. They banked on their defense snuffing Valdosta—or maybe on Ryan backsliding again—and getting one last shot. The game would come down to what Gillespie said it would come down to: which team could out-tough the other.

So Valdosta went to Swoll, handing him the football seven straight times. Malcolm limped off at one point, the trainer groping his ankle on the sideline, but everybody's eyes stayed fixed on the field.

Facing third down and inches with a little more than a minute left,

Ryan again planted the ball in Swoll's belly. The former Wildcat ball boy, who once went to the house of a dude named Charles and paid him ninety dollars to tattoo SWOLL clear across his back, had waited his whole life to play in a game like this and hold a football in exactly this kind of situation. So Phillip "Swoll" Moore—too small, too slow, too banged up—sliced right through the prettiest boys in Georgia and iced the game.

He'd heard a voice in his head all night, too.

His own.

"I've seen a whole lot of seniors walk out after their last game not getting past the second round," he said afterward. "Every time I step on the field and tote the ball, that's what I think about."

The 'Cats swarmed the field, danced around, broke into one of their chants.

"Turn me up a little—"

"Higher!"

"Just a little—"

"Higher!"

Suddenly, a Gatorade bottle flew out of the end zone bleachers. Then some McEachern kids started their own chant when they spotted Big Terry: *"Prehhh-cious! Prehhh-cious!"* It was hard to know in all the commotion if any of the Wildcats caught or understood the reference to the movie *Precious*, whose title character was an obese, illiterate black girl. Dashay looked ready to go just on principle. A couple of coaches jumped in and herded the players away. No harm, no foul.

Fans who'd road-tripped from Valdosta now milled around the field, too. Stan lurched from out beneath the stands and headed straight for Jay. LaVerne shook her head behind him. "I told him," she said, "'You are such a *wimp*.'"

David Waller nodded his graying wise man's head as he clasped Gillespie's hand. He'd seen too many epic Wildcat victories over the last six decades to get too worked up by a second-round win, but he was clearly pleased. Like a lot of folks on the field, he sensed something he hadn't sensed in a while.

"Every game I feel better," he said, light from the stadium's tall towers bouncing off his bifocals. "I think luck's with us. I think the good Lord's with us."

Gillespie gathered his players for their prayer. The moment they finished, someone yelled, "We're goin' back to the *house!*" Word had already spread that North Gwinnett lost. The Lowndes game was over, too: Vikings won. For that matter, so did Colquitt County. Three of the eight remaining playoff teams were from the same little region in South Georgia.

The SEC of high school football was back.

"You never quit," Gillespie shouted out to these Wildcats, who now looked worthy of that old 'Cat's words, "and that says a lot about who you are."

He glanced over at where that earlier yell came from.

"And you're right," he said, "we *are* going back to our house!"

Everybody on the field cheered and hugged together, a town within the town. Little kids broke into their own football games, as if they'd annexed the place following the 'Cats' fifth thumping of McEachern in the last twenty years and declared it a part of Bazemore-Hyder's turf. Valdosta kids just kind of intuited that stuff.

"Hey! Hey!" Gillespie shouted again as his players trailed off to hoot and holler a little longer before they boarded the buses. School was out all next week. "Monday morning! Practice 9:00 A.M.! You be there at eight!"

Kennedy finally ran up and gave Rance her hug. So did Claudette. The two of them were already plotting Thanksgiving. They knew this routine cold.

"While Rance is at practice, we'll lay around in pajamas, watch the Macy's Day Parade, and then Kennedy will be so glad when her daddy comes home and smells like football," Claudette said.

She looked across the field. It was still covered with kids and parents and grandparents—white and black, blue-collar and white-collar, Republican and Democrat. It was getting toward midnight, and they all had a five-hour drive home; a bunch of them would run into each other in a little while at a Waffle House south of here off I-75. It was like they had some Waffle House homing device sewn in their heads.

Here they still stood, on the coldest night of the season, looking like they didn't want to be anywhere else in the world—except, of course, inside their own gorgeous, ghost-filled stadium.

Now they'd be back there next week. They'd finally get to gather again at Bazemore-Hyder in late November.

Claudette just smiled.

"That stinking smell," she said again of the whiff of football practice her husband would carry home with him Thursday—the stink, she knew, of a successful season. "It's the greatest smell on Thanksgiving."

21

Shooting Deer, Giving Thanks, Waging War, Moving On

or The 229 Forever

A white pickup pulled behind the practice field bleachers Thanksgiving morning, the driver in camo eager to show off what he had. Dead as a doornail in the back of his truck: an eleven-point buck.

A nearly forgotten Valdosta tradition.

"It's Thanksgiving," said Trevor Shaw, a Hyder 'Cat in the '80s who shot the deer in Hahira, not far north. "You have deer hunting and you have practicing football."

The two dozen folks there to watch the Wildcat practice bunched around Shaw's truck bed and nodded approvingly.

"Those are some pretty feet," Matt Stephenson cooed over the carcass.

Shaw turned to look out onto the field. Footballs sailed through a lingering fog. The water tower beside the school was hardly visible.

"How they lookin'?" Shaw asked.

"Good, good."

He'd take their word for it. He climbed back in his truck, leaving his daughter behind to watch the rest of practice with her girlfriends, who were there with their own daddies.

"I'm gonna run off before it hardens up," Shaw said, meaning the deer, then spun on out of the lot.

Dead deer and football: Winnersville, baby!

It had been a smooth if largely uninspired week of practice. With school out and players on the field by 8:30 A.M., the usual buzz was missing.

Nobody was in the halls to "My *dawg!*" the players or talk up the next game. 'Cats left practice around noon and had the whole day left to fill. They slept, played video games, did chores, hung out, caught up with girlfriends. A few studied. "Hey IB, you literally, no joke, have ruined my life," James Eunice posted, trying to keep up during the off-week with his seven college-prep classes. Others ran off to jobs. Some smoked a little dope.

Practice also lost a bit of pizzazz without Malcolm. The injury he limped off with at the end of the McEachern game turned out to be a high ankle sprain. The Wildcats trainer said he'd be good to go by Friday, but Malcolm didn't practice, on offense or defense.

Fresh off the season's most impressive win, Gillespie felt good about how far his team had come since spring. Back then he'd looked out across the practice field as the Wildcats flew around and allowed, "We have a lot of athletes but not a lot of football players. There's a difference."

Now he saw football players. These kids could hold their heads up around town again. There were things that troubled him, though. Some players still needed to be reminded too often to pick up their pace, put on their helmets, lift harder in the weight room.

"They're not mentally ready for a fifteen-game season," Gillespie said. "You just kind of keep waiting for the ax to fall. It's the nature of the beast."

Coaches never know whether their perpetual doomsday worrying is for nothing or if the chronic paranoia is justified. One of Gillespie's Peach County teams had an inexperienced, undersized offensive line that he expected all season to crack. It never did; in fact, it got better, and the team ran the table all the way to a title.

"Here, it's the mental transition," he said, explaining his concerns. "The cultural transition. I worry about discipline, work habits."

Gillespie knew that the team that finished on top at the end of the playoffs didn't just play on Fridays. It worked with focus and brio all week. With this bunch, he worried that some of the same things that got them this far might keep them from going farther.

"Teams like this drive me crazy," he said. "There's a calmness to them. I don't know if it's confidence—it's almost like they just don't know better. Football kids are like that. They know how to play the game. But there's more to it. Good as we are on Friday nights, we could be better. We're not machinelike yet."

Gillespie worried how that would play against this Friday's opponent, who he knew would be unlike any this Valdosta team had faced.

Grayson High had opened only ten years earlier to sop up the overflow from other schools bursting at the seams in sprawling Gwinnett County, where between 1996 and 2005 teams had won as many titles in the state's highest classification as had teams from South Georgia. One county coach even boasted that "the road to the state championship now runs through Gwinnett."

Mickey Conn, a walk-on for Alabama's 1992 national title team, grew up in Gwinnett and was the team's first and only coach. When he started the football program, the school had fewer than 1,500 students and no stadium, no field house, no concession stand, and no weight room. Players shared lockers with gym classes.

Now the school had almost 3,000 kids, its own stadium, its own Touchdown Club, and its own youth football pipeline. Grayson ran the Wing-T like clockwork—except for the occasional you-never-know-when long-bomb surprise. The Rams had gone unbeaten the two previous regular seasons and made it at least as deep as the Elite Eight in the playoffs three straight years. Their three losses this season were all to quality opponents. Grayson was big and rough, and they got at it. They'd become machinelike.

"I respect the way they play," Gillespie said. "Football at its core is a physical game. It's a tough game made for tough people. And people who try to compromise that, it catches up to them sooner or later.

"The most exciting thing this year is we've jump-started the program. I want them to take pride in that, but we're not there yet. When it's time to get two yards, or to stop the other team from getting this much"—he held two fingers inches apart—"I want them to be able to feel like we're the baddest [team] on the block and we're going to get it.

"We have the ability to be there," he repeated, "but we're not there yet."

Gillespie grabbed his whistle and headed out to the practice field. It was his first Thanksgiving practice in Valdosta, and Valdosta's first in eight years. He loved everything about it. He ate his first fried turkey during a Thanksgiving week at Peach; a guy from the local coroner's office showed up behind the bus barn with an embalming needle and injected birds with a concoction of lemon juice and hot sauce. He hadn't tasted a better fried turkey since, though he'd eat one again this afternoon with Claudette and Kennedy over at the Loudermilks' house—sans embalming needle.

Right now he had to go give hell to a bunch of hungry teenagers.

"I'm trying to cut through their collective desire to split and go eat."

The fog burned off by 9:30. Practice flew by. During breaks, players chattered about last week's stay in a hotel the night before the game ("Dashay snored like a sixty-five-year-old grandpa"), the possibility of meeting Lowndes again for state ("That would be the biggest game in the history of games"), and old country cures for Malcolm's ankle, including wrapping it in red clay and vinegar.

Of that last, Malcolm said he'd tried it without success. "That junk didn't work."

Ryan's dad stood watching beside the bleachers, not far from Alex's dad. Hal Whilden was low-key and smiled easily; it wasn't hard to tell who Ryan got his man-of-few-words genes from.

Hal's busy season was over. He and a partner had 2,600 hives that they could drop, two to an acre, on any farm in this neck of South Georgia that needed bees to pollinate its crops—cucumbers, squash, cantaloupes. This time of year, except for feeding the bees sugar water and monitoring their health, Hal was pretty much through until spring.

"Farmers will start hollering for them again in April and May," said Hal, whose own father was a beekeeper.

Hal was finally enjoying the fruits of this football season. It hadn't always been easy—he still remembered that night early on when fans booed Ryan—but last Friday's win at McEachern was a highlight. He was proud of what Ryan had done and who he had done it for. Hal grew up in a little town north of Valdosta but knew what the Wildcats meant back then to this town. It wasn't until Ryan played this year that he saw what it still meant.

"I've watched little kids coming up to Ryan after the games," Hal said. "I've seen old people—one eighty-year-old woman with tears in her eyes—hugging him. You see stuff like that, you start to get it."

The flip side, of course, was the criticism. Hal understood it came with the job.

"You're always going to hear things," he said. "It's always going to be the quarterback's fault. It was harder on his mom than it was on me. But I never doubted what he could do, and about halfway through the season you didn't hear anything anymore. Everybody started looking at them as a team."

He paused, shrugged, grinned.

Like Ryan.

"Winning cures everything, though, don't it?"

Gillespie blew his whistle and called it a day at 10:22. Players rushed to circle him.

"All right, hey, listen," he said. "Men, this is a great opportunity for you. Make sure you make the most of every opportunity in life. This is a big one."

Before they ran off, Rodemaker stopped his defense. He had something to add. He was hot.

"You can't take a day off practice like you did today," he said in his now permanently shredded voice. "Ain't nobody here ever played in a Game 13 and I have to scream and holler to get your attention? You traded a whole week's vacation, the work you put in all year—think how it's going to feel at 10:30 Friday night if you're not successful.

"I'm leaving here with a different feeling than I wanted to on Thanksgiving," he said. "It's an honor and an opportunity to practice on Thanksgiving. You're *right there*."

Geese honked overhead. The last of the fog smeared the sun.

"So men," he added, "tighten it down. Get your head locked in. We're going to find out tomorrow night. If you wait until you're 14 points down to lock in, it's going to be over."

Rodemaker stared at their chastened faces.

"I love you all," he told them. "Tell your mama you love her. Enjoy the day. But for the next twenty-four hours be locked and loaded."

They broke up and trotted off, jawing about turkey and greens and cornbread.

Rodemaker still didn't feel right.

"Thing is, they'll all regret it," he said. "Friday night, if they don't do it, it'll be a river of tears."

●

Edrae stood in front of a table piled with turkey and stuffing, ham, baked chicken, mac and cheese, green beans, potato salad, cornbread, four different kinds of cakes . . . it went on and on.

That was just one grandparent's house. When he finished there, Edrae stopped with his newest family at another grandparent's home, where the dining room table groaned with a second meal as over-the-top as the first.

By early evening, Edrae was stuffed. He sat back on a couch inside a small, cozy living room. The flower wallpaper was tacked everywhere with family photos. Outdoor plants filled the floor and every available space, brought inside in case the temperature dropped.

Denise Mathis sat across from Edrae in her mother's well-used chair. She'd taken Edrae into her own house almost two months ago. Edrae now called her Mom. He called Denise's mother Grandma.

The distance from where Edrae was two months earlier to where he was now kind of blew his mind.

"Yesterday after practice, Coach Dixon said, 'I know you're staying with Marte's family, but Thanksgiving's coming up and if you need a place to eat you can come to our house,'" Edrae said. "And I told him, 'Thank you but, Coach, I got a family now. And I'm going to be spending Thanksgiving at both grandparents.'"

As Edrae talked, the men in the house sat in another room and watched the Saints-Cowboys game on TV. The house's other teenagers, including Marte, drifted out to the driveway to talk among themselves. Denise's mom rattled dishes in the kitchen.

"For me when I was growing up, I'd always see families on TV get together and eat on Thanksgiving," Edrae said. "Most of the places I stayed at didn't have Thanksgiving. So for me to witness what I always looked at on TV . . ."

His wide almond eyes blinked with a kind of onlooker's amazement. It was like he was still watching what he'd done today on a TV screen.

"I don't know," he summed up. "It's a blessing."

David and Sharon had moved from town a few years earlier out here to Kinderlou Forest, a rolling, upscale golf club community developed by the Langdales. Lowndes coach Randy McPherson lived two doors away. David didn't play golf, but he liked to watch the deer and armadillos from his front porch. He'd filled an entire upstairs room with Wildcat memorabilia; there used to be more before he donated it to the Wildcat museum.

Out in the county, off Highway 84, beyond the Gloryhill Cowboy Church and about halfway to Quitman, David Waller pushed away from his own Thanksgiving groaning board and moved to his spacious living room. The Patriots-Lions game rolled across a big-screen TV that was usually tuned to Fox News.

David and Sharon had moved from town a few years earlier out here to Kinderlou Forest, a rolling, upscale golf club community developed by the Langdales. Lowndes coach Randy McPherson lived two doors away. David didn't play golf, but he liked to watch the deer and armadillos from his front porch. He'd filled an entire upstairs room with Wildcat memorabilia; there used to be more before he donated it to the Wildcat museum.

David now sat back in a favorite living room chair. Nub, whose family was out of town to visit relatives while he stayed behind for tomorrow night's game, sat beside him. It had been a while since they'd talked on Thanksgiving about the Wildcats' next game. They liked Valdosta's chances of going all the way—if not this season, they both agreed, then soon enough. They'd finally found the right coach.

Then a different topic came up: What would you give for another championship?

Being a businessman, David thought about the answer in terms of monetary worth.

"Ten thousand dollars," he said. Then he thought about it some more. "Fifty thousand," he said this time. "Does that sound crazy?"

From the man who once vowed never to give the program another dime if a black kid pulled on a Wildcat jersey, it sounded almost miraculous.

Nub pondered the same question. Being a one-armed painter, he thought about the answer in terms of limbs. He raised the glass of water in his one and only hand and gave the same answer he always gave.

"My left arm," he said, grinning.

◆

Game day unreeled with a kind of slow-motion, underwater quality.

Early in the afternoon, defensive players filtered in and out of the freshman locker room, a dank, echoing cement-scape where Rodemaker stood beside a cinder-block wall that flickered with last week's Grayson game. Players wore ball caps every way but straight and sat and watched from any hard surface they could find.

"They're going to come off the line better than anybody we've played this year," Rodemaker told them, pointing at a row of flat backs crouched along the Rams' big offensive front.

Then the screen filled with a kind of Goliath in pads and helmet. He folded himself into a three-point stance. It looked like he'd been Photoshopped into the film.

"Number 90 is their best football player—and he's a sophomore," Rodemaker noted of 6'5" 260–pound Robert Nkemdiche (the *N* is silent). Some recruiters already considered the massive but athletic defensive end, who spot-played at running back, the South's best prospect since Herschel Walker and Bo Jackson back in the '80s.

Still, Rodemaker chuckled. "He tried to friend Willie and Freak on Facebook," he said.

Rodemaker then peppered his players with a few questions, to see if they'd paid attention at all this week. His voice clanged around the room like he'd dropped it down a manhole.

"Every down's a majority run except *what*?"

Players: "Third and long."

"They run with motion *when*?"

"Ninety-three percent of the time."

"Men," Rodemaker then told them, watching as Grayson ran yet another sweep across the cinder-block wall, "when a team likes to run, we all brag, 'Bring it on!' Well, tonight's the proving ground."

The horn to let school out bleated up and down Valdosta High's empty halls, right at 2:30. Players shuffled off to the cafeteria for their pregame feed and devotional, just like usual.

Loudermilk took on the devotional duties again, just like he did before MLK. His wind-up was another long one, this time about Joshua before God called him to take his people to the Promised Land. He quoted passages about being "strong and courageous" and not deviating from "the right or the left." It could've fit any game this season.

Halfway through he got more to the point. He talked about being tired, something that seemed to catch a general mood in the room, whether anybody wanted to admit it or not. He thumbed in his Bible to Galatians.

"So let's not get tired of doing what is good," he read. "At just the right time we will reap a harvest of blessing if we don't give up."

He looked out at the 135 or so players seated at the long lunchroom tables. Grayson's buses were rolling into town right about now. They'd driven past the green sign that welcomes visitors to Winnersville. They were the kind of team that could not have cared less.

"You feel sorry for yourself and want to give up, but the opportunity is here," Loudermilk went on. Players blinked back at him, waiting. So he thundered, *"Make sure you want it more than they do!"*

Gillespie stood off to the side. A slow grin animated his face as players lined up to toss out their chicken bones and shake Loudermilk's hand on their way out the cafeteria door.

"If he goes 2-0," Gillespie cracked of Loudermilk's record following devotionals, "I might have to hire him."

●

The sky was blue and the sun still blazing when the Wildcat buses pulled out of the high school. People waved and cheered from a Huddle House parking lot. A warm drizzle fell by the time the team reached the stadium, with big, dark clouds rolling in fast from the west. The Wildcats still strolled through the Cat Walk, lined on both sides with folks shaking their hands, snapping their pictures, exchanging fist bumps and high fives.

Nub gave each 'Cat some nub.

Yet before the last player reached the stadium's brick entrance, the whole sky fell in, driving parking lot tailgaters back into their trucks and shooing David Waller inside the Wildcat museum. Players, already soaked, sprinted for cover under the stands.

The rain let up a few minutes later and a number of Wildcat seniors again stepped out to midfield to kiss the yellow paw. Some cheerleaders knelt and kissed it, too.

"It keeps the tradition alive," senior Carly Cangelosi said. "You feel like you're part of something bigger here than yourself. Part of a family that never changes."

Kathryn Cody, the cheerleader who'd worried about all those big, pretty, shiny Indians up at McEachern, worried about tonight's game, too. Still, she allowed, "I always psych myself out."

Doubt was a habit unique to this generation's Wildcats.

The mood in the coaches' room was warier even than usual.

"I ain't been nervous about a game all year," Pruitt said, "but my stomach's in knots tonight."

Part of it was Grayson. They stepped onto the Bazemore-Hyder turf for pregame drills in their basic green-and-gold uniforms and looked utterly unaffected and locked in.

Then there was that number 90 . . .

"He looks as pretty in person as he does on film," Pruitt observed.

"He's a grown man," offensive assistant Keith McConnehead added. "He's what an NFL tight end looks like when he's a sophomore in high school."

It was a universal coaches' tic always to think that the other teams' players looked more beautiful than their own. Something else unsettled them tonight: Malcolm didn't sound like he wanted to play.

"I think he's afraid of going out there and not being dominant," Pruitt said.

"All he's got to do is push through it," said Gillespie. "If it was anybody in this room, it would've been, 'Coach, I'm going.' But boys, we ain't there yet."

Then he added as an afterthought, "And he ain't but two catches away from breaking the record."

"The record" was the most hallowed mark in Valdosta's hallowed history: Stan Rome's 75 catches during his sophomore season, Bazemore's last. It had withstood every talented, hungry, never-quit Wildcat to play receiver for almost four decades. After last week's dazzling game, Malcolm now had caught 74.

"I played my whole senior year with *two* high ankle sprains," Henderson, an all-state Wildcat tackle in '97, said matter-of-factly.

Added McConnehead, a Hyder 'Cat in the early '90s, "It ain't like it used to be."

Malcolm was going to play. He just hadn't practiced all week and had no idea yet how his ankle would react tonight. He'd played before with bruises and pulls and sprains, but he'd never dealt with anything so full of unknowns as this. He just needed some time to wrap his head around it.

He'd play.

The black clouds, the rain, a gimpy Malcolm—the foreshadowing was too handy to take seriously.

In fact, even after the Grayson Rams charged into the stadium through a four-cheerleader-high banner (HASTA LA VISTA VALDOSTA!) to the roaring delight of their fans, the Wildcats looked pretty freaking beautiful themselves. When Grayson handed the ball on the game's first play to their sophomore Goliath, a swarm of black jerseys and yellow hats stuffed him before he gained a yard.

"*That's* not going to work," Pernell Bee said, standing in the drizzle with the rest of Valdosta's sideline mafia. "It's a little too . . . *simple* for us."

Grayson kept grinding, machinelike, and with the help of an awkward catch, an inches-long quarterback sneak, and a pass interference call, they lumbered up to midfield.

Then that was that. Valdosta held, and Grayson punted. The 'Cat offense sprinted out. Valdosta fans, in their slickers and rain hats and war paint smeared from the weather, went crazy.

Then . . .

Needing 9 yards on third down from their own 24, Ryan floated back, searched the middle for his favorite receiver, and coolly fired a high strike.

As the ball spiraled toward Malcolm, the voice in his head suddenly hemmed and hawed, or at least that was the effect. It seemed to be saying too many things at once. When a pass came Malcolm's way before, the voice would tell him to turn around, catch the ball, and then "Go! Go as far as you can go!"

This time, with Malcolm's ankle killing him, the voice sounded unsure of what to say next, like it was still furiously working out all the calculations. "What are you going to do after you catch it?" it asked. Because Malcolm knew he couldn't do much once he got the ball. He knew he couldn't spin, couldn't stick his foot in the turf when he landed and cut to his right. His ankle wasn't up to that. If somebody came up on him from his left? He didn't know what he'd do then, either.

"When a ball's coming at you full speed and you're not focused 100 percent on catching it, you're going to drop it," Malcolm would say later. "When all those things register in your head, that's what happens.

"So my focus was off. And the next thing I know the ball is coming out of my hands."

Ryan's pass indeed slipped through Malcolm's outstretched hands and into the waiting, unconflicted grasp of a Ram defender. Three plays later Grayson ran a sweep and scored.

Still, Valdosta blocked the extra point, and fans all over the stadium turned to each to say some variation of the same thing: At the end of the night, that point would save the Wildcats.

Then . . .

Valdosta got the ball back, crossed midfield, looked ready to roll—and then Dashay fumbled. "He's in a whole 'nother world," Stan said.

Yet the Wildcats defense held again. Forced Grayson to punt.

Then . . .

As Reggie tried to gauge the ball's flight while it spun up in the lights, with the rain now blowing sideways in big, gusting sheets, he had trouble distinguishing the voices in his own head.

During big plays all season, Reggie had talked out loud to his cousin Sidney, gunned down almost exactly a year earlier but still his most trusted friend. Reggie held those conversations with Sidney right out on the field. He'd say aloud, "What would you do, Junior?" Or "This is a big one, Junior. Let's fly."

Now other voices had crowded in. All week at practice coaches had yelled at Reggie to *get every punt, get every punt*—over and over.

Reggie got every punt he could get his hands on this year, even ran a handful back for touchdowns. He electrified the crowd every time he touched the ball. Even Gillespie's mother hugged him after one game and told him he was her favorite player. As much as he loved to run back kicks, though, Reggie also knew that some kicks you just had to let go.

This one he wanted to let bounce. It was raining too hard and he couldn't get a good line on it. Except those coaches were screaming in his head, *"Get every punt!"* so Reggie ran up to get it. Then the damn thing slid right through his hands.

Grayson recovered. Two plays later, their Wing-T quarterback looped a dead-eyed 35-yard touchdown surprise over the Wildcats' stunned heads.

13–0.

Then . . .

Deep in Grayson's end of the field, Ryan spotted Jay. He never did spot the Grayson kid who idled nearby, just waiting to jump the moment that Ryan released the ball. Kid then picked the pass clean and lugged it 65 yards for Grayson's third touchdown.

20–0.

Then . . .

Son of a *bitch*. Valdosta rolled all the way to the Grayson 12-yard line with just seconds left in the half, looking like the Comeback 'Cats again, cool as cucumbers—when Ryan got clobbered in the backfield and lost the ball.

Again.

🏈

The locker room was Sunday service quiet. Players looked lost in their own heads, trying to make sense of what just happened. It felt dizzying. They'd been down before but this was different.

Gillespie huddled with his coaches, scanned his play sheet. Didn't see much there.

"There ain't a whole lot of adjustments to make," he said. Valdosta had outgained Grayson. "Man," he added, "five turnovers . . ."

Stan hobbled into the locker room and saw the rows of hanging heads. He rapped his cane on the floor, a ghost of 'Cats past, one almost literally back from the dead.

"Y'all can *win* this ball game," Stan called out. "It's going to take some guts and it's going to take some heart. You got to hit 'em in the mouth! You got to quit playing like you're scared! You got to quit turning the ball over!"

Tyran leaped up. "I ain't ready to go home!" he shouted. "I wanna keep going, baby!"

Players started to stir.

Gillespie strode in going straight to the whiteboard. He asked players what they thought was available; he drew up schemes to help them out.

"We shot ourselves in the foot more than they beat us," he told them. "Ain't nothing says you can't score 21 points and win this freakin' ballgame. But men, we got to score and we got to score quickly."

The kids who'd gone to war for him so many times this season looked like they wanted to believe him.

"Keep battling your ass off and I guarantee y'all will feel good at the end of this football game," he finished. *"You're the better football team!"*

●

They weren't.

Not tonight.

Rain washed out the band's halftime show, and it still hadn't let up. Fans who hung around looked washed out themselves—except for Nub, of course. He was from that generation that just *knew* the Wildcats were going to win.

"We're going to be all right," he assured everybody after his halftime cig. "I'm really not worried about it now."

Grayson sacked Ryan twice on Valdosta's first posession, and a grim tone was set.

The 'Cats picked up yards all night long but too often looked discombobulated; all those talented but awkward adolescent parts that had been made to work together so artfully over the course of spring practice and summer camp and eleven hard-fought games now seemed to shoot off in different directions at once, each trying to do too much on its own and mucking up the works.

They kept plugging. By this point, these players didn't know how not to—Gillespie's first long-term victory. Still down 20-0 in the fourth quarter, Ryan fearlessly floated a ball down the middle that Jay turned into a pirouetting 43-yard grab. Jay then transformed a routine catch into another balletic display, spinning away twice from tacklers and leaving them to grab at the night's damp air.

Malcolm played until the end. He finished the night with three catches—breaking Stan's record—but the rain and score muted any congratulations. One catch went for nine yards . . . on a fourth and 10. It was that kind of night.

Reggie returned his final punt 30 yards. A clipping penalty brought it back.

Ryan got hammered in the second half, including three sacks by Nkemdiche in the final few minutes. One sack resulted in a safety. It was only then that Gillespie conceded that the jig was up and slipped his homemade play sheet into a back khakis pocket, right beside his tin of Grizzly.

Game over.

22–0.

The scoreboard lights snapped off the instant time expired, wiping the result from the stadium, if not from the record book. Several Valdosta players yelled out curses; one threw his helmet. Most of the Wildcats just stood on the sideline silently, stunned, their helmets still on so that no one could see them crying. Cheerleaders huddled together and bawled. Swoll's girlfriend came onto the field and put her arm around him as he took slow, bow-legged steps down the sideline, his head lowered to his chest. His father stood nearby.

"This isn't the end," he said of his warrior son. "His heart is there."

Stan draped an arm over Jay's shoulder as the two stood alone in an end zone. Tears brimmed in Jay's eyes.

"It hurts. I know it hurts," Stan told him. "But this will pass."

Jay looked inconsolable. Stan scanned the all but deserted stadium, then looked across the field as the Wildcats slowly formed a line to shake their opponents' hands.

Suddenly, he lit up and turned back to Jay.

"That pass you caught, all that spinning and turning," he said, referencing one of the night's few highlights. "You looked like . . . *me*."

A quick smile creased Jay's face.

"Now go out and shake hands," Stan told him, clapping him on the pads. "Show some sportsmanship."

Players circled Gillespie in the end zone for a last prayer. The coach then told his weeping, still-stunned team, "I know it didn't end the way we wanted it to. But I'm proud of you."

Parents and boosters lined up for one last time this season to tell Gillespie that they were proud of him, too, win or lose. Ryan's dad, with his wife crying beside him, leaned in and said softly to Gillespie, "I appreciate you believing in him." Another player's mother whispered to the coach, "You can't play better than from your heart. I can't wait until next year."

David Waller had watched the game from inside the museum, standing behind its long glass window like he was watching the neighborhood kids play on his front lawn. He'd have to wait another year for that one more championship.

The moment the game ended he slowly walked the length of the field and clasped Gillespie's hand, too. Gillespie brightened when he saw David—he always did—and told him, "Appreciate it."

The two of them had come a long way since their Tour of Dead Coaches. David's offer of those free cemetery plots still stood: 11 victories down, only 189 more to go.

"I'm okay," David said later. "I'm old, I have a cold. I'd have felt better if we won. But I'm okay."

Then someone came up behind him.

"Hey, Coach," Nub croaked, giving Gillespie a full nub.

Three months earlier, the night before the season's first game, Nub had sat inside the same locker room the players now cleared out of, channeling the enormity of Wildcat football and the possibilities this new coach brought. "You might be the head coach now," he'd texted Gillespie that same night, "but you better make our asses happy."

Now, even with this loss, Nub's ass felt just fine.

"You did good," he drawled to Gillespie. "We're proud of this football team."

After nearly everyone else had left, Claudette and Kennedy came up one more time. Tears streaked Claudette's face. Rance wiped one or two of them away. Then he told her what he always told her when her heart was broken: "Everything's going to be okay."

"I *swore* I wasn't going to cry," Claudette said. "I don't know what I'm going to do. I wasn't ready for it to end."

Then, as always, she rallied with her next breath.

"But it *didn't* end," she said, her mountain girl smile spreading wide and bright. "This is the beginning. This is the beginning of putting this program back to the way it was. You just have to go through growing pains."

A dozen young kids in black-and-gold jerseys, many of them the same ones who'd run around up in suburban Atlanta after the McEachern game, already were playing football again out on the Bazemore-Hyder turf. They wanted to get in one last game before the lights went out—heaving passes, juking tacklers, raising their arms in mock signals for touchdowns.

With the scoreboard dark, they'd moved on.

Back at the high school, players packed it up for the season. Ryan looked almost lost as he wandered the locker room, like it was his first time in there. His eyes were raw and red. His mother said it was only the third time she'd ever seen her cool-cat son cry: once after losing a Little League baseball game, once after a loss in middle school, and tonight. Ryan hardly spoke. He just kept walking around, hugging teammates, taking big, deep breaths.

Jay stopped him as he passed his locker.

"You did your shit this year," Jay told him, highest praise from Valdosta's bluest blood.

Ryan nodded, then headed out to his Silverado. Gillespie grabbed him before he could duck out the door. The spent-looking coach put both hands on his senior quarterback's shoulders and looked him straight in the eye.

"I am so proud of you," he told him. "From where you started to all that you accomplished . . ."

The beekeeper's kid with no experience, no arm, and no college offers finished the season with 30 touchdown passes and 3,019 passing yards—both Valdosta records.

Dashay sat undressing on a bench at an end of the locker room. He didn't say a word, barely moved, never lifted his big liquid-brown eyes. He'd been crying, too, sobbing on the bus the whole way back from the stadium, one teammate said. His long lashes were wet, his face streaked.

He rolled down a sock; blood smeared his shin. He pulled off the sock, grabbed his jersey and a couple of pieces of equipment, and got up and dumped it all in blue plastic bins. He then sat back down and dropped his head between his knees. Players and coaches came by, patted him on the back, gave him hugs. Dashay didn't move, didn't say a word.

"It's the same thing I did my last playoff game," said his uncle Emanuel Williams, who'd taken Dashay to his first Wildcat games as a kid and whose framed photograph in a Valdosta uniform, wearing number 27, still sat inside Dashay's grandmother's house.

Williams had a pretty good idea of what Dashay was feeling. He'd been in the street with Dashay last spring when those shots were fired. Before he enlisted in the navy, he was one of those kids for whom Wildcat football looked like *the end.*

"I sat and cried," Williams remembered of the last time he took off his Valdosta uniform. "You don't want to leave. It's like your favorite thing you've done. I couldn't believe it was my last game. I felt empty. It was like, 'What am I going to do now?'"

"I still think about it," he said. "Every time I see kids playing football, I wish I could play. Some people in the city still follow you, like you're a local celebrity. Kids want your autograph. You'll hear them say to each other, 'He used to play for the Wildcats!' You're a Wildcat and you wore the black and gold."

Now, almost a decade later, Williams talked like those memories were still raw.

"You don't completely get over it," he said.

Dashay pulled some pants over his bloody shin, slipped out the door, and disappeared into the night.

"They're all upset right now," Pruitt said after Dashay split and the last players finished up, "but they'll look back and have a lot to be proud of."

There was one piece of good news tonight: Lowndes lost. All that rooting for the Vikings so that the Wildcats could get a rematch with them in the Dome ended the moment Valdosta was eliminated.

"Good," one coach blurted when he heard the Lowndes score. "Now I don't have to hear *that* shit."

Gillespie finished his rounds inside the locker room. He thanked every player he could find, told each of them how much he appreciated everything he'd done.

Then he thanked his coaches. Together, they'd gotten through Year One.

Now it was on to Year Two. Then, hopefully, Year Three, Four, Five . . .

There wasn't much time to linger over tonight.

"Every class is unique. Every kid is different," Gillespie said. "Then it's time for the next group."

He walked back to his office, got whatever it was he needed. Told Kennedy it was time to go.

"I feel . . . empty," he said. "It's like you've worked for so much and then you come up a little short."

He closed the door to his office. Pulled out his keys.

"I'm a little anxious to go back to work Monday," he then said. "It's 365 days. It never stops."

Then he called out to everybody.

"I'm lockin' it down!"

Outside, the rain had stopped. Rance and Kennedy tiptoed around puddles in the parking lot, got in the one vehicle out there that wasn't a pickup, and headed home in the black Saturn sedan that still had the tire with the slow leak.

He never did get it fixed.

Maybe Monday.

❦

Next day broke damp and cold, and the town seemed to wake with a collective hangover—not from too much booze but from a thing here that's far stiffer: losing.

Tables were still crowded inside Bynum's and the Gold Plate and, yeah, the Waffle House. Folks still picked up their dozen glazed from the counter at the Dixie Cream Donut Shop on North Oak, even though the neighborhood wasn't what it used to be.

Yet those who ventured out appeared mostly just to sit and stir their coffee and pick at their eggs. Daily life felt a little hollower than it had just twenty-four hours earlier.

Morgan Long, the junior cheerleader, stayed at home and summed up the next-day ennui on her Facebook page: "Good morning reality."

Big Terry went even deeper. His was a one-word post: "Over."

Pruitt was right, though. Devastated as they were Friday night and through the weekend, players soon understood what they'd just been through, what they'd accomplished, the lineage they'd finally attached themselves to, maybe even reignited.

The receiving record Malcolm set got lost in the shock that followed Friday's shutout, but it wasn't long before he grasped the hugeness of what he'd done. The kid who two years earlier had landed in juvie after a stolen car incident and wanted to quit football now realized he'd achieved a kind of immortality.

"I don't know how I'll be portrayed after I leave here," Malcolm said one afternoon, catching a ride after school to his house across town, out near the airport. "But I got my way into the museum—into the history books. I got to the point where I'll always be remembered. And it can't be taken away. It doesn't matter if the record is broken next year. It won't be as important as breaking Stan Rome's record."

The road Malcolm rode over now was the same one he once walked along after practices, miles south to his house in a neat, modest neighborhood just past a cypress pond with an alligator.

Habitat for Humanity built the sweet little four-bedroom when Malcolm was in the eighth grade—first house his mother, Pratina McKinnon, a supervisor for a satellite TV service, ever owned.

"Our first yard ever," Malcolm said proudly as he nodded toward the postage-stamp front yard. He nodded again. "Our first mailbox ever."

This clearly was not the end for him. He was headed to the next biggest stage, going from the SEC of high school football to the SEC.

He'd signed with Georgia. No telling where he'd go from there.

"Maybe if I make it to the NFL it'll be bigger than this," he said. "Maybe if I make it to the Hall of Fame. But right now, people will remember me here for this, no matter what."

It was crazy, really, this trajectory from nowhere to somewhere, from nobody to somebody. It's what everybody here was after. Malcolm couldn't explain it or justify it, other than to say, "I'm just one of the players that came through that's good."

Kids in Valdosta still got rewarded for that.

Reggie was doing better, too. He soon forgot about that muffed punt, finally got the voices in his head back in order. He also had been handed a kind of immortality.

A year ago, he should've been dead, put down by one of those two dozen bullets that missed him but found his cousin on that lazy Sunday afternoon. Now, the season over, he strolled down a sidewalk lined with the low brick apartments of the Ora Lee West housing project. He stayed with his mom in 244. His grandma stayed next door in 246. His dead cousin Sidney stayed across the street in 612.

Reggie's mother finally saved enough to move out, but he still had kin here—it's where his dad grew up—and he came to visit his favorite aunt almost every day. Crossing a street to her apartment, he pointed out the "trap fences" that cops put up between buildings to help them corner bad guys. He nodded at the "bootleg house" where folks here got liquor. He laughed to himself when he saw three cars parked in a row along the curb, each with a temporary tag. "The 'hood, man," he said. "Get their income tax check, get a new car. Have to give it back by May."

These were the streets that almost took Reggie.

"On this strip," he said outside his auntie's house, across from his old place, "I seen all the drugs you can see, all the guns you can see, all the fights you can see. It was like a whole other ball game. Guys pressuring you all the time, 'Have a smoke with me,' 'Pop a bean [ecstasy] with me.' Guys tell you they're your homey but they're not. I found that out the hard way. In the projects, the only way to be different is be good."

On this warm late night in early February, Reggie had the glow of somebody who played his way out. He'd just signed a letter of intent with Albany State, a historically black university about an hour away. Nobody else in his family had ever graduated high school. He had nephews still running these streets. Cops could point them out.

"It feels good to be a McQueen right now," he said.

A block away, a handful of guys stood under a streetlight. It was hard to tell what they were up to. From where Reggie stood, it looked like they were up to nothing.

"I seen people standing on that same corner all my life," he said, shaking his head for what seemed like the hundredth time tonight.

As he made his way down the sidewalk, sidestepping some little kids on bikes, Reggie looked a lot like those guys under the light down the street. He wore baggy jeans and an oversized watch and dreads that poured from a sideways-turned baseball cap.

Reggie wasn't those guys anymore, though. In this cracked patch of deepest South Georgia, he was after something beyond that corner. He didn't know what yet. He just knew it was beyond that corner.

The fellas on the corner hadn't moved. They checked him out, waited to see if he'd walk on down. They'd be there after he left.

"You can Google me," Reggie finally said, looking at them but not going their way. "You can't take anyone on this street and Google them. But you can Google me."

It was nearly midnight. His cell phone purred. A text from Jay.

Four words, 'Cat to 'Cat.

"I love you bruh."

Jay was at home, seven miles north from where Reggie stood and about a million miles from Ora Lee West in every demographic line item: No kids riding bikes down sidewalks on a school night at eleven in these landscaped cul-de-sacs; no fellas loafing under the streetlights in this gated community. You could grow mighty old out there on the corner of Creekwood and Sweetwater waiting for somebody to ask you to "pop a bean."

Yet they still shared an area code, 229. Jay knew what that meant better than anybody. He'd been schooled to know it, to appreciate it—to understand that it could be yanked away in the time it takes somebody to lift a .22 from 30 yards away and go *click*.

He'd been schooled to inherit it.

While he understood all that, this was the first season Jay *felt* it. He'd never worked harder and never been happier. He and the rest of his *boys,* Reggie and Malcolm, Dashay and Ryan, Swoll and Freak, Justin and Jarquez and Zach and Bee and Yontell and Eunice and Odell and all the crazy rest of them who'd fly off in every direction and meet every fate (James Eunice, tragically, drowned that January, falling from a boat while duck hunting)—they'd all finally, *finally* felt connected to that part of this team that remains this town's one-of-a-kind inheritance.

Once a Wildcat, always a Wildcat.

"Even though we lost, it's been the best season," Jay said. "Just feeling that tradition, that history—I felt like I was part of something bigger, not just the team of 2010. I finally feel like I was part of something that's been here for the last hundred years."

As Jay talked, his big frame sank into a long, comfy couch inside his house's soaring living room, the bounty of Stan's complicated, harrowing, ultimately redemptive narrative. A few weeks earlier, Jay also had signed to play at Georgia, live on ESPN.

His future looked set: limitless.

Itchy as he was to get out of here and test those limits, though, Jay wasn't ready to let Valdosta go just yet. Not now. Not ever. He was too rooted in this place to believe his future would ever eclipse his past. He'd been lucky enough to play ball all over the country but never anyplace like this—up or down, win or lose.

It was . . . *unexplainable.*

"There's something about that feeling when you step in the 229," Jay said. "Wherever I'm at, if I have kids, I'm going to send them back to Valdosta. They're coming back to stay with somebody to be in Valdosta. To be in the 229."

229.

Great tattoo.

EPILOGUE

A year later.

I'm seated on the tailgate of a pickup parked in Gillespie's front yard, drinking iced-down beer under tall pines and an October moon.

Maybe thirty or forty people are there when I show up a little after midnight, mostly assistant coaches with their wives and sleepy-eyed kids. They roam the lawn like it's a Sunday afternoon picnic. The music is a little loud and a little twangy, but the other ranch houses on this subdivision's quiet street stay dark and uncomplaining. Rance and Claudette can play their music as long and loudly as they want tonight.

Valdosta just beat Lowndes.

"I'm not leaving until I see the sun!" Alan Rodemaker declares beside me in his rubbed-raw rasp, raising a beer as Gillespie hops up next to us on the tailgate.

Our feet dangle like little boys'. Rodemaker's hair is still damp with sweat and exuberance. So is Gillespie's.

"Maybe we'll celebrate this good again if we win state," Rodemaker adds. "Or *almost* this good."

It would be hard to top tonight's miracle comeback for the state championship of Valdosta, played across town inside the sold-out Concrete Spittoon. The Wildcats trailed Lowndes by 10 with less than a minute remaining. Some fans left. They had to wonder, after seven straight losses and now losing by two scores with time virtually all gone, if their storied but besieged school could ever again beat the county behemoth. Maybe consolidation *was* the answer.

Then . . .

The Wildcats channeled some of that old never-quit mojo to score 2 touchdowns in the final 48 seconds and pull out a 21–17 stunner.

It was a scene, man. Grown men and women wept as they wandered the field. A player dropped to his knees, closed his eyes, then lifted his head to the heavens while his mouth moved soundlessly in some deep, monkish prayer. A cheerleader threw up.

Stan Rome spun me around near midfield and grinned his beautiful, lop-sided grin.

"Greatest win," he blurted, "in Valdosta history."

David Waller grinned, too. It wasn't the state title he'd been waiting for, but it was close. He nodded slyly toward Gillespie.

"That win was worth another year for him, don't you think?"

Soaked and smiling, Gillespie stood in the middle of his ecstatic players. The sideline mafia of Bazemore 'Cats and Hyder 'Cats who stood sentinel behind the present bunch now included one more class of exalted alumni: Gillespie 'Cats.

Jay was there and still towered over everyone else. He came home for the weekend from Georgia, where he'd been redshirted his freshman season. Reggie roamed the field, too. His scholarship at Albany State fell through at the last minute, so he returned to Valdosta to pursue another career: rapper.

Dashay and Ryan left the stadium together in Ryan's pickup to beat the traffic back to the high school, where a delirious crowd was growing. Dashay never did graduate, and Ryan attended Valdosta State but planned to transfer, tired of everybody asking him why he didn't play football anymore. Yet there they both were.

Swoll and Justin showed up a little later in the locker room. They both played at Valdosta State now, yet each had spent the night at home watching the Wildcat game on TV, then drove straight here as soon as it ended, unaware the other was on his way, as if guided by the same ancient homing instinct.

They all shared in this win. It was every 'Cat's win. Finally, it became clear to everyone out here tonight, the torch had been passed.

"I can't tell you how proud I am of this football team," Gillespie shouted so he could be heard above the pandemonium on the field. "Hey, when it didn't look real good you never, ever, ever quit. That's what Valdosta football is all about. Never quitting. Keep battling. I wouldn't take it any other way."

Then the coach punched the air with a hard right cross, knocking out something that nobody else could see.

"That's awesome!"

●

I left the field with tears in my own eyes. I'd come to love these folks and this place, gnats and all. I'd spent most of a year here. Early on I commuted, making the five-hundred-mile round-trip from Atlanta several times a week. Except for the tickets I piled up, I never minded the drive at all.

When a neighbor in Atlanta learned I was writing a book about a season in Valdosta, he told me that he'd journeyed down there twice with his high school football team in Athens to play in the early '90s.

"Scaredest I've ever been in my life," he said, still able to summon the sound of those Wildcats banging the tin, "was when I got off the bus in Valdosta."

Those trips were pilgrimages of sorts. Pilgrims—players, fans, recruiters, journalists—had come down here and talked about what they'd seen for more than half a century. I came for the first time two decades earlier, while traveling the length of the Georgia-Florida line for a different story. Finished with work one Friday afternoon in a tiny town near the bottom of the big swamp, I drove two hours out of my way to catch a game that night in old Cleveland Field. At the time, I didn't know much about Valdosta except that football there was supposed to reside in a place somewhere between iconic and mythic.

That's what I found. Seated in the visitors' bleachers, the only spot where I could fit, I looked across the grass at a whole town that turned out to watch its kids play football like nowhere else in Georgia—or maybe the rest of the known world.

I didn't come back again until 2009, a week after that 57–15 drubbing from Lowndes. It was Valdosta's *annus horribilis,* and I was there to write a story for *The New York Times* on the fall of the greatest high school football team in America. When I stepped inside the spiffed-up new stadium this time, I could've sat anywhere I wanted: The stands were two-thirds empty.

The team had lost its town.

The folks I met were anxious to talk about what they'd lost and whether they could ever get it back. That's when I first met Stan Rome. He came as advertised, damaged and enlightened to an almost sagelike degree. Like Woody Harrelson, I also was introduced right away to Nub. Apparently I didn't freak him out the way Woody did; he not only offered to take me in his boat down the Withlacoochee, he escorted me through the town's more peculiar cultural byways.

I met Rance and Claudette a couple of months later at a Touchdown Club meet-and-greet. Rance, who'd never set eyes on me, didn't hesitate when I proposed spending a season with him. I'd never met a man more comfortable in his own skin, more confident in his ability, or more humble about his place in the universe.

🏈

I eventually found a permanent address in Valdosta, a green bungalow with white trim in the middle of town. It was within spitting distance of at least three churches and two tattoo parlors. It had a front yard pecan tree and a little porch where Nub could come over mornings and smoke. The next-door neighbors kept a key for me in an old soccer shoe on their back porch. If it wasn't there, I'd just open the back door and search the key rack in their kitchen.

I called it "Mama's House." Kay Powell, an Atlanta colleague, grew up in it—she remembered a young, dashing David Waller installing the air-conditioning back in the '50s—and Kay and her sisters kept it after their mother, Juanita, a lifelong Wildcat fan, passed a few years earlier.

Nothing was updated. Kay gave me detailed instructions on how to prepare a bath in the ancient tub. There was no shower.

"Turn the hot water all the way on," Kay began in a slow-rolling South Georgia drawl that not even decades in Atlanta could hurry up, "then go make yourself a cup of coffee. Enjoy it. When you finish, your bath should be about ready."

The place was perfect. My twin eight-year-olds wanted to live there forever. They still tell friends in Atlanta about their "Valdosta house," like others might go on about their "Paris pied-à-terre." They chose which dining room chair to sit in by the vegetable rendered on it in needlepoint: radish, carrot, eggplant, corn.

After the kids' first weekend in Valdosta, they knew everyone and everything they needed to know. They played football in the Bazemore-Hyder end zone with Jay Rome's little brother Justin. They played on a fishing boat parked in Nub's backyard. They ordered "Georgia ice cream" when they wanted grits. They spat gnats out of their mouths instead of waving them away with their hands, the way outsiders do. They learned that cotton bites back when you pick it. They said "yes, sir" and "no, ma'am" without prompting. They never, ever quit.

"He's like a . . . *Southern me*," my son Frankie said of Nub's wide-open young boy John, not seeing the irony in the fact that he and his sister, Mary Louise, were born and raised in the heart of Atlanta, capital of the South.

To them, Valdosta was capital of the *real* South.

●

My heart got broken here, too.

I was back in Atlanta after the season, sitting in my living room one Saturday afternoon in January, surrounded by friends and kids, when Nub called.

You need to get back down here, he said. James was duck hunting and fell out of a boat. They can't find him.

A blond kid with warrior eye black and a million-watt smile, James Eunice was one of my favorites. He hardly played, got his butt kicked every practice—I'd wink at him before he'd go up against a bigger, meaner, more talented kid, then he'd wink back after he picked himself up off the grass—and yet nobody loved being a Wildcat more.

Just two weeks earlier, the day after New Year's, he posted on Facebook: "Miss Bazemore-Hyder's lights."

When I arrived at Ocean Pond, a 525-acre former sink hole a dozen miles south of Valdosta, it seemed like the whole town, most of the school, and every rescue squad in the region were already there. So were the Wildcat coaches.

"First one I've lost in nineteen years," a solemn Gillespie said to me by the water's edge. James was one of his favorites, too. "I'm not supposed to bury them. They're supposed to bury me."

The community came together like family for one of its own. Inside the white two-story, century-old, tin-roofed house that belonged to the Ocean Pond Fishing Club, big tables piled quickly with covered dishes, homemade desserts, gallons of coffee, all of it brought up a canopied dirt road by friends, neighbors, local restaurants. Volunteers fed weary divers around the clock.

Standing on the wraparound porch or in the shade of a stately oak, James's parents, John and Tammy Eunice, talked with everybody. Tammy, especially, displayed an unusual, awe-inspiring strength in the face of this unspeakable tragedy. *She* comforted folks who didn't know what to say: *She* reassured friends who wondered how something this terrible could happen.

"She did that for me, too," Drew Pipkin, James's friend who hunted with him that day on the pond, told me in utter amazement.

James had dropped Drew off on a reedy bank and steered the boat around a small spit of land to flush ducks his way. A little while later, Drew spotted the boat again, spinning in the water, empty.

Nobody knows what happened. Likely as not, James took his hand off the engine for a brief moment, the boat jerked, and he was tossed into the pond. You couldn't struggle long in that cold, grass-filled water.

At sunset that first Sunday, as the lake turned gold and Spanish moss waved like an ancient hand in the wind, a couple of hundred people formed a prayer circle down by the water while search boats continued to loop and switchback off shore.

"This is what Northerners think of when they think of the South," Nub whispered to me of the sweet, sad, sepia-toned scene. "Heck, it's what *Southerners* who've moved away think of when they think of the South."

A diver found James's body seventeen days later. At the packed church funeral service inside a converted Winn-Dixie, Jay and Malcolm presented John and Tammy with a Georgia football jersey that bore their son's name and his Wildcat number, 23. James had already been accepted to Georgia and planned to walk on to the football team. Mark Richt issued him a uniform and put him on the roster.

I saw John and Tammy often after that. They traveled to every county in Georgia and Florida that sent somebody to Ocean Pond, just to thank them. They visited churches and schools all over the region to spread the story of James's intensely exuberant spiritual life. They came to Valdosta High baseball games to cheer James's former teammates.

We talked again outside Bazemore-Hyder Stadium before the Wildcats' next season opener. They'd showed up early for the Cat Walk, which James loved. John told me about all the money they'd raised to buy wet suits that would let rescue team divers work longer in the kind of frigid waters James had been lost in. He told me about the scholarship fund they'd started. He related, almost offhandedly, the countless miracles, large and small, that they'd witnessed since James died.

Then I saw them again as I walked off the field after the Lowndes game. We hugged like everybody hugged that night, deliriously. All around us Wildcat players who'd dedicated the season to James repeatedly shouted out, "Two-three! We did it for two-three! *For real!*"

John and Tammy knew James was looking down tonight on Winnersville's singular craziness.

Beaming from ear to ear.

The win over Lowndes echoed beyond the playing field, as it always does is in Valdosta.

Four weeks later, Valdosta residents swarmed the polls to vote on a referendum to repeal their school charter and have their system taken over by Lowndes County.

On paper, the proposal looked like a lock. The powerful consolidation forces—the chamber of commerce, the industrial authority, prominent lawyers, influential preachers—amassed a $300,000 war chest. Their billboards blanketed the town. One radio commercial invoked Martin Luther King Jr. and featured an actor hired to sound like Morgan Freeman. They hired strategists and pollsters from out of state, printed glossy fliers, opened an office in a downtown storefront, and employed a small army of organizers.

I went door-to-door with them one blistering spring evening as they gathered signatures from registered voters to get their referendum on the ballot. Every person who opened the door in the white, middle-class neighborhood we canvassed expressed support for merging the schools.

That included the guy in khakis, striped polo, and loafers. His shirt collar half hid a tattoo that ringed the bottom of his neck. I asked him what it said. He smiled and opened his collar wider. It revealed the inked image of a bald eagle clutching a shield, and then these words: HATED AND PROUD.

The group needed 7,400 signatures by July. They turned in more than 10,000.

I also sat with the man behind the crusade, a former Bazemore Wildcat who worked most days out of his barn on Skipper Bridge Road, just outside town.

Barn: There wasn't a horse turd or hay bale or spider web in sight. Set at the end of a long winding drive, behind a glowing white house topped with a green tin roof that looked torn straight from the pages of *Southern Living,* the "barn" included a loft office and soaring atrium used to host events. Hung high on the walls were trophies from an African hunting expedition: oryx, kudu, impala, and blue wildebeest.

Rutledge A. "Rusty" Griffin was perhaps the wealthiest man in Valdosta not named Langdale. The barn had been Rusty's base of operations since he sold his $400 million pesticide company in 2003 to the global chemical behemoth DuPont. Tall, ruddy, kind of hangdog, Rusty had kept busy in his retirement, serving on a bunch of boards, including the Georgia Board of Regents, and running (and losing) a race for state senate.

Now he wanted to consolidate the schools. He talked to me about it for hours in front of a big fireplace, told me about the business it would help bring in, the reforms it would help streamline, the poor black children it would help educate.

As he spoke, I couldn't keep from glancing at the portrait that hung above the mantel: General Robert E. Lee.

Opposing this hostile takeover of Valdosta's schools, at least at first, was mostly just Nub and anybody else he could round up. Their ragtag group spent about $20,000, most of it on yard signs, bumper stickers, and buttons. The preservation of Valdosta football was their concern at the start, yet for Nub and his growing group of followers, the game soon took a backseat to the belief that their maligned school system, with a new superintendent shaking things up academically and Gillespie shaking things up athletically, was poised for a revival. Reading scores, graduation rates, wins—all were way up.

Nub had set up a folding table with T-shirts and buttons outside the stadium during the Lowndes game. I bet him a steak dinner at Shorty's that he'd lose in a landslide.

It was a landslide: A month after Valdosta upset Lowndes, and a year after Gillespie had arrived to reignite the program, consolidation was turned down by nearly 80 percent of the city's voters.

Nub became the toast of the town. The one-armed painter had helped slay Valdosta's wealthiest, most connected, most powerful institutions. While those he defeated would argue otherwise, the overwhelming majority believed he had also helped save the school, the town, and the team. The president of the local NAACP chapter even asked him to run for the at-large seat on the board of education.

Would wonders here ever cease?

"When the president of the NAACP asks you to run, it's time to look in the mirror and see who you are," the perpetually sunburned Nub allowed. "It's time to pinch yourself and see if you're white."

He laughed his wheezy laugh. "They had the money and these professional consultants who do this every week, and we were just a bunch of country boys who didn't know what we were doing."

Didn't matter. Underestimate folks here at your peril.

"We were just fightin' for our lives!"

●

By 3:00 A.M., Rance and Claudette's lawn is all but empty. The handful of us still left move inside to watch a replay of the game on a flat screen. The final minute looks just as insane the second time around. A junior transfer from Moultrie threw the 'Cats' winning touchdown. Alex, the starter until he got hurt two games ago, didn't play a down.

He never started for Valdosta again, and a month later he transferred to Lowndes. Matt believed Lowndes was now the best place for Alex to showcase his talent for the next level.

Three A.M. turned to 5:00 A.M.: Time to go. Claudette, God bless her, is up but ready to crash; even first ladies need to sleep sometime. Rance, meanwhile, has officially crossed the no-sleep line. He has to swap game film someplace in less than three hours.

I step outside into the cool morning air with Rodemaker and another coach. Still no sun.

"C'mon, Drew," Alan calls over his shoulder as he heads for his vehicle. "We're going to the Waffle House. We'll watch the sun come up there."

I think about it a minute. I could go from there straight to Mama's house. Then I think about that bathtub. I tell Alan I'll pass. Seeing the sun come up means a lot more to him than it does to me.

I'm ready to leave anyway. Perfect game, perfect night, and the most important question finally answered. Valdosta was back.

So I pull out of Rance and Claudette's silent subdivision, the moon a white wafer in the black sky, and roll out of town on North Valdosta Road. I pass Shorty's Steak House, Cass Burch's car lot ("Drive it like you stole it!"), the Smokin' Pig's neon embers—thanks a lot, Pig, I want to shout, for the extra ten pounds.

Then I crest a hill and see I-75. Even at this hour there's traffic. I slow for the ramp, then accelerate at the bottom and make a smooth, swift liftoff. My car's pointed north. Up and out of the Gnat Lands.

Away from home.